SECTION 1031 EXCHANGES

for Real Estate Investors and Professionals

BRADLEY T. BORDEN

Section 1031 Exchanges for Real Estate Investors and Professionals

Bradley T. Borden

Published by:

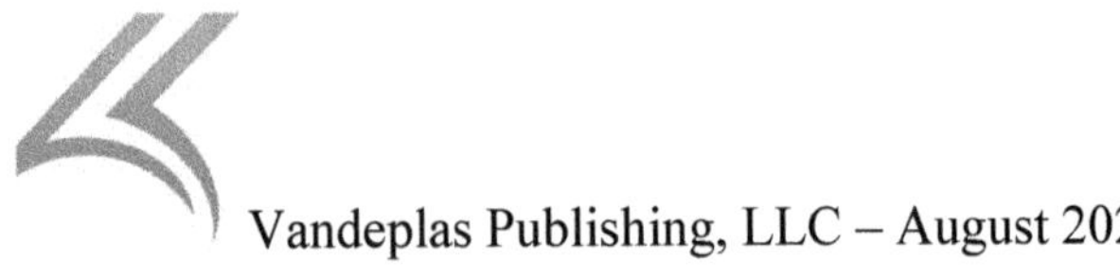
Vandeplas Publishing, LLC – August 2021

801 International Parkway, 5th Floor
Lake Mary, FL. 32746
USA

www.vandeplaspublishing.com

978-1-60042-539-4

TABLE OF CONTENTS

ACKNOWLEDGMENTS

This book reflects the contributions of many people. My wife Samantha and daughter Claire have supported and encouraged me in this endeavor. I dedicate this book to them.

Stanley Blend introduced section 1031 to me when I was in law school. His suggestion that I study reverse like-kind exchanges inspired my master's thesis and led to my first publication. Practicing law with him provided additional exposure to section 1031 and gave me the opportunity to spend numerous hours with him in practice, over lunch, or otherwise to discuss emerging issues and planning opportunities that section 1031 presents. His creativity as a tax lawyer demonstrates the problem-solving skills needed to structure many of the transactions discussed in this book. His interest in tax law, continuous pursuit of knowledge, and efforts to contribute to the legal community inspire me. I thank him for getting me started in the law and in section 1031.

Many section 1031 practitioners have influenced me and helped me gain a better understanding of section 1031 through one-on-one discussions, presentations, or articles they have written. I thank each of them. I also thank the numerous people in the section 1031 industry, the intermediaries and exchange specialists, with whom I have worked and with whom I continue to work. I count them as good friends and treasure the association I share with them.

Several people read earlier drafts of this manuscript and made comments that improved the text. These people include Kelly Anders, Samantha Borden (who is also a certified public accountant), Kent Corkum, Helen Crow, Katy David, Pat Dowdall, Rachel Flaschner, Alex Glashausser, Alex Hamrick, Jeff Jackson, Todd Keator, Ali Khan, Sang Lee, Stephen Mazza, Joe McKinney, Bill Merkel, Susan Miletta, Rob Rhee, Megan Rustand, Michael Schwartz, Joshua Stein, and Joline Wang. Tammy Thiessen helped make the numerous diagrams more appealing to the eye and display complicated information in an accessible manner. Patty Cates and Erica Soto helped prepare the manuscript through the numerous revisions that writing demands. I thank all of these people for the time they spent with the manuscript and discussing needed changes with me. Any errors that remain are my own.

About the Author

Bradley T. Borden is a Professor of Law at Brooklyn Law School and the principal of Bradley T. Borden PLLC. He teaches Federal Income Taxation, Partnership Taxation, Taxation of Real Estate Transactions, and LLCs and Partnerships. He frequently works as an expert witness and consultant in cases related to Section 1031 and helps his clients navigate complex tax aspects of real estate transactions. He has been working with Section 1031 for more than two decades.

Brad is the author or co-author of several books and at least 125 articles in leading tax and legal journals, and he has given more than 300 presentations at major tax conferences and other professional settings.

Brad is a fellow of the American Bar Foundation and the American College of Tax Counsel, an active member of the Section of Taxation of the American Bar Association, and a past chair of the Sales, Exchanges & Basis Committee of that Section. He earned a B.B.A. and M.B.A. from Idaho State University and a J.D. and LL.M. in taxation from University of Florida Fredric G. Levin College of Law, he is licensed to practice law in New York and Texas, and he is a certified public accountant.

Law School Website: www.brooklaw.edu
Firm Website: www.bradborden.com
LinkedIn: www.linkedin.com/in/bradley-t-borden-24681634/

Introduction

Section 1031 is a tax-saving tool. It allows property owners to exchange qualified property tax free for like-kind property. Contrast this with a property owner who sells or exchanges property in a taxable transaction. If a property owner sells a $300,000 piece of property in a taxable transaction and pays $30,000 of income tax, the property owner will have only $270,000 to reinvest. In contrast, a property owner who does a section 1031 exchange pays no income tax on the exchange and has the entire amount of the exchange proceeds to reinvest in other property. Thus, section 1031 preserves the property owner's $300,000 investment in replacement property. By eliminating the tax on the exchange, section 1031 allows the property owner to preserve net worth.

Unlike other tax-saving tools, section 1031 is available to a large cross-section of property owners. Large international corporations and other large property owners use section 1031 to avoid tax on the transfer of multi-million-dollar assets. The largest section 1031 exchanges may involve thousands of properties, the aggregate value of which may be in excess of billions of dollars. On the other end of the spectrum, individual property owners of average means use section 1031 to avoid tax on the transfer of single-family residential rental property worth less than $100,000. Section 1031 is a widely available tax-saving tool.

The tax-saving benefits of section 1031 fuel its popularity. As a result, section 1031 has grown significantly over the past few decades. Now, it seems everyone has heard of it. A business owner may have heard a friend or family member talk about how to save tax dollars doing a section 1031 exchange. A reader of national newspapers may have seen the advertisements for section 1031 exchange property and services or read articles covering section 1031. A property owner may have heard about section 1031 from a tax advisor or may have read about it in a book on investing. A real estate agent, real estate attorney, or CPA may have attended a continuing education seminar that covered section 1031. A person's relative or friend may be an exchange specialist at a major exchange company. In fact, with the popularity and spread of section 1031, a person may have heard about it (or one of its synonyms—tax-free swaps, tax-free exchanges, like-kind exchanges, or *Starker* exchanges) in a casual conversation with another person. Undoubtedly section 1031 is becoming ubiquitous and is now a part of our common vocabulary. Even so, many people are unaware of the benefits section 1031 provides; fewer are aware of its breadth; and fewer still are aware of its intricacies. This book helps introduce the benefits of section 1031 and demonstrates its scope.

PURPOSE OF THE BOOK

This book is for anyone interested in developing a working knowledge of section 1031. A working knowledge of section 1031 requires at least a basic understanding of its source and industry. Section 1031 grew out of a relatively simple idea—Congress believed that property owners who exchange into like-kind property should not pay tax on the exchange. The reason for this is that a like-kind exchange represents a continuation of an investment, and U.S. income tax law does not tax the continuation of an investment (*e.g.*, homeowners do not pay income on the appreciation in the value of their homes). Section 1031 grew from that simple continuation-of-investment principle. The principle dictates the types of structures an exchanger may use to do a section 1031 exchange. It also dictates the limits of section 1031. A person who understands that concept is prepared to consider the numerous exchange structures that open section 1031 to a broad array of transactions.

This book provides a significant description of section 1031 and the section 1031 exchange structures. It balances technical description with presentation. Thus, the detail in this book is much less specific than that found in a section 1031 treatise. Nonetheless, the book presents the fundamental structure of the most complicated exchanges. It provides a definite flavor of the various exchange structures, which have become the heart of section 1031. This will help property owners prepare for exchanges and provide an overview for advisors and exchange specialists who are becoming familiar with section 1031. After reading about some of the more complicated exchanges, some readers may find themselves sympathizing with James Herriot, the Yorkshire veterinarian and storyteller. In one of his timeless books, *All Things Wise and Wonderful* (Bantam Books, 1976), Mr. Herriot described an occurrence with which many of us can relate.

James Herriot tells of an event that occurred a few months after he was qualified as a veterinarian. He had successfully attended to several animal ailments during his few months of practice. One day, he was called to examine a horse and found that it had a very bad case of canker of the foot. He described what he saw as follows:

> The sole was a ragged, sodden mass with a stinking exudation oozing from the underrun horn, but what really bewildered me was the series of growths sprouting from every crevice. They were like nightmare toadstools—long papillae with horny caps growing from the diseased surface. I had read about them in books; they were called ergots, but I had never imagined them in such profusion. My thoughts raced as I moved behind the horse and lifted the other foot. It was the same. Just as bad. (p. 254)

It was the first such case Mr. Herriot had seen, and although he was familiar with the ailment and knew what would happen if he did not cure it, he was unsure what to do. His first thought was that he would lay the horse over and simply cut away the growth. Thankfully, he first spoke with his boss Siegfried, a seasoned veterinarian who had seen canker of the foot many times and knew how to operate on it. Mr. Herriot describes the discussion with Siegfried and the subsequent operation.

> My boss lifted the hind foot and whistled softly. Then he moved round and examined the other one. For a full minute he gazed down at the obscene fungi thrusting from the tattered stinking horn. When he stood up he looked at me expressionlessly.

It was a few seconds before he spoke. "And you were just going to pop round here on Monday, tip this big fellow on the grass and do the job?"

"Yes," I replied. "That was the idea."

A strange smile spread over my employer's face. It was something of wonder, sympathy, amusement and a tinge of admiration. Finally, he laughed and shook his head.

"Ah, the innocence of youth," he murmured . . .

. "You mean I couldn't do it at one go?"

"That's exactly what I mean. There's six weeks' work here, . . . and there'll be three men involved. We'll have to get this horse in to one of the loose boxes at Skeldale House [the veterinary] and then the two of us plus a blacksmith will have a go at him. After that his feet will have to be dressed every day in the stocks."

"I see."

"Yes, yes." Siegfried was warming to his subject. "We'll use the strongest caustic—nitric acid—and he'll be shod with special shoes with a metal plate to exert pressure on the sole." He stopped, probably because I was beginning to look bewildered, then he continued in a gentler tone. "Believe me, James, all this is necessary. The alternative is to shoot a fine horse, because he can't go on much longer than this."

* * *

Bobby (the horse) came in to the yard at Skeldale House (the veterinary hospital) the following day and when I saw the amount of sheer hard labour which the operation entailed I realised the utter impossibility of a single man doing it at one go.

Pat Jenner the blacksmith with his full tool kit was pressed into service and between us, taking it in turns, we removed the vegetations and diseased tissue, leaving only healthy horn. Siegfried applied the acid to cauterize the area, then packed the sole with twists of

> tow which were held in place by the metal plate Pat had made to fit under the shoe. This pressure from the two was essential to effect the cure. (p. 258-260)

Mr. Herriot later reports the operation was a success. The story provides a backdrop for discussing section 1031 exchanges. First, Mr. Herriot's graphic description of Bobby's canker of the foot may aptly describe what many people perceive when they are first exposed to a complicated exchange structure. The most complicated exchange structure has several parties, several moving parts, and significant documentation. The first time a person is exposed to such an exchange, the structure may appear to be a "ragged, sodden mess with stinking exudation." Unlike Bobby's ailment, however, section 1031 exchange structures, no matter how complicated, can be wonderfully beneficial to property owners.

Second, much as Mr. Herriot had seen many routine matters and successfully handled them, many property owners have bought and sold property and many advisors have counseled clients about the purchase and disposition of property. Other people have heard about section 1031 and understand some of its concepts. Still others have done one of the more routine exchanges, such as a multi-party deferred exchange (Chapters 4 and 5). All these things will help a person better understand section 1031, but having the opportunity to read about a particular exchange structure will better prepare any party better deal with the exchange. This book can thus save property owners, tax advisors, exchange specialists, and others the embarrassment that would otherwise result from a naïve underestimation of section 1031's requirements, demonstrated by a statement revealing one's "innocence of youth."

Third, people familiar with routine section 1031 multi-party deferred exchanges but unfamiliar with the more complicated exchange structures may be tempted to use the structure of a routine multi-party deferred exchange to handle complex exchange needs. Such attempts would be analogous to Mr. Herriot tipping Bobby on the grass and operating on the canker of the foot alone. Just as the results of operating on Bobby alone would have been disastrous, using an inappropriate structure for a section 1031 exchange could be financially disastrous. Exchange structures such as reverse exchanges (Chapter 6), improvements exchanges (Chapter 7), exchanges and proximate business transactions (Chapter 8), and related-party exchanges (Chapter 9) can be very complex and may require a significant amount of planning and the services of several parties, and certain types of replacement property such as DSTs and triple-net properties (Chapter 10) present unique legal and tax issues that require careful consideration. The alternative to operating on Bobby would have been fatal; the alternative to using a complicated section 1031 exchange structure should not be fatal, but could be financially significant, as an exchanger may lose the benefits of section 1031.

This book can help many people avoid the financially harmful decision of using an inappropriate exchange structure. A reader will also be less likely to underestimate the requirements of certain structures. Readers will be introduced to exchange structures and presented with the general requirements of each. This book will describe transactions and tell what the various exchange structures require. Nonetheless, it cannot empower readers to handle particular transactions alone. Just as the operation on Bobby required more than one party, many of the exchanges require multiple parties. Perhaps the most common party required to complete a section 1031 exchange is a qualified intermediary. This book describes when such parties are needed and the types of services such parties perform and prepares the reader to participate in section 1031 exchanges.

Finally, Mr. Herriot's story had a happy ending. He and the others were able to remove the grotesque growth of Bobby's canker foot. Unfortunately, this book cannot remove the grotesque complexity of some section 1031 exchanges. Section 1031 complexity results from formalistic rules that have grown out of section 1031's original continued-investment rationale. Instead, the book explains the possible reasons for the complexity. This should help make such exchanges less mysterious and more manageable. By describing the section 1031 industry, the book also illuminates how exchange companies are able to help simplify the exchange process by spreading the costs of handling complexity over thousands of exchanges. The processes such companies develop help reduce the complexity of each individual exchange.

The book will introduce the uninitiated to section 1031 and provide them with a working knowledge of section 1031. It will add depth and breadth of knowledge to people who have some exposure to section 1031 but seek more. The book will benefit property owners, attorneys, CPAs, real estate agents, closing agents at title companies, loan officers at banks, financial advisors, and any other of the many people who come across section 1031 in their work. Some readers will benefit from reading the book cover to cover to gain a general understanding of section 1031 and the working vocabulary used in the section 1031 industry. Section 1031 presents many technical terms. To address these terms, the book includes a glossary that some readers may find useful while reading the book. After reading the book, readers may retain it as a reference to access when specific questions arise regarding an exchange structure. Others will buy the book to use as a reference manual to gain an understanding of section 1031 issues as they arise. Either use will benefit the reader.

USE OF EXAMPLES IN THE BOOK

The book uses examples liberally to explain aspects of section 1031. In many of the examples, participants are given a voice. Although actual conversations between property owners and advisors may not precisely mirror the hypothetical discussions presented in this book, property owners and practitioners will recognize similar discussions as they participate in section 1031 exchanges. Thus, for the novice, especially, the examples provide an introduction to the types of discussions that are common in the section 1031 industry.

To avoid monotony, the book uses names to identify exchange participants and generally changes the names with each new example. Some examples involve several different participants and multiple properties. Although the names of specific parties typically change with each new example, the examples adopt the key, which makes party- and property-identification easy.

Example Key

The examples throughout the book use the following letters to help identify the parties.

If the first letter of a name is:	Then the party/ property is:
A	**Attorney**
B	**Buyer**
C	**CPA**
D	**Party Related to the Exchanger**
E	**Exchanger**
O	**Owner of a Legal Entity**
Q	**Relinquished Property**
R	**Replacement Property**
S	**Seller**
QI	**Qualified Intermediary**
EAT	**Exchange Accommodation Titleholder**

Readers may refer back to this key, but after considering a few examples, the reader should be able to easily identify the participants and property.

With that, the discussion begins.

CHAPTER 1:
THE HISTORY OF TAX-FREE EXCHANGES

If one were to graph the number of section 1031 exchanges that have occurred each year from the date of section 1031's inception in 1921 until the present day, the graph would most likely show a steady but modest increase in exchanges between 1921 and the 1980s. Beginning in the 1980s, the number of exchanges would begin to increase in frequency and then show a pronounced increase beginning in 1991. Since 1991, the graph would show a sharp turn upward representing a significant increase in the number of exchanges during each of the past several years with no sign that the number will level off anytime soon.

A review of the history of section 1031 shows that key developments in tax law, the section 1031 industry's growing size and

History of Section 1031 Popularity
(Illustration only, exact data not available)

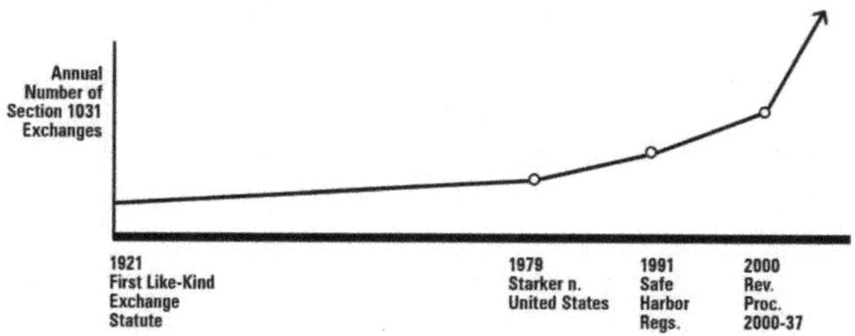

sophistication, and taxpayer awareness contribute to the upswing demonstrated by the graph. The early history of section 1031 is marked by a struggle with fundamental income tax concepts—realization and recognition. After section 1031 was enacted, lawmakers struggled to define what types of transactions qualify for section 1031. Several court decisions helped define the term "exchange" and establish the breadth of section 1031. In 1979, a key case, *Starker v. United States*, opened the door for deferred exchanges, and Treasury's subsequent promulgation of regulations in 1991 spawned the growth of the section 1031 industry and made section 1031 accessible to most property owners. Over the same period of time, tax practitioners discovered uses of section 1031 that provide tax-saving opportunities to property owners in diverse situations. Today, section 1031 is an accessible tax-saving tool for a significant part of the tax-paying population and the industry is vibrant and growing.

REALIZATION, RECOGNITION, AND THE INCEPTION OF SECTION 1031

Income tax concepts that now seem commonplace were once the subject of serious debate. In 1913, when Congress enacted the first income tax law following the ratification of the Sixteenth Amendment (which unequivocally made an individual income tax constitutional) the concepts of realization and recognition were not solidly a part of the U.S. tax system. Several early court decisions considered the place of both realization and recognition, laying a framework for the taxation of property transactions generally and section specifically.

Source of U.S. Tax Law—Constitution, Statute, Case Law

United States tax law derives from several sources. First, the Sixteenth Amendment of the Constitution grants Congress the authority to impose a tax on individual income. Second, with the authority granted by the Constitution, Congress enacts statutes imposing income tax on individuals. Congress also imposes income tax on corporations, trusts, and estates. Federal tax statutes are found primarily in the Internal Revenue Code and form the primary source of U.S. tax laws. Third, if a dispute arises between the government and a taxpayer regarding the interpretation of a statute and the dispute is tried before a court of law, the court will decide the legal interpretation of the statute. The decision of the court becomes case law. Constitutional issues infrequently arise with respect to income taxes. Thus, two important sources of U.S. tax law are statutes (the Internal Revenue Code) and case law (the decisions of courts).

Another source of U.S. tax laws is regulations promulgated by the Department of Treasury. Treasury promulgates regulations when a statute is unclear and when directed to do so by Congress. Regulations are law only if they reasonably interpret statutes. Taxpayers may challenge the validity of a regulation (claiming it is not a reasonable interpretation of the statute), but regulations are binding on the IRS because the IRS, as an agency of Treasury, is subject to rules Treasury adopts.

Tax law is also in rulings published by the IRS. As an agency of Treasury, the IRS is charged with administering the U.S. tax law. To help taxpayers understand its position on specific issues, the IRS will often publish revenue procedures. Revenue procedures, such as Rev. Proc. 2000-37, describe the IRS's administrative position with respect to certain issues. For example, in Rev. Proc. 2000-37, the IRS provides that it will not challenge the tax treatment of certain aspects of title-parking reverse exchanges if the exchanger satisfies all of the requirements in the revenue procedure. The IRS also publishes revenue rulings that provide guidance on specific substantive issues. Finally, the IRS publishes private rulings that only the addressee of the ruling may rely upon. Although available to the public, private rulings are not legal authority.

Realization

The concept of realization considers whether property owners should be taxed on the appreciation of their property. As the U.S. income tax evolved, it provided that property owners generally would not be taxed on the appreciation in value of their property until they disposed of the property. The disposition of property is a realization event. With few exceptions (for certain publicly traded securities), increases in a property's value are not subject to income tax without a realization event. The significance of this is that it allows property owners to experience a tax-free increase in net worth so long as they hold property.

For example, if Erin purchased a vacant lot for $100,000 and it appreciated in value to $150,000 over a one-year period, she should not owe federal income tax on that $50,000 increase in value, assuming she does not dispose of the lot. This is significant because her net worth increased by $50,000 tax free. Compare this to Shelby who earns $50,000 for services over the same one-year period. Service providers are subject to income tax when they receive compensation. If the tax rate is 20 percent, Shelby will owe $5,000 of tax on her $50,000 of compensation income. Thus, she will only have a $45,000 increase in net worth after taxes while Erin has a $50,000 increase.

The stated justification for not taxing appreciation in value without a realization event is that valuing property each year to assess such a tax would impose a significant administrative burden. Also, such a tax may force property owners to sell property to pay the taxes on appreciation. People dispute these justifications of the realization requirement. Some believe it is unfair because it allows property owners to increase their wealth tax free while service providers must pay tax on their annual compensation. Regardless of the debate over the realization requirement, it is firmly ingrained in the U.S. income tax system. Thus, most property owners do not realize gain before they dispose of property.

The disposition of appreciated property will, however, trigger gain realized. Thus, if Erin were to sell her lot, she would realize $50,000 of gain. Realization is a requirement for taxing most property appreciation, but the law does not tax all gain realized. Gain realized is taxed only if the law requires that it be recognized.

Recognition

The recognition requirement builds on the realization requirement. The U.S. income tax law generally requires all property owners to recognize all gain realized. Stated simply, a property owner recognizes gain by reporting it on a tax return. Thus, if Erin sells her property for $150,000 and realizes gain of $50,000 on that sale, she generally must report $50,000 gain on her tax return. The U.S. tax system, however, provides several exceptions to the general rule of gain recognition. One of the most significant exceptions is section 1031.

Section 1031 provides that if a property owner disposes of one piece of investment property in exchange for like-kind business-use or investment property (the exchange is a realization event), the property owner does not recognize gain on the transaction. Thus, if Erin exchanges her vacant lot for a duplex worth $150,000, she would realize gain of $50,000 on the exchange. Because a vacant lot and a duplex are like-kind, however, she would not recognize that $50,000 of gain. Section 1031 grants this nonrecognition. Section 1031 nonrecognition is a property owner's goal when structuring a section 1031 exchange.

The rationale for section 1031 is that a person who uses sale proceeds to invest in like-kind property is similar to a person who does not sell property. That rationale relies upon equity. Because a person who does not sell property is not subject to income tax, a person who exchanges into like-kind property similarly should not be subject to income tax. In both situations, the property owners have property before and after the exchange. Thus, to preserve equitable tax treatment for both types of property owners, section 1031 grants the exchanging property owner nonrecognition. This is the rationale for section 1031, upon which Congress relied when it enacted the predecessor to section 1031 in 1921.

As with many laws, the devil is in the details of section 1031. Although the concept is straightforward and simply stated, as the other chapters of this book reveal, the technical requirements of section 1031 can be very complex. Satisfying those requirements generally requires careful planning and an understanding of the details of the law. Those details began to emerge shortly after Congress enacted the law in 1921.

The first wave of lawmaking came in the form of judicial interpretation of the term "exchange."

The Judicial Interpretation of the term "Exchange"

Section 1031 has changed over the years, but all versions of section 1031 have required property owners to exchange property. The statute, however, does not provide a definition of the term "exchange." Thus, property owners and the IRS were left to struggle to find the definition. Consequently, disputes arose between individual property owners and the IRS over the definition of the term "exchange." From 1935 until 1979, courts considered the definition of exchange in different contexts at least seven times. This series of judicial decisions provides a fairly clear definition of exchange and identifies several types of structures that satisfy the section 1031 definition of exchange.

Direct Swap Not Required—
The Birth of Multi-Party Exchanges

Early case law established that section 1031 does not require a direct swap. That case law established that a property owner could transfer property to a buyer and the buyer could acquire other property from an unrelated party and transfer it to the property owner. To illustrate, assume that Eastland Corp (the exchanger) owns an office building. Big Ltd (the buyer) offers to purchase the office building from Eastland Corp, and Eastland Corp agrees to sell only if it can sell the office building as part of a section 1031 exchange. To facilitate Eastland Corp's exchange, Big Ltd agrees to acquire replacement property from Sam (the seller) and transfer it to Eastland Corp. Courts held that this type of indirect exchange may qualify for section 1031 nonrecognition. Because this type of transaction involves three parties, some refer to it as a three-party exchange or a three-corner exchange.

Three-Corner Exchange

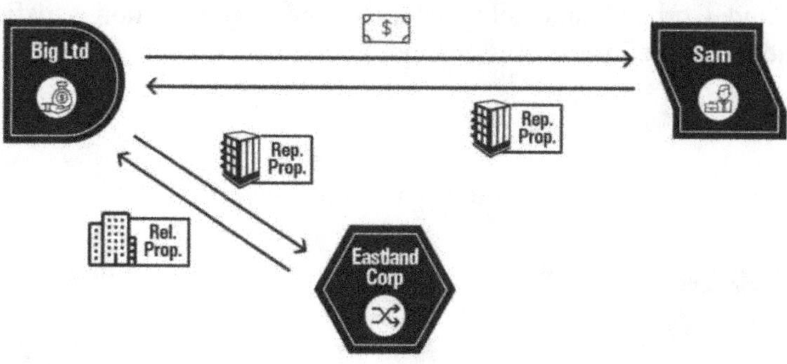

Basic Exchange Terminology

Exchanger: A party seeking section 1031 nonrecognition.

Relinquished Property: Property an exchanger transfers as part of a section 1031 exchange.

Replacement Property: Property an exchanger acquires as part of a section 1031 exchange.

Exchange Proceeds: Proceeds from the sale of relinquished property

Another type of indirect exchange the courts allowed is the four-party or four-corner exchange. An exchange facilitator participates in a four-party exchange. Thus, if Big Ltd is interested in purchasing Eastland Corp's office building but is not interested in facilitating Eastland Corp's exchange, Eastland Corp may hire an exchange facilitator to assist with the exchange. The exchange would be completed by (1) Eastland Corp transferring the office building to the exchange facilitator and the exchange facilitator agreeing to transfer replacement property to Eastland Corp, (2) the exchange facilitator transferring the office building to Big Ltd in exchange for money, (3) the exchange facilitator using the money to acquire replacement property from Sam, and (4) the exchange facilitator transferring the replacement property to Eastland Corp. Courts held that this type of transaction satisfies the section 1031 definition of exchange.

Four-Corner Exchange

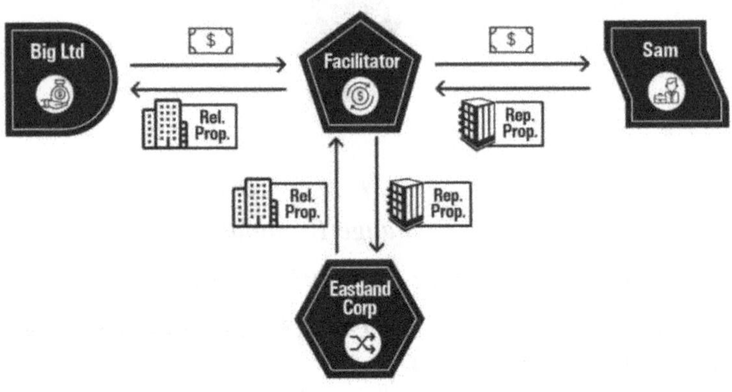

Simultaneity Not Required—The Birth of Deferred Exchanges

In the most famous section 1031 exchange case (*Starker v. United States*), a court held that a property owner completed an exchange for section 1031 purposes even though the property owner did not acquire all of its replacement property until two years following the transfer of the relinquished property. The court held that simultaneity is not a requirement of section 1031 and the exchange was valid. A few years after the *Starker* decision, Congress enacted a statute that allowed deferred exchanges but required the exchanger to acquire replacement property within 180 days after the transfer of relinquished property. Thus, section 1031 does not require simultaneity, and deferred exchanges are a vibrant part of the exchange business.

Property-for-Property Transfer Required

Although courts interpreted the definition of exchange broadly in allowing property owners to do three- and four-party exchanges, they have restricted the type of consideration property owners may receive as part of an exchange. Specifically, courts prohibit property owners from receiving anything other than like-kind property. Thus, in one famous case, the court held that husband and wife property owners had not completed a valid section 1031 exchange because they received money from the sale of a ranch, even though the property owners clearly intended to do a section 1031 exchange and used the proceeds to purchase like-kind replacement property on the same day they sold the ranch. The decision in that case demonstrates that to complete a valid section 1031 exchange, property owners must receive other property, not money. The receipt of money will destroy section 1031 nonrecognition.

Subsequent case law establishes that if a property owner constructively receives money or other property, the transaction will not qualify as a section 1031 exchange. Thus, a property owner may not merely direct its attorney to receive the proceeds from the sale of relinquished property. In such a situation, the property owner will be deemed to be in constructive receipt of the money and will not satisfy the section 1031 definition of exchange. Based on this series of cases, avoiding the actual or constructive receipt of money must be a principal objective in structuring a deferred or multi-party exchange.

Property-for-Property Requirement

An important discussion between members of the House of Representatives drives home the property-for-property requirement. In this 1924 discussion, Representative LaGuardia and Representative Green discuss the property-for-property requirement.

La Guardia: "Under this paragraph is it necessary to exchange property? Suppose the property is sold and other property immediately acquired for the same business. Would that be a gain or loss, assuming there is greater value in the property acquired? . . . "

Green: "If the property is reduced to cash and there is a gain, of course it will be taxed."

La Guardia: "Suppose that cash is immediately put back into the property, into the business?"

Green: "That would not make any difference."

Source: 65 Cong. Rec. 2799 (1924)

Thus, to satisfy the section 1031 definition of exchange, the exchanger must transfer property and acquire property. The exchanger cannot transfer property and receive money. This is the property-for-property requirement.

THE SECTION 1031 DEFERRED EXCHANGE SAFE HARBORS

In 1991, Treasury promulgated regulations that help property owners structure three- and four-party exchanges to avoid actual or constructive receipt of money or non-like-kind property. These regulations set forth special rules that create safe harbors for structuring like-kind exchanges. If a property owner can satisfy the rules in the safe harbor, the property owner will not be in actual or constructive receipt of money held in the safe harbor and can satisfy the property-for-property requirement.

The most popular of the safe harbors is the qualified intermediary safe harbor. As discussed in detail in Chapter 5, an exchange with a qualified intermediary requires the exchanger to enter into an exchange agreement with the qualified intermediary. Pursuant to the agreement, the exchanger transfers relinquished property to a buyer, and the buyer transfers the exchange proceeds to a qualified intermediary. Because the qualified intermediary, and not the exchanger, receives the exchange proceeds, the exchanger does not actually or constructively receive the proceeds. When the exchanger identifies and is prepared to acquire replacement property, it directs the qualified intermediary to transfer the exchange proceeds to the replacement property seller. The exchanger then receives title to the replacement property.

The regulations provide that with such a transaction, the exchanger will be deemed to have transferred property to the qualified intermediary and to have received replacement property from the qualified intermediary. This satisfies the property-for-property requirement. Although this transaction is complicated, it provides a safe harbor for doing multi-party exchanges and professional qualified intermediaries greatly simplify the transaction, with streamlined processes and expert knowledge.

THE SECTION 1031 REVERSE EXCHANGE SAFE HARBOR

Another significant section 1031 structuring development is the creation of the section 1031 reverse exchange safe harbor in 2000. As stated above, a deferred exchange is an exchange in which the exchanger transfers relinquished property and subsequently receives replacement property. Thus, for a period of time, the exchanger owns neither relinquished property nor replacement property. A reverse exchange is just the opposite. With a reverse exchange, the exchanger acquires replacement property first and then transfers relinquished property. There is no law that specifically provides that such reverse exchanges qualify for section 1031 nonrecognition. The concern is that the concurrent ownership of both replacement property and relinquished property may violate the section 1031 definition of exchange. To avoid the threat that reverse exchanges may not satisfy the section 1031 definition of exchange, tax advisors developed title-parking arrangements to accomplish reverse exchanges. The goal of title-parking arrangements is to ensure that the exchanger does not hold relinquished property and replacement property at the same time.

A typical title-parking reverse exchange requires that an accommodator take title to replacement property and hold that title until the exchanger sells the relinquished property. At that time, the exchanger acquires the replacement property from the accommodator. If done correctly, this transaction can qualify for section 1031 nonrecognition. To help exchangers successfully structure title-parking reverse exchanges, the IRS published Rev. Proc. 2000-37, which provides a safe harbor for title-parking reverse exchanges.

CHAPTER 2: THE SECTION 1031 PLAYERS

Since the promulgation of the safe harbor regulations in 1991, which created the qualified intermediary, the section 1031 industry has witnessed significant growth. Although intermediaries and section 1031 experts practiced prior to the promulgation of the safe harbor regulations, the regulations opened the door for more rapid growth. Today, the professionals in the industry include attorneys and CPAs, title companies and financial institutions, qualified intermediaries, exchange accommodation titleholders, TIC and DST promoters and dealers, and real estate professionals. At times, the roles of these various players may overlap.

ATTORNEYS AND CPAS

Attorneys and CPAs (certified public accountants) provide legal and tax advice to exchangers and exchange facilitators (*i.e.*, qualified intermediaries and exchange accommodation titleholders). An attorney can provide both legal advice and tax advice. A CPA is not licensed to provide legal advice but may provide tax advice. Exchangers are best served when they hire an attorney or CPA who is an expert in section 1031 and who is familiar with the section 1031 industry. Every major accounting firm and every law firm with a sophisticated tax practice has experts in section 1031. These experts know the section 1031 rules, are familiar with the section 1031 industry, and have extensive section 1031 experience. An experienced section 1031 attorney or CPA will help an exchange occur efficiently because they will be familiar with the exchange process and know the roles of the section 1031 players.

TITLE COMPANIES AND FINANCIAL INSTITUTIONS

Title companies generally provide closing documents and help close the sale of the relinquished property and the acquisition of the replacement property. Financial institutions provide financing for exchanges. Many title companies are familiar with section 1031 and willingly work with exchangers to help them successfully complete section 1031 exchanges. Many financial institutions understand the section 1031 process and will work with exchangers and other parties as needed. At times, however, financial institutions are unable to provide exactly what an exchanger requests. In such situations, exchangers may have to restructure a transaction to satisfy the financial institution. For example, exchangers must structure some reverse exchanges as exchange-first transactions to ensure that the exchanger takes title to the replacement property immediately (exchange-first transactions, a form of reverse exchange, are discussed in Chapter 6). With good planning, an exchanger can often generally satisfy both the financial institution's requirements and the section 1031 requirements. Many title companies and financial institutions have created affiliated entities that serve as qualified intermediaries.

QUALIFIED INTERMEDIARIES

Qualified intermediaries come in all sizes and can be found throughout the United States. Under the rules, an individual may serve as a qualified intermediary, but most qualified intermediaries are companies that employ exchange specialists. Qualified intermediaries serve the important function of facilitating deferred multi-party exchanges. Professional qualified intermediaries also bring a wealth of experience, expertise and resources to an exchange, all of which can help make the exchange process more efficient. Having said that, not all professional qualified intermediaries provide competent services. The best professional qualified intermediary companies expend considerable resources to prepare quality documents and processes, invest time and energy to educate their exchange specialists in section 1031 law, and provide exceptional customer service. Such companies provide valuable services to exchangers.

Definition of Qualified Intermediary

Treasury regulations define qualified intermediary b[illegible] *excluding from the definition disqualified persons. Any person who does not come within this definition of disqualified person may serve as a qualified intermediary. A disqualified person is any one of the following: (1) the agent of the exchanger, (2) a party related to the exchanger, and (3) a party related to the exchanger's agent.*

Disqualified Person

Agent of the Exchanger

An agent of the exchanger may not act as qualified intermediary. The regulations provide generally that the exchanger's agent includes the exchanger's employees, attorneys, accountants, investment bankers and brokers, and real estate agents or brokers. A person is not an agent of the exchanger, however, if the person only provides services for the exchanger with respect to a section 1031 exchange or has provided no services to the exchanger within the last two years.

Party Related to the Exchanger

A party related to the exchanger may not act as qualified intermediary. Related parties include family members, entities of which the exchanger owns more than 10 percent, and other entities if the exchanger and other entities are under common control. Chapter 9 provides an in-depth discussion of the definition of related party. That definition applies here, but 10 percent is used instead of 50 percent to determine whether an entity is a party related to the exchanger.

Parties Related to Agents of the Exchanger

Parties related to agents of the exchanger are disqualified. Thus, an entity wholly owned by the exchanger's attorney generally may not serve as the exchanger's qualified intermediary. Similarly,

of the exchanger's CPA may not serve as

st exchange may cause some anxiety and termediary becomes an important step. Most who regularly provide section 1031 advice know competent qualified intermediaries and should be able to provide several references. Property owners can also learn a great deal about qualified intermediaries from the internet. In addition to the individual websites of numerous qualified intermediaries, the Federation of Exchange Accommodators (FEA) lists its members at www.1031.org.

Federation of Exchange Accommodators

The FEA is a professional organization of exchange accommodators. The vast majority of its members provide qualified intermediary services. The FEA provides a network for qualified intermediaries to discuss common concerns, offers continuing education seminars to its members, and grants Certified Exchange Specialist designation to members who have provided exchange services for a required period of time and pass an exam. The FEA also lobbies lawmakers and administrators on behalf of its members and exchangers to influence legislation that would affect the section 1031 industry and the scope of section 1031. Because of the FEA's efforts to certify its members and provide them with continuing education, membership in the FEA provides some evidence that an exchange accommodator is familiar with section 1031.

Things to Look for in a Qualified Intermediary

In addition to membership in the FEA, property owners should consider (1) the qualified intermediary's policies and processes for protecting exchange proceeds it holds, (2) the experience of the qualified intermediary and its exchange specialists, (3) the qualified intermediary's fees, and (4) the qualified intermediary's ability to deliver timely services. Exchangers should be particularly concerned about whether their exchange proceeds will be safe while held by a qualified intermediary.

Exchange Proceeds Security

A qualified intermediary generally holds exchange proceeds for exchangers. To complete successful section 1031 exchanges, exchangers must be able to access exchange proceeds and direct their distribution at short notice. Thus, it is imperative that the qualified intermediary has immediate access to the proceeds and be able to distribute them as directed by exchangers. The vast majority of qualified intermediaries carefully guard exchange proceeds they hold, but a few qualified intermediaries have breached the trust given them by exchangers. For example, in one infamous case, a qualified intermediary commingled exchange proceeds with personal funds, invested the proceeds unwisely, and used the funds for personal enjoyment. In another case, a qualified intermediary invested exchange proceeds that became illiquid. The result in both cases was that the qualified intermediary was unable to provide funds for exchangers to complete exchanges within the required time limits. The exchangers in both cases thus lost section 1031 nonrecognition and recovered exchange proceeds after prolonged litigation.

To avoid this possibility, property owners should inquire about a qualified intermediary's practices, policies, and procedures regarding exchange proceeds. Many exchange companies provide a guarantee from a parent or affiliated company, if affiliated with a large bank or title company. Many exchange companies are bonded up to a certain amount and carry errors and omissions insurance, providing some security that exchange proceeds will be available.

Exchangers should also find out where qualified intermediaries deposit exchange proceeds. The qualified intermediary should deposit funds in segregated accounts with a trusted financial institution and not in the qualified intermediary's operating account. To help ensure that exchange proceeds are protected, exchangers must exercise due diligence in choosing a qualified intermediary. For added protection from failure of a qualified intermediary, exchangers should consider having proceeds deposited in a qualified escrow account or with a qualified trust (discussed in Chapter 5).

Experience

Several exchange companies have been in operation since 1991, when Treasury gave life to the qualified intermediary, and employ very experienced exchange specialists. If the exchange specialists are active in the section 1031 industry, participate in section 1031 seminars, keep abreast of changes in the law, and otherwise possess professional competence, they will provide valuable services.

Other qualified intermediary companies may be fairly new but have experienced and competent exchange specialists. For example, an attorney with considerable section 1031 experience may leave private practice to form an exchange company. Although the exchange company will be new, the attorney's vast section 1031 experience provides the company with instant credibility. Exchange specialists also may leave a qualified intermediary company to form or acquire another company. Although such newly formed company will have a short history, the experience the exchange specialist brings to the company makes such company competent to provide quality exchange services. In choosing a qualified intermediary, exchangers should consider the qualified intermediary's experience.

Fees

Qualified intermediaries make money in two ways: (1) they charge a transaction fee for exchanges and (2) they make interest on exchange proceeds they hold. Exchangers should discuss fees with qualified intermediaries. Many qualified intermediaries charge a small transaction fee and rely upon interest for a bulk of their revenue. Therefore, exchangers should find out what amount of interest they will earn on exchange proceeds while the qualified intermediary holds them.

Timely Service

Because section 1031 exchanges are time sensitive, qualified intermediaries must be able to deliver timely services. This requires that they do simple things, such as answer telephones, reply to e-mails, and watch the fax machine. A qualified intermediary company that is unable to provide these basic services may not be able to deliver exchange proceeds in a timely manner and may cause an exchanger to lose section 1031 nonrecognition. If a qualified intermediary company places exchange proceeds on deposit with another institution such as a bank or other financial institution, the qualified intermediary must be able to access those proceeds easily. Some qualified intermediaries request that exchangers notify them a few days in advance of the day they need exchange proceeds. Such requests are not unreasonable, as exchangers should be making preparations to close on replacement property long before the closing date arrives. Nonetheless, qualified intermediaries must be prepared to act on shorter notice in some unusual circumstances.

Qualified Intermediaries as Tax Advisors

Many exchange specialists employed by qualified intermediaries are section 1031 experts. A question often arises, however, about whether qualified intermediaries should provide tax advice. The income tax regulations allow qualified intermediaries to provide legal and tax advice with respect to section 1031 exchanges. If the advice covers more than section 1031 exchanges, the company employing the exchange specialist would lose its qualified intermediary status. Furthermore, providing advice would constitute the practice of law, so the exchange specialist and qualified intermediary must have a license to legally provide tax or legal advice. Nonetheless, market forces often pressure qualified intermediaries to offer legal and tax advice through their exchange specialists. Both exchangers and qualified intermediaries must consider the ramifications of qualified intermediaries providing advice.

Qualified intermediaries must consider the effect providing advice will have on their status as qualified intermediaries, the legal consequences of providing advice without a license, and the market impact of providing advice versus not providing advice. As long as qualified intermediaries limit their advice to matters related to section 1031 exchanges, they should not lose their qualified intermediary status.

Almost any communication to a client about the law, an interpretation of the law, or application of the law is tax and legal advice. Thus, if an exchange specialist tells an exchanger that the identification period (Chapter 5) is 45 days, the qualified intermediary, through the exchange specialist, has arguably provided tax and legal advice. The advice relates to a section 1031 exchange, so it should not affect the qualified intermediary's status as a qualified intermediary, but it is a statement of the law (states that the exchanger must identify replacement property within 45 days), an interpretation of the law (provides that the identification period begins on the day after the transfer of the relinquished property and ends at midnight on the 45th day after that), and an application of the law (identifies the specific date on which the identification period ends). If the qualified intermediary is not licensed to give such advice, then such advice would be the unauthorized practice of law. The unauthorized practice of law is a crime in most, if not all, states. Additionally, a person who engages in the unauthorized practice of law is held to the same standard of care as a licensed practitioner, and in some states to a higher standard of care. Thus, if a client ever sues the qualified intermediary for malpractice, the qualified intermediary would be treated as a lawyer or CPA in determining whether the qualified intermediary was negligent in providing advice.

Even with the potential for practicing law without a license and for an enhanced standard of care, the market pressures qualified intermediaries to provide tax advice. If one qualified intermediary holds itself out as providing tax advice, then other qualified intermediaries feel pressure to offer such advice to attract and retain clients. Because of this pressure, a significant number of qualified intermediaries provide tax advice with respect to exchanges.

Exchangers should be concerned about three things when receiving advice from qualified intermediaries. First, the exchanger must ensure that the advice is related to the section 1031 exchange. This helps ensure that the qualified intermediary retains its qualified status. Second, exchangers must understand that they will enter into a contract with the qualified intermediary and that the qualified intermediary's interests may not always align with the exchanger's. Thus, the qualified intermediary may not be in a position to provide unbiased advice to the exchanger. Finally, the exchanger must consider the cost of seeking advice elsewhere. Attorneys and CPAs generally charge an hourly rate for providing advice. Qualified intermediaries often provide services at a fixed rate, regardless of the amount of advice they provide. To minimize the cost of an exchange, some exchangers will be pressured to seek advice from qualified intermediaries.

In the end, a qualified intermediary's decision to provide tax advice and an exchanger's decision to accept tax advice from a qualified intermediary requires a judgment call. Both parties must weigh the several factors discussed above. Often economics will drive the decision. If the size of an exchange is relatively small, exchangers will often choose to work exclusively with the qualified intermediary, and the qualified intermediary will provide the required services. If the exchange is a larger, complicated transaction, exchangers will seek legal and tax advice from licensed practitioners, and qualified intermediaries will encourage such efforts and may refuse to serve as qualified intermediary if the exchanger does not have competent counsel.

The one aspect that may trouble exchangers, qualified intermediaries, and others is the legal significance of providing advice without a license. Concerned parties should be actively involved in finding a way to change the law to allow qualified intermediaries to provide tax advice. Some of the most competent section 1031 practitioners in the country work for qualified intermediaries. The FEA is taking steps to ensure that all of its members obtain professional competence through certifying qualified members as exchange specialists. Things should continue to progress in that direction to help make section 1031 exchanges more accessible and less cumbersome. The qualified intermediary industry is becoming more sophisticated; the law should adapt to reflect this.

Types of Qualified Intermediaries

There are several types of qualified intermediaries, providing exchangers numerous choices when preparing for an exchange. The discussion below makes some general statements about each type of qualified intermediary. Ultimately, the type of qualified intermediary is not as important as the quality and competence of the qualified intermediary. Many of the professional qualified intermediaries are excellent. Those who provide qualified intermediary services on the side may have difficulty providing such services well.

Bank-Affiliated Qualified Intermediaries

One common type of qualified intermediary is the bank-affiliated qualified intermediary. Such qualified intermediary companies can be separate legal entities owned by a bank holding company or bank affiliate or be part of a bank's operations. Many of these qualified intermediaries have a name that includes the name of the bank.

Bank-affiliated qualified intermediaries are generally large companies. Their clients include many of the largest companies in the world, but they also serve small companies and individual taxpayers. Bank-affiliated qualified intermediaries may have exchange specialists throughout the country with a central location to process exchange documents and handle the company's administrative matters. Because such companies are associated with a bank, many exchangers take comfort that their exchange proceeds are secure. This class of qualified intermediary generally provides excellent service, but they are generally large corporations. The general perception is (and perhaps unjustifiably so) that such companies may seem more aloof than a smaller private intermediary company that appears to provide more of a personal touch.

Title Company-Affiliated Qualified Intermediaries

Title company-affiliated qualified intermediaries are similar in many respects to bank-affiliated qualified intermediaries. Both types of companies are generally large and are affiliated with even larger companies who may provide financial support to the qualified intermediary. Title company-affiliated qualified intermediaries seem to be more inclined to have regional offices. Some maintain one location that processes all of the company's exchanges; others have several regional offices that individually process exchanges. The regional offices allow exchange specialists to be close to their client base. This in turn provides a personal feel that some exchangers seek. Like bank-affiliated qualified intermediaries, this class of qualified intermediary serves both large and small taxpayers. Some of the largest qualified intermediaries are affiliated with title companies.

Private Qualified Intermediaries

Many qualified intermediary companies are stand-alone, privately-owned companies. Some are owned by a single individual; others are owned by several individuals. These companies can be as sophisticated as any of the large bank-affiliated or title company-affiliated qualified intermediaries but have private ownership. Some of these companies have very successful practices assisting large companies with very complicated exchanges or to process a significant volume of exchanges. Others focus more attention on facilitating smaller exchanges but will occasionally assist with very large exchanges. Although many such qualified intermediaries have a single office, many of them have a national clientele. For those with smaller volume, it is not unusual for exchange specialists to become familiar with their clients and provide the sense of very personal service.

Attorneys and CPAs as Qualified Intermediaries

Some attorneys and CPAs act as qualified intermediaries. Some have largely or entirely given up the practice of law or accounting and focus primarily on providing qualified intermediary services; others practice law or accounting and provide qualified intermediary services for roughly the same amount of time; others primarily practice law or accounting and provide qualified intermediary services on the side. The risk is that the attorney or CPA will be treated as the exchanger's agent and be disqualified from acting as qualified intermediary. If this is not the case, there is no reason why an attorney or CPA cannot provide excellent qualified intermediary services.

As with any qualified intermediary, an attorney or CPA should be familiar with section 1031 and be able to help ensure that all of the section 1031 requirements are satisfied on each exchange. Unless the person does a significant number of exchanges, however, the company's processes may not be as developed as other qualified intermediaries who facilitate hundreds (or even thousands) of exchanges each year. Furthermore, simply because someone is an attorney or CPA does not mean that the person is competent in section 1031. Thus, the attorney or CPA credential may not mean that the person is competent to assist with section 1031 exchanges.

An exchanger should never allow an individual to act as qualified intermediary, regardless of the person's credentials. An individual is subject to too much potential liability. An attorney or CPA could run into individual financial difficulty or family problems that could tie up the accessibility of exchange proceeds. Thus, an attorney or CPA should be a qualified intermediary through a separate entity.

Friends as Qualified Intermediaries

Generally, asking an individual friend to serve as qualified intermediary is a bad idea. One can imagine a situation where a friend agrees to act as intermediary, the parties draft exchange documents (due to the complexity of such arrangements, such documents may not satisfy all of the section 1031 requirements, unless a section 1031 expert helps draft them), and the friend takes possession of the exchange proceeds. Thereafter, the friend is sued or divorced, and the exchanger's money is subject to the legal proceedings and not available to complete the exchange. That would destroy the possibility of the exchanger completing the exchange, not to mention the detrimental impact it would have on the relationship with the former friend. To avoid these possibilities, property owners would be wise to seek someone other than a friend with no exchange experience to act as qualified intermediary. Of course, professional qualified intermediaries and their employees have friends and business associates. Such qualified intermediaries should be capable of providing excellent exchange services.

The regulations disqualify most family members from serving as qualified intermediaries, so family members are never a good choice.

Exchange Accommodation Titleholders

Exchange accommodation titleholders facilitate reverse exchanges and improvements exchanges. Stated generally, in a reverse exchange, the exchanger acquires replacement property first and later transfers relinquished property (Chapter 6). Exchange accommodation titleholders take title to replacement property and hold it until the exchanger transfers the relinquished property or they take title to relinquished property and hold it until the exchanger finds a buyer. At that time, the exchanger acquires the replacement property.

Most qualified intermediary companies have affiliated entities that serve as exchange accommodation titleholders. As discussed in Chapter 6, the exchange accommodation titleholder should always be a legal entity separate from the qualified intermediary to help protect exchange proceeds and the qualified intermediary operation from potential liability that may arise with respect to property to which the exchange accommodation titleholder holds title. To provide further protection from liability, the exchange accommodation titleholder will form a separate legal entity each time it takes title to a piece of property. This tends to add complexity to reverse exchanges, and, consequently, they generally cost more than deferred exchanges.

Example of Typical Exchange Company

A typical exchange company is comprised of three entities: (1) a holding company, (2) a qualified intermediary, and (3) an exchange accommodation titleholder. The holding company generally is the sole owner of the qualified intermediary and of the exchange accommodation titleholder. The qualified intermediary facilitates indirect exchanges (Chapter 4) and deferred exchanges (Chapter 5). The exchange accommodation titleholder facilitates reverse exchanges (Chapter 6) and improvements exchanges (Chapter 7).

Typical Exchange Company

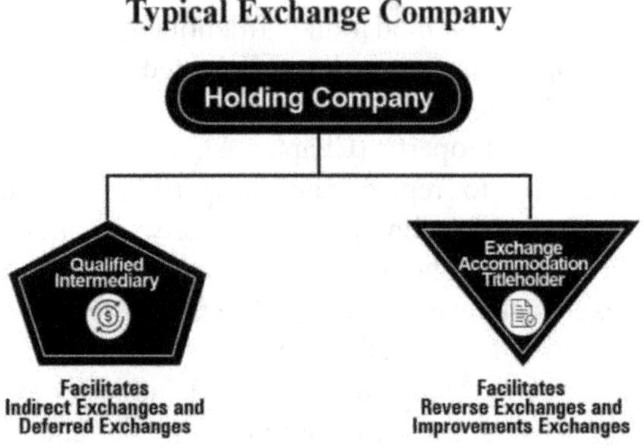

If the exchange company is affiliated with another company (a title company for example), the other company will likely be the sole owner of the holding company. As a policy matter, some companies do not act as exchange accommodation titleholder or they limit the type of property to which they take title. For example, a bank holding company may have an affiliated qualified intermediary that facilitates indirect exchanges and deferred exchanges. The bank holding company may, however, have a policy that neither it nor any of its affiliates take title to property for the purpose of facilitating exchanges. In such situations, the bank holding company's affiliated qualified intermediary will work with unrelated exchange accommodation titleholders to facilitate reverse exchanges.

DST AND TIC PROMOTERS AND DEALERS

DST (and formerly TIC) promoters and dealers are also a significant part of the section 1031 industry. This group of professionals offers and brokers Delaware statutory trust (DST) and tenancy-in-common (TIC) interests as section 1031 replacement property. As discussed in Chapter 10, DST and TIC interests provide owners with interests in real property. Such interests provide property owners the opportunity to sell a small piece of real property and acquire a fractional interest in larger, professionally managed property. Thus, a person may sell a small apartment complex and reinvest the proceeds in a fractional interest of a high-rise office building in a major metropolitan area. DST promoters help property owners by syndicating the acquisition of the larger piece of property and selling interests in it. Broker-dealers market DST interests through their registered representatives. Most DSTs are classified as securities under federal and state securities laws. Thus, most DST brokers should be licensed broker-dealers and the individuals selling the interests should be registered representatives. Syndicated DST interests are often acquired as replacement property. While investors can find both syndicated DST and TIC interests, the predominant form of syndicated replacement property is the DST, as of the writing of this book.

There is a growing number of developers and real estate fund sponsors who are willing to make accommodations for investors with section 1031 funds to allow them to join their real estate ventures. A typical accommodation is to allow section 1031 investors to join a venture by acquiring a TIC interest in the venture property. Such structures provide an opportunity for section 1031 investors to participate in real estate ventures. Managers of such ventures typically take a promote as a profit share. As discussed in Chapter 10, a TIC requires proportionate sharing of revenue and expenses, and a promote would be a disproportionate sharing of revenue and expenses and would most likely disqualify TIC interest from section 1031. Thus, section 1031 investors who are considering such investments should work carefully with a competent advisor to ensure that the acquired interest will qualify for section 1031 nonrecognition.

Chapter 3: Deciding Whether to Hold, Sell, or Exchange

Section 1031's allure is so powerful that some property owners are tempted to structure a property disposition as a section 1031 exchange without carefully considering whether it will provide a benefit. Before considering the section 1031 requirements, property owners should consider whether section 1031 would justify doing an exchange. This analysis requires property owners to compare the results that would obtain alternatively if the property owner were to hold the property, sell the property, or exchange the property. Many factors may impact the decision, but this discussion focuses mainly on the financial factors by comparing the effect each alternative may have on the property owner's net worth. Net worth is the amount by which the value of the property owner's property exceeds the property owner's liability.

Generally, a property owner will decide to hold property if the alternative use of the capital invested in the property will not provide the return the property owner is realizing by holding the property.

If the property owner decides to transfer property, however, the property owner then must decide whether to sell the property or exchange it as part of a transaction that qualifies for section 1031 nonrecognition. In making that decision, the property owner must compute the potential tax liability of selling the property and the costs of exchanging the property. If the potential tax liability is greater than the costs of exchanging, the property owner will most likely prefer to exchange the property. Otherwise, the property owner will sell the property and pay the tax. If the property owner realizes loss on the transfer of the property, section 1031 will prohibit the loss recognition if the transfer is part of a section 1031 exchange. Thus, a property owner will try to avoid doing an exchange if the transfer will otherwise result in a loss. Because of this, the following examples consider the decision assuming the property owner will realize gain.

COST OF SELLING: POTENTIAL TAX LIABILITY

Earl had been mulling the decision for weeks now, but could not make up his mind. Like most property owners, Earl knew that he would part with his property only if he could be convinced that the financial return was sufficient to justify the sale. Deciding whether to sell property is difficult when the property is returning a positive cash flow. Nonetheless, Earl had just received an offer on a medium-sized office building, the Quake Building that he had owned and leased for about four years. Before making a decision, Earl had to know how the transaction would affect his net worth.

Barney offered Earl $500,000 for the Quake Building. While Earl could think of many things that he could do with that amount of cash, he knew only a fraction of it would go to him. Before taking a penny out of the transaction, Earl would have to satisfy the $200,000 mortgage on the Quake Building. Additionally, Earl estimated that he would have closing costs of approximately $50,000. Thus, he anticipated having no more than $250,000 cash left after the sale. This would be a nice return on the initial $70,000 he paid to acquire the Quake Building plus the $20,000 he invested to improve the property. He remained uncertain, however, about how much tax, if any, he would owe on the sale. Earl had made up his mind that if he had to pay too much tax, he would not sell the property. Up to now, he had the following information on a notepad:

Estimated Before-Tax Return on Initial Investment

Estimated sale price	*$500,000*
Outstanding mortgage	*($200,000)*
Estimated closing costs	*($50,000)*
Estimated cash before tax	*$250,000*

Earl's investment	*$ 90,000*
Estimated return	*$160,000*

Earl knew that any tax he might owe on the sale would reduce this estimated return. Earl called his CPA, Claire, told her about the offer he had received and asked her for an estimate of how much tax he would owe if he sold the Quake Building. Earl told Claire that he had purchased the Quake Building for $280,000. To do so, he had borrowed $210,000 and invested $70,000 of his own money. At the time he bought the Quake Building, Earl also paid an additional $20,000 to improve the property. Over the seven years he owned the Quake Building, Earl was able to deduct $45,000 of depreciation. This information, along with the information Earl provided about the sale price, helped Claire determine the amount of tax Earl would owe if he sold the Quake Building in a taxable sale. Claire told Earl that computing the amount of tax was a six-step process.

Step One: Determine Amount Realized

Claire said that the first step was to determine the "amount realized." She explained that this is a tax term that is defined in the Internal Revenue Code, but it generally is the amount in the sales contract minus closing costs. In this case, Barney offered to buy the Quake Building for $500,000, so that would be the amount in the sales contract, and closing costs would be $50,000. Thus, subtracting $50,000 from $500,000, Claire estimated an amount realized of $450,000.

Amount Realized

Amount realized = contract price – closing costs
OR
$450,000 = $500,000 - $50,000

This came as quite a surprise to Earl. He asked, "How can my amount realized be $450,000? According to my estimates, I will walk away with no more than $250,000 in this transaction, but you are telling me that I will have an amount realized of $450,000. Didn't you forget to subtract the amount of debt that I have to repay on the sale?"

"I know that seems intuitive," she said, "but there is a well-established rule in income tax law providing that the amount realized includes not only cash received, but also the amount of liability from which you are relieved on the sale. In your case, you will receive $250,000 cash and be relieved of $200,000 of liability."

"Are you telling me that when I receive cash and pay off the liability on the sale of the property, I am treated as receiving all of the sale proceeds and paying down the outstanding balance of the liability?" Earl asked, "Why is that?"

Claire replied, "When you purchased the Quake Building, you borrowed $210,000 to help finance the acquisition. You added that amount to your cost of the building and the depreciation deductions you took were based upon that amount. You were not required to include the $210,000 in income when you borrowed it. Thus, when you sell the Quake Building, tax law treats you as selling for cash equal to the total $500,000 contract price and then using $200,000 to pay off the liability."

"So I'm treated as selling the property for $500,000 of cash, even though I don't get to keep $200,000 of it?" Earl asked.

"That's right," Claire said. "But you do subtract the $50,000 of closing costs from that amount, so your amount realized is $450,000."

Step Two: Compute Adjusted Tax Basis

After determining the amount realized, Claire then determined the Quake Building's "adjusted tax basis." She did this by identifying the original $280,000 purchase price, adding the $20,000 spent by Earl to improve the property, and subtracting the $45,000 of depreciation deductions. Thus, Claire informed Earl that he had a $255,000 adjusted tax basis.

Earl was now a little bit confused. "Slow down, Claire, I need to make sure I understand this." Earl then put the following numbers on his pad of legal paper:

Adjusted Tax Basis

Original purchase price	*$280,000*
Plus improvements	*$20,000*
Minus depreciation	*($45,000)*
Adjusted tax basis	*$255,000*

"Did I do that right?" Earl asked Claire.

"Your numbers match mine," replied Claire.

Earl considered his numbers for a minute or two and then asked Claire, "Now that I have the amount realized and adjusted tax basis, what do I do with these numbers?"

"Let's move to the next step and determine the amount of gain you will realize," Claire said.

Step Three: Compute Gain Realized

Claire told Earl that computing the amount of gain realized is a fairly simple step. To compute gain realized, simply subtract the adjusted tax basis from the amount realized.

Claire told Earl, "Since we already know both the amount realized and adjusted tax basis, computing the gain realized is relatively easy. We simply subtract the $255,000 adjusted tax basis from the $450,000 amount realized. This gives us $195,000 of gain realized."

While Claire was saying this, Earl wrote the following amounts on his notepad:

Gain Realized

Amount realized	*$450,000*
Minus adjusted tax basis	*($255,000)*
Gain realized	*$195,000*

Step Four: Determine Gain Recognized

"What do we do with the gain realized?" Earl asked. "Do we use that to compute the potential tax?"

"Not necessarily," Claire said. "Tax is imposed on gain recognized, not gain realized."

"What is the difference between gain realized and gain recognized?" Earl asked.

"Gain realized is the economic gain, and gain recognized is the amount of gain you report on your tax return," Claire said. "Generally, gain realized becomes gain recognized, but some exceptions apply. For example, if you transfer the Quake Building as part of a section 1031, you will have gain realized of $195,000, but you may have no gain recognized."

"If I have no gain recognized, I wouldn't report gain on my tax return, so I wouldn't owe any tax on a section 1031 exchange. Is that right?" Earl asked.

"That is correct," Claire said. "That is the difference between the tax consequences of selling and the tax consequences of doing a section 1031 exchange."

"So, if I sell for cash, I'll have $195,000 of gain realized and that amount of gain recognized?" Earl asked.

"Yes. If you sell for cash, you will have $195,000 of gain recognized and use that amount to compute your potential tax liability."

Step Five: Determine the Appropriate Tax Rate

"Claire, I think I understand how you calculated gain realized and, I know that I report gain recognized on my tax return. What rate do we use to compute the tax liability?"

Claire said, "Because we are considering an income tax, we compute the amount of tax you will owe by multiplying your gain recognized by your tax rate."

"That sounds simple enough. What's my tax rate?"

"Your tax rate depends on several factors," Claire replied.

"There is never an easy answer with tax, is there?"

"The more you work with this type of transaction, the easier the answers are to come by," said Claire. "In your case, you are selling property you leased to business owners. You also held the property for more than twelve months. Therefore, any gain you recognized should be subject to no more than 20 percent of federal tax, with an exception."

"20 percent? Are you kidding me?" Earl wanted to know. "That sounds awfully low."

"Currently, the long-term capital gain rate is 20 percent, and that is the general rate you will use to compute tax on the gain from selling the Quake Building. That rate fluctuates from time to time, but it is now 20 percent. Remember, however, that I said there is one important exception to consider. That important exception is unrecaptured section 1250 gain."

"Unrecaptured section 1250 gain? I have no idea what that means, but I would guess it isn't good."

Claire explained, "Unrecaptured section 1250 gain is the amount of gain recognized from the sale of certain real property that is attributable to depreciation. Currently, that amount is taxed at 25 percent. In your situation, you took $45,000 of depreciation, so that amount would be taxed at 25 percent. The remaining amount of gain recognized would be taxed at 20 percent."

Determining Tax Rates

This example limits the discussion to federal capital gain rates for simplicity. Property owners must also account for any state or local taxes imposed on gains and other federal taxes. In some locations, the combined tax rate on capital gains can approach 40%.

Step Six: Compute Tax Liability

"We can apply these rates to the appropriate gain recognized and come up with the following potential tax liability," Claire said.

Potential Tax Liability		
Section 1250 gain	*$45,000 x 25% =*	*$11,250*
Remaining gain	*$150,000 x 20% =*	*$30,000*
Total potential tax		*$41,250*

Thus, on the sale of the $500,000 piece of property, Earl would have to pay $41,250 of tax.

Effect on Net Worth and Investment Return

Earl considered how that $41,250 would affect his ability to purchase other property. If Earl kept the Quake Building, his net worth attributed to the property would be $300,000 (the property's $500,000 value minus the $200,000 liability). If he sold the property and paid the tax, instead of having $300,000, he would have only $208,750 ($300,000 net value of the Quake Building minus both the $50,000 paid in closing costs and $41,250 paid in tax). Thus, the taxable sale of the property would reduce his net worth by the amount of closing costs and income taxes.

Estimated After-Tax Return		
Net Worth before Taxable Sale		
Value of Quake Building		*$500,000*
Liability		*($200,000)*
Net worth		*$300,000*
Net Worth after Taxable Sale		
Cash proceeds		*$300,000*
Closing costs	*($50,000)*	
Potential tax liability	*($41,250)*	
Total costs		*($91,250)*
After-tax net worth		*$208,750*

Earl's investment	*$90,000*
Estimated after-tax return	*$118,750*

"That is a significant difference," Earl said. "If it wasn't for the tax liability, I would sell the Quake Building for sure. I think the offer is above market, and I am ready to look for a new investment. There is property in other parts of the town that I think are undervalued. I would like to consider some of those properties. The tax hit will set me back several years, however."

"Not only that," Earl continued, "the tax also reduces my investment return. Instead of getting $250,000 for the $90,000 I invested seven years ago, I would only get $208,750. That reduces my IRR from about 14 percent to about 11 percent. I can't live with that."

"Because you want to use the proceeds from the sale of the Quake Building to acquire other like-kind property, perhaps you should consider a section 1031 exchange," Claire suggested. "If you do a section 1031 exchange, you can avoid paying the $41,250 in tax."

"It sounds like that would leave me with the $250,000 to reinvest," Earl said.

"You will definitely save in taxes if you do a section 1031 exchange," Claire said. "You will, however, have section 1031 transaction costs. We need to consider what those will be and compare them to the potential tax liability and to your staying invested in the Quake Building. After that, you can make a decision."

Costs of Exchanging

In deciding whether to do a section 1031 exchange, a property owner must consider both the transactional and non-financial costs of exchanging. The non-financial costs include the costs of satisfying the section 1031 requirements.

Section 1031 Requirements

Section 1031 has five basic requirements: (1) the holding and use requirement, (2) the real-property requirement, (3) the like-kind property requirement, (4) the exchange requirement, and (5) the qualified asset requirement. If a property owner has to significantly alter a transaction to satisfy these requirements, the property owner must determine whether such alteration is more costly than selling the property and paying the taxes. If a property owner would otherwise enter into a transaction that satisfies the section 1031 requirements and the amount of potential gain is sufficient to justify the transaction costs, the property owner should seriously consider doing a section 1031 exchange.

Section 1031 Requirements

Section 1031 has five basic requirements: (1) the holding and use requirement, (2) the real-property requirement, (3) the like-kind property requirement, (4) the exchange requirement, and (5) the qualified asset requirement.

The Holding and Use Requirement

Section 1031 requires that an exchanger hold relinquished property for productive use in a trade or business or for investment. It also requires that the exchanger acquire replacement property to be held for productive use in a trade or business or for investment. An exchanger may satisfy this requirement by exchanging business-use property for investment property, and vice versa. The holding and use requirement is actually two requirements: (1) the holding requirement and (2) the use requirement.

The holding requirement focuses on whether the exchanger is the owner of property for federal tax purposes. Ownership for federal tax purposes may not mirror ownership for state law purposes. For example, state law may look at who holds title to property, but federal tax law may consider legal title along with several other factors. Thus, an exchanger may not be deemed to hold property for tax purposes even though the exchanger holds legal title to property. This was the outcome of a case in which a partnership transferred legal title of property to a partner. After the transfer of legal title, the partner and partnership continued to treat the partnership as owner of the property for accounting and tax purposes, and the partnership negotiated the disposition of the property. Thus, the partnership was the owner for federal tax purposes, even though the partner held legal title to the property. Because the partnership was the owner of the property for federal tax purposes, the partner did not satisfy the holding requirement and could not do a section 1031 exchange with the property.

The use requirement focuses on whether the exchanger held relinquished property for productive use in a trade or business or for investment and acquires replacement property for productive use in a trade or business or for investment. This requirement excludes from section 1031 nonrecognition property that is held for resale. For example, a property dealer's inventory is held for resale, not held for productive use in a trade or business or for investment (Chapter 12 discusses dealer property). The requirement also excludes personal-use property such as principal residences and vacation homes.

The holding and use requirement generally excludes from section 1031 nonrecognition property that an exchanger acquires with the intent to transfer. For example, if an exchanger acquires replacement property with the intent to transfer it to a family member as a gift or to a charity, the replacement property will not qualify for section 1031 nonrecognition. The use requirement becomes important when considering a proximate business restructuring (Chapter 8) because the exchanger (an entity) may exchange property and immediately distribute the replacement property, or a member of an entity may receive property from the entity and immediately exchange it. Both types of transactions raise questions about whether the exchanger held, or intends to hold, exchange property for productive use in a trade or business or for investment.

Earl appears to satisfy the holding and use requirement with respect to the Quake Building. He owns the property, leases it, and manages it. This comes within the definition of holding property for productive use in a trade or business. If he acquires replacement property to hold for productive use in a trade or business or for investment, he will satisfy the holding and use requirement.

The holding and use requirement applies at the time of the relevant transfer. Thus, if Earl acquires property with the intent to hold it for investment and later changes his holding purpose (*e.g.*, converts the replacement property to personal use), the exchange should still satisfy the holding and use requirement. In fact, section 1031 does not impose a holding period requirement; it applies based on the exchanger's intent at the time of the relevant exchange. Although an immediate transfer of the property following an exchange may indicate intent to transfer the property at the time of the exchange, intervening events may demonstrate a change of intent following the exchange.

The holding and use requirement could become a non-financial cost to Earl if he plans to use the proceeds from the sale of the Quake Building to acquire personal use property or dealer property. He will incur a non-financial cost if he adjusts his intent merely to come within section 1031. Changing his intent to come within section 1031 may not be worth the tax savings that section 1031 will provide. Earl would have to weigh these considerations before deciding whether to exchange.

Real-Property Requirement

Following the Tax Cuts and Jobs Act of 2017, section 1031 only applies to real property. Section 1031 does not provide a definition of real property to establish its scope. It should, however, apply to land and fixtures. It should also apply to other real property interests that qualified for section 1031 treatment prior to the 2017 Act, such as air rights, development rights, certain oil and gas rights, and other such partial interests in real property. When dealing with partial interests in real property, exchangers should consult their advisors to ensure that there is support for treating such interest as real property and like-kind to the other exchange property.

Regulations define real property for section 1031 purposes as (1) land and improvements to land, (2) unsevered natural resources, and (3) water and air space superjacent to land. Additionally, the regulations provide that real property under state and local law is real property for section 1031 purposes. Property also comes within the section 1031 definition of real property if it is specifically listed in the regulations or determined to be real property under one of the multiple-factor tests in the regulations.

Improvements to land include inherently permanent structures such as a building or other structure that is permanently affixed to real property and will remain affixed for an indefinite period of time. Structural components of inherently permanent structures are also real property. Structural components include assets such as walls, partitions, plumbing systems, HVAC systems, elevators and escalators, and similar property. The regulations list factors, including the following, that help determine whether property is an inherently permanent structure or structural component: (1) the manner, time, and expense of installing and removing the item; (2) whether the item is designed to be moved; and (3) the damage that removing the item would cause the item or structure of which it is a part.

Intangible assets such as fee ownership, co-ownership, leaseholds, options to acquire real property, and easements can also come within the section 1031 definition of real property. Other intangible property that derives its value from real property or an interest in real property and is inseparable from that real property or interest in real property also comes within the section 1031 definition of real property.

Property that comes within the section 1031 definition of real property must also be like-kind to the other exchange property to qualify for section 1031 treatment.

Like-Kind Property Requirement

To qualify for section 1031 nonrecognition, an exchanger must acquire property that is like-kind to the relinquished property. The section 1031 definition of like-kind property considers a property's nature or character, not its grade or quality. Real property and personal property are of a different nature or character and therefore are not like-kind. Similarly, intangible property is not of the same nature or character as real property, so the other types of property are not like-kind to real property. To be like-kind, therefore, properties must be the same type, i.e., real property can only be like-kind to other real property.

Real Property, Personal Property, and Intangible Property

Real property

Real property is tangible and immovable and provides the holder of the property rights in the property that run into perpetuity, or for several years at a minimum (generally at least thirty years for section 1031 purposes). Real property includes land, buildings attached to the land, and partial interests in such property, such as a lease, a life estate, and certain mineral interest.

Tangible personal property

Tangible personal property is property that a person can touch and that is movable. Personal property includes such things as equipment, automobiles, computers, machinery, rolling stock, artwork, and collectibles.

Intangible property

Intangible property is property that a person cannot touch but that grants rights to the holder of the property. Intangible property includes such things as copyrights, patents, stock, and trademarks. Some intangible property is evidenced in tangible property. For example, stock may be evidenced by a stock certificate. The property in such a case is not, however, the piece of paper that can be touched; the property is the intangible rights that stock ownership confers on the stockholder.

As a general rule, all real property is like-kind. The Quake Building is real property, so almost any other kind of real property would be like-kind. Obvious types of like-kind real property include raw land, a warehouse, an apartment complex, and a hotel. Earl would satisfy the like-kind property requirement by exchanging into any such properties. Certain less obvious real property interests are also like-kind to the Quake Building. For example, a leasehold of thirty years or more in real property is treated as real property. Therefore, Earl could acquire a thirty-one-year leasehold in an office building and satisfy the like-kind property requirement. Other interests, such as certain conservation easements and certain water rights may also be like-kind to the Quake Building. Several rulings indicate that such interests, if perpetual, are like-kind to other real property. Perhaps such interests, if longer than thirty years, would also be like-kind. Certain mineral interests, such as oil and gas leases and royalties, may also be like-kind to the Quake Building. Because the specific rights granted by particular interests may vary from property to property, an exchanger should always seek professional advice when deciding whether to do an exchange involving such property.

Section 1031 specifically provides that U.S. property and foreign property are not like-kind. Apparently, the basis for this rule is the difference between depreciation rules that apply to foreign property and the depreciation rules that apply to U.S. property. Thus, exchangers who own U.S. property must swap for U.S. property and exchangers who own foreign property must swap for foreign property to qualify for section 1031 nonrecognition. The status of real property is determined based on its location; real property located in the United States and its territories is U.S. property, all other real property is foreign property.

The Qualified Asset Requirement

Section 1031 specifically excludes from nonrecognition exchanges of real property held primarily for sale (Chapter 12). The section 1031 regulations defining real property also exclude bonds, notes, and most stock; other securities or evidences of indebtedness or interest; interests in a partnership; certificates of trust or beneficial interests; and choses in action. An exchange of such properties will not qualify for section 1031 nonrecognition. Therefore, an exchanger may neither transfer nor acquire such property as part of a section 1031 exchange.

Boot

If Earl does not reinvest all of the Quake Building sale proceeds in like-kind property, any money or non-like-kind property he receives will trigger recognition. Any money or property Earl receives that is not like-kind to the property transferred will be boot. Liability from which Earl is relieved may also be boot. Consider a possible discussion between Earl and Claire, his CPA, regarding boot and how it can trigger gain recognition.

Boot

Boot is any consideration an exchanger receives as part of an exchange that is not like-kind to the relinquished property. Boot includes money, liability relief, services, and property that is not like-kind to the relinquished property.

Receipt of Cash or Non-Like-Kind Property

"Earl, another thing you have to understand in deciding whether you want to do a section 1031 exchange is that you will recognize gain if you receive any money or property that is not like-kind to the Quake Building."

"So you're telling me if I receive $25,000 of cash at closing on the sale of the Quake Building I will recognize gain?" asked Earl. "How much gain will I recognize?"

Claire stated, "The section 1031 boot rules provide that you will recognize one dollar of gain for each dollar of boot you receive up to the amount of gain realized. Since you will have $195,000 of gain realized, the $25,000 of boot would trigger $25,000 of gain recognition."

Earl thought about this. He was somewhat bewildered. Claire had just explained the concept of basis and that when a property owner sells a piece of property in a taxable transaction, gain realized equals amount realized minus the property's adjusted tax basis. Earl had just learned, however, that under section 1031 every dollar of boot triggers gain recognition up to the amount of gain realized.

"What if I receive boot in excess of the $195,000 of gain realized? For example, what if I receive $200,000 of boot?" Earl asked.

"Section 1031 cannot require you to recognize more gain than you realize. Therefore, if you receive $200,000 of boot and have $195,000 of gain realized, you will only recognize $195,000 of gain. In other words, section 1031 requires you to recognize gain equal to the lesser of the gain realized and the boot received," Claire explained.

"That makes sense," Earl said, "but I would have thought that I could recover some basis for each dollar of boot I receive."

"That may make sense," Claire said, "but the rule clearly requires a dollar of gain recognition for each dollar of boot you receive, up to your gain realized."

Liability Relief

"In fact," Claire explained, "for you to defer all of the gain on the disposition of the Quake Building, you have to acquire like-kind replacement property worth at least $450,000—your amount realized."

"You seemed to imply that earlier when you told me that I have to include the $200,000 Quake Building liability in my amount realized. I don't understand why I can't simply replace the $250,000 of equity in the property. That is all the property is worth to me," Earl said.

"That does seem intuitive to property owners who think in terms of cash invested and return on the investment, but section 1031 treats liability relief as money received. Thus, if you had $450,000 amount realized and reinvested $250,000 (the net cash after paying for closing costs and repaying the Quake Building liability), tax law would treat you as having received $200,000 of cash, the amount of liability relief. Recall that tax law generally treats you as receiving the $200,000 and using it to pay down the debt. Section 1031 does the same thing.

"Another way to think about this," Claire continued, "is that you are selling the Quake Building for cash and someone is assuming your liability. Thus, you have liability relief, which is part of what you receive in exchange for your property. Liability relief is not like-kind to the Quake Building. Because liability relief is not like-kind to the Quake Building, debt relief would be a form of boot. We call that liability-relief boot."

Liability Relief

Liability relief is any reduction in the exchanger's liability as a result of an exchange. Thus, liability relief occurs if the purchaser assumes the exchanger's liability, the purchaser pays down a mortgage on the relinquished property, or the purchaser takes the relinquished property subject to a liability. This may become liability-relief boot if the exchanger does not offset it by assuming liability on the acquisition of the replacement property or by investing additional money in the replacement property.

Claire continued, "To avoid liability-relief boot (or any other form of boot for that matter), you must acquire replacement property that is worth at least as much as the relinquished property."

"Does that mean that if I acquire replacement property worth $450,000 that I will have to borrow $200,000 to acquire it?" Earl asked.

"Not necessarily. We are talking now about liability-relief boot," Claire stated. "You already know the first rule: liability relief is treated as boot. Three other rules are important.

"First, liability assumed offsets liability relief. Therefore, if you acquire a piece of property subject to $200,000 of liability, you are treated as assuming $200,000 of liability. Because this liability you assume offsets your liability relief, you will have no liability-relief boot. You can satisfy this rule by acquiring replacement property worth at least $450,000 and subject to a $200,000 liability."

"Does that mean that I have to find replacement property that is already subject to a $200,000 liability? That might be very difficult," Earl worried.

Liability Assumed

An exchanger assumes liability by either borrowing to acquire the replacement property, taking property subject to a liability, or assuming the seller's liability.

Claire responded, "You will be treated as assuming liability if you borrow to purchase the replacement property. You might find replacement property worth $450,000, use $250,000 of exchange proceeds and borrow $200,000 from a bank. By doing this, you will be treated as assuming $200,000 of liability, and you will avoid liability-relief boot.

"The second rule provides that any cash you invest, in addition to the exchange proceeds, will offset liability relief. Therefore, if you acquire replacement property worth at least $450,000 using the $250,000 of exchange proceeds and an extra $200,000 of your own money, you will not have liability-relief boot.

"These first two rules simply support what I said earlier— if you acquire replacement property worth at least as much as your amount realized, you will not have liability-relief boot."

Liability-Relief Boot Offset Rules

To avoid gain recognition under section 1031, an exchanger must acquire replacement property with a value equal to or greater than the amount realized on the disposition of the relinquished property. To do this, the exchanger must offset liability relief on the disposition of the relinquished property with liability assumed on the acquisition of the replacement property or with out-of-pocket money added to the exchange proceeds.

Claire continued, "The third rule simply provides that debt assumed does not affect cash received. If you receive cash in an exchange, you will have boot, even if your liabilities increase as part of the exchange. This rule is more complicated than the other rules. To be safe, you should be certain any cash you receive at closing is loan proceeds, not exchange proceeds. For example, if you were to borrow $300,000 to acquire the replacement property and receive $100,000 at closing, you need to be able to show the cash you received came from the loan and all exchange proceeds went to acquire replacement property."

"It sounds like there is some risk that cash received at closing could be treated as boot. To minimize that risk, I guess I must reinvest all $250,000 of the equity from Quake Building." Earl wondered aloud, "What if I later want to borrow against the replacement property—you know, take advantage of the equity in the property?"

Claire replied, "Generally, borrowing is not a taxable transaction. Therefore, if you borrow against replacement property after the exchange, the borrowing should not be a taxable event, even if the borrowing dips into the equity of the property."

"How long do I have to wait to borrow against replacement property?" Earl asked.

"If the borrowing is a transaction separate from the exchange, you could borrow against the replacement property immediately following the exchange," Claire said. "To make sure the borrowing is separate from the exchange, however, you will need separate loan documents. This means that you can't merely tell your lender to lend you enough to acquire the replacement property and then advance more after the exchange closes. The loan to acquire the replacement property must be separate from the loan to borrow against the equity of the replacement property."

Claire summarized these rules: "First, liability relief will be treated as cash received and thus could trigger gain recognition. Second, to avoid liability-relief boot, acquire replacement property worth as much as the amount realized on the disposition of the relinquished property. Third, cash received at closing may be treated as boot. Be certain that if you receive cash at closing you clearly identify it as loan proceeds and ensure that you have reinvested all of your exchange proceeds in the replacement property. To avoid this issue, borrow against the equity in replacement property after the exchange in a separate transaction."

FINANCIAL COSTS

Gain Deferral—Not Gain Exclusion

Another financial cost of section 1031 is gain deferral. The section 1031 basis rules preserve unrecognized gain, which an exchanger may recognize on a subsequent transfer. Those rules also limit depreciation available on the replacement property.

"Earl," Claire said, "in making the decision whether to sell the Quake Building or exchange it, you have to understand that section 1031 does not exclude the gain forever—it merely defers it."

"Are you saying that if I don't pay the tax now, I will have to pay it later anyway?" Earl asked. "If so, why bother doing a section 1031 exchange?"

Claire explained, "Deferring tax generally provides financial benefits to you. Between the time of the exchange and the time you subsequently sell the replacement property in a taxable transaction, you can reinvest the tax savings. By putting the tax savings to work you benefit from that amount. Thus, gain deferral is a good thing.

"The cost of gain deferral is that you take a lower basis in replacement property than you would take if you used exchange proceeds to acquire replacement property by purchase," Claire continued. "Also, the benefit of gain deferred depends upon how long you will hold the replacement property. The longer you hold it, the more value gain deferral provides. In fact, if you hold the replacement property until you die, the person who inherits the property would take a basis equal to the fair market value in the property at the time of your death under our current estate tax laws. Thus, the gain would disappear at the time of your death."

Assessing the Benefits of Tax Deferral

A sophisticated analysis of the benefits of a section 1031 exchange requires the property owner to determine any depreciation that will be lost on the replacement property and how long until the replacement property will be disposed of in a taxable transaction. The property owner should compare the future tax benefit lost because of lower depreciation and the present value of the future taxable gain to the current tax savings minus the transaction costs. Because real property is depreciated over a long period of time, depreciation savings are generally minimal. Thus, with real property, if a property owner intends to hold the replacement property for more than a few years, a section 1031 exchange generally is advisable if the deferred gain is somewhat greater than the transaction costs.

"What are the section 1031 basis rules and what do you mean when you say depreciation deductions for the replacement property will be lower if I do a section 1031 exchange?" Earl asked.

Exchanged Basis

Claire explained, "Section 1031 has a special mechanism for deferring gain: exchanged basis. The result of exchanged basis is that your section 1031 replacement property will take the same adjusted tax basis that you have in the Quake Building. Since you have an adjusted tax basis of $255,000 in the Quake Building, you will take that basis in the replacement property if you do a section 1031 exchange. That basis is the exchanged basis."

Continuing, Claire said, "The exchanged basis defers gain because if you later sell the replacement property in a taxable transaction, you will recognize the gain at that time. For example, assume you exchange the Quake Building for like-kind property worth $450,000. You would take a $255,000 adjusted tax basis in that replacement property. If the replacement property increases in value by $100,000 and you sell it one year later for $550,000 (assume the property was raw land and not subject to depreciation), you would recognize $295,000 of gain ($550,000 amount realized minus $255,000 adjusted tax basis). This would include the $195,000 of gain deferred on the section 1031 exchange and the additional $100,000 of appreciation realized while you held the replacement property. Thus, section 1031 merely defers gain by carrying the adjusted tax basis of relinquished property over to the replacement property."

If Earl plans to hold the replacement property for a short period of time and then dispose of it in a taxable transaction, the current tax savings may not justify his structuring the sale of the Quake Building as a section 1031 exchange. As a general rule, gain deferral is very attractive to taxpayers. The use of money that would otherwise be used to pay taxes is like an interest-free loan from the government. A taxpayer would hesitate to enter into a transaction that defers gain if the gain would be deferred for a short period of time and the transaction cost of deferring the gain exceeds the tax benefit to be gained from deferral.

Adjustments to Exchanged Basis

The amount of gain deferred depends upon the exchanged basis. As stated above, section 1031 provides that the exchanger's basis in replacement property is the exchanged basis. It also provides that the exchanger must adjust this basis for certain items. Earl did not have any of these items, but they arise in many exchanges. The rules provide that an exchanger must increase a property's exchanged basis by the amount of any gain the exchanger recognizes on the transaction. The exchanger must reduce the exchanged basis by the amount of any boot received and by the amount of any loss recognized. Although section 1031 provides that an exchanger may not recognize loss on a section 1031 exchange, the exchanger may recognize loss if the exchanger transfers non-like-kind property. For example, if Earl had transferred the Quake Building and a truck in exchange for raw land, Earl could recognize loss on the transfer of the truck, if its fair market value was less than Earl's adjusted tax basis in it.

To illustrate the adjustments to exchanged basis, assume that Earl transfers the Quake Building in exchange for Raw Land worth $400,000 subject to $100,000 of liability. Because Earl does not offset the full $200,000 of liability relief with liability assumed, he will have $100,000 of boot. This is less than his realized gain of $182,000, so he must recognize $100,000 of gain. In determining his basis in Raw Land,

Earl would begin with the exchanged basis of $255,000, increase that amount by $100,000 of gain recognized, and decrease it by the $100,000 of boot received in the form of the liability relief. Therefore, Earl's basis in Raw Land would be $255,000 exchanged basis.

Basis in Replacement Property

Basis in Quake Building	*$255,000*
Gain recognized	*$100,000*
Loss recognized	*$ - 0 -*
Boot received	*($100,000)*
Basis in Raw Land	*$255,000*

Transaction Costs of Structuring an Exchange

In deciding whether to do a section 1031 exchange, an exchanger must consider the transaction costs in structuring an exchange. In addition to the traditional closing costs of disposing of the relinquished property and the acquisition of the replacement property, the exchanger will generally have to pay an exchange facilitator (qualified intermediary and perhaps exchange accommodation titleholder) and tax advisor on an exchange. For a routine deferred exchange, the exchanger will generally have to hire a qualified intermediary. Most professional qualified intermediaries charge a flat fee for facilitating deferred exchanges. That fee will generally be in the low to mid four figures (e.g., $2,000), regardless of the size of the transaction. In addition, the qualified intermediary will generally earn some interest on exchange proceeds it holds. Qualified intermediaries could provide consulting services in addition to acting as qualified intermediary. Such qualified intermediaries may charge more than the typical flat fee to cover the consulting costs.

Exchange accommodation titleholders charge more for facilitating reverse exchanges and improvements exchanges. Such fees may run anywhere from a few thousand dollars to tens of thousands of dollars depending on the size of the transaction and the transaction's complexity. Such transactions may become extremely complicated and costly. Thus, exchangers doing smaller transactions may not be able to justify the costs required to do one of these more complicated exchanges.

Often, an exchanger will wish to employ an attorney or a CPA to provide advice with respect to an exchange. Fees paid to either an attorney or a CPA will vary depending on the party's expertise, the complexity of the transaction, and the advisor's involvement. An attorney or CPA may charge a few thousand dollars to assist with a routine exchange. If the exchange structure is complicated or the transaction is large, the advisors' fees may run into the hundreds of thousands of dollars.

An exchanger should not base a decision to exchange upon the absolute dollars of transaction costs. Exchangers should instead be concerned about the comparative amount of the transaction costs. If the transaction costs are considerably less than the tax to be deferred, then the exchanger may decide to do the exchange. If the tax to be deferred is less than the transaction costs or only slightly greater, the exchanger will likely decide not to do an exchange. As stated above, the exchanger must also consider how long it will hold the replacement property to determine the tax benefit the exchange provides.

Tax Risk

"In your situation, the final thing you will have to consider is the tax risk of doing an exchange," Claire said. "Several factors will affect the tax risk of an exchange you might consider. For example, the type of replacement property you acquire, the exchange structure you choose, and the facilitator you hire may all affect the tax risk of the exchange."

"Tax risk doesn't sound like a positive thing to me," Earl said. "As you know, I won't do anything that breaks the law. I want to know what the law is and arrange my affairs within the law."

"I understand that, and I wouldn't be interested in working with you otherwise," Claire said. "The law specifically provides guidelines for planning transactions for which the law is unclear. Remember that although tax law is very extensive, it isn't comprehensive. There are many areas where the tax law hasn't developed. The law doesn't prohibit people from entering into transactions in such areas, but the tax outcome of such transactions will have varying levels of uncertainty, depending on several factors."

"Aren't there areas where the law is clear?" Earl asked. "Isn't section 1031 one of those areas?"

Relationship of Tax Risk to Probability of Prevailing

"Indeed, there are areas of the law that are clear and well established," Claire answered. "Section 1031 is a very large body of law. Parts of it are well established and clearly defined. Other parts are not fully developed."

Claire continued, "If the law is clear with respect to a certain issue related to an exchange, the tax outcome is fairly clear. For example, section 1031 clearly provides that replacement property must be like-kind to relinquished property. If replacement property is not like-kind, the tax outcome is certain— the transaction will not qualify for section 1031 nonrecognition.

"On the other hand, if you satisfy all of the requirements of section 1031, the transaction will qualify for section 1031 nonrecognition. The tax outcome in both of these situations is clear— nonrecognition if you satisfy the requirements, recognition if you do not."

"That covers the two extremes," Earl said. "Is there something in the middle?"

Claire answered, "Yes, the law doesn't clearly provide whether certain properties are like-kind. For example, many practitioners believe that a building attached to land is real property and like-kind to other real property. The IRS appears to take the position that a building is like-kind to other real property only if its title is transferred along with the legal title of the land on which it sits. There is no authority that directly addresses this issue. Thus, if you exchange the Quake Building, which includes the underlying land, and receive title to a building as replacement property without taking title to the underlying land, tax law does not definitively answer whether the Quake Building is like-kind to the replacement property. Because the law does not definitively answer whether the two properties are like-kind, whether that transaction would qualify for section 1031 nonrecognition is not certain."

"What exactly do you mean when you say that nonrecognition is not certain?" Earl asked.

"Certainty in this context, refers to the probability of prevailing on a particular issue if the issue were presented to a court and the court decided the case on the merits," Claire said. "For example, if your exchange does not satisfy the requirements of section 1031, it will not qualify for section 1031 nonrecognition. That is fairly certain. If you report the transaction as a section 1031 exchange, the probability of your prevailing in a court if that issue were litigated is extremely low. In fact, there is no chance that you would prevail on the merits. If you satisfy all of the requirements of section 1031, however, the probability of prevailing if you claim nonrecognition is high. The probability of prevailing is close to 100 percent if you rely upon the law and the probability of prevailing approaches 0 percent if you take a position contrary to the law."

"What does this have to do with tax risk?" Earl asked.

"Tax risk is a function of the probability of prevailing and the amount of tax and penalties you would owe if you didn't prevail," Claire said. "It would also consider the risk of more severe punishment in the case of tax fraud."

"So if I claim section 1031 nonrecognition on a return and my probability of prevailing is high because I satisfy all of the section 1031 requirements, then my tax risk would be low," Earl said.

"That's correct," Claire confirmed. "You should never owe tax with respect to that transaction. Thus, the tax risk of reporting it as a section 1031 exchange is low."

"I understand," Earl said. "If I claim section 1031 recognition when I do not satisfy the section 1031 requirements, I would lose if the reporting position were litigated. Then I would have to pay the tax, so the tax risk is high."

"Tax risk is very high if your probability of prevailing is low," Claire said. "In addition to having to pay the tax, you may have to pay penalties and could even get jail time."

"I definitely don't want that," Earl said, "but I do see that there is an indirect relation between probability of prevailing and tax risk."

Relationship of Probability of Prevailing to Tax Risk

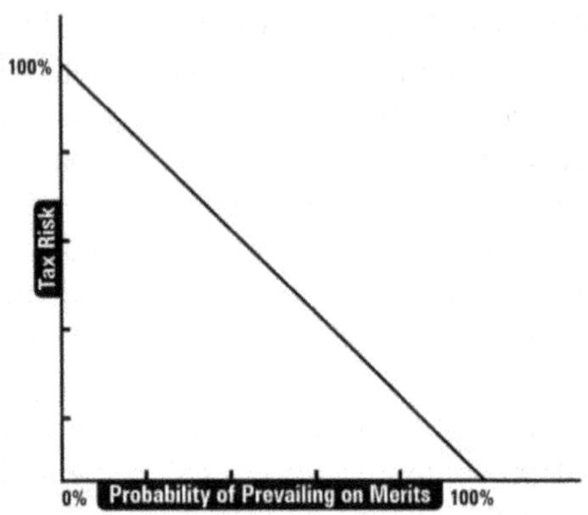

Tax Penalties

"It sounds like in my situation, the tax outcome won't be certain," Earl said. "How will I be able to make decisions in such a situation? For instance, if we are not certain whether a transaction will satisfy the section 1031 requirements, how do I decide whether to do the transaction and how to report it?"

Earl's question raises complicated issues. The answer to his question requires consideration of the tax penalty rules.

Claire told Earl, "If the law is uncertain, the important question is whether you may be subject to penalties for a position you take on a tax return. This requires examining the level of legal support you have for your position."

"What type of penalties are you talking about?" Earl asked.

"There are several potential penalties that the IRS may impose," Claire replied, "but one of the most significant is the substantial understatement penalty. Let's discuss the substantial understatement penalty to discover how the potential for tax penalties may affect your decision. If it applies, the IRS may impose a penalty equal to 20 percent of the tax that you should have paid."

"If my transaction doesn't qualify for section 1031 nonrecognition, I would owe $41,250 of tax, based on our earlier estimates," Earl said. "If the IRS can impose the accuracy related penalty, I would owe an additional 20 percent of that amount (or $8,250) in penalties? That's pretty steep."

"You're correct," Claire replied. "The penalty is a significant deterrent for most taxpayers. If you would have to pay that penalty, you wouldn't take the position on your return. You would be better off paying the taxes than claiming section 1031 nonrecognition."

"Does the substantial understatement penalty always apply if I am unsuccessful in defending a tax position I take on a return?" Earl asked.

"No. The IRS may challenge a position you take on your tax return and prevail in court. Thus, you would have to pay the taxes. Nonetheless, you may not be subject to the substantial understatement penalty," Claire explained. "The IRS may not try to impose the penalty, or the court may hold that you don't owe the penalty. If you don't owe the penalty, you would have to pay the tax plus interest."

"What rate of interest would I have to pay in such a situation? Is it usurious?" Earl asked.

"No, the interest rate reflects a market rate of interest—an amount similar to what you should get from a fairly conservative investment," Claire said.

"If I lose in court and just have to pay the taxes and interest on the taxes," Earl said, "it sounds like I would be better off taking the position on the return and then fighting the IRS if they challenged the position. Paying tax now or paying tax later with a market rate of interest should be the same from a financial perspective."

Earl continued, "Furthermore, if the probability of prevailing on the merits is reasonably high, I may never owe the taxes. Thus, I could pay the tax now for sure, or perhaps pay them later with interest. It sounds like if the IRS cannot impose a penalty, I am better off taking the position on the return that favors me. For instance, if I have an 85 percent chance of prevailing, I probably would never owe the tax. In the unlikely event that I do, I will only owe the tax plus interest."

"That's the thought process that you have to go through in assessing tax risk," Claire said. "You also must consider the potential cost of challenging the IRS. Before you get to court, you will work with the IRS at the administrative level to try to determine the appropriate treatment of the challenged item. That will most likely cost you something to hire an attorney or CPA to represent you before the IRS. You will incur more costs to litigate the issue, including non-economic costs such as any stress that may accompany the process. At any time during the process, you could settle with the IRS and pay the taxes they claim you owe plus the interest and avoid incurring more costs of challenging the IRS."

"That's a good point," Earl said. "It sounds like tax risk requires me to consider the possible outcome of an uncertain reporting position. If the reporting position may result in penalties, I don't want to take the position because I may have to pay tax plus the substantial understatement penalty, which is very significant."

"You will also have to pay interest," Claire said.

"At any rate, I don't want to take a position on a tax return if I may have to pay the substantial understatement penalty," Earl said. "If the reporting position won't result in my having to pay the substantial understatement penalty, I think I would take the position. If the IRS challenges it, I will then have to decide whether to incur costs to work the issue out with the IRS and possibly litigate the issue, or pay the tax plus penalties at that point."

"That sounds right," Claire said.

"How do I know if a reporting position may subject me to the substantial understatement penalties?" Earl asked.

"The probability of your prevailing on the merits of a reporting position should shield you from being subject to the substantial understatement penalty, if it is high enough," Claire said.

Probability of Prevailing on the Merits

Claire continued, "Tax law provides that the substantial understatement penalty does not apply if (1) a return position is supported by substantial authority or (2) if a transaction and the reporting position are disclosed and the taxpayer presents a reasonable basis for the position. Substantial authority and reasonable basis refer to the probability of prevailing on the merits in a court on a particular issue."

"Explain to me what you mean when you refer to prevailing on the merits in a court on a particular issue," Earl requested.

"Prevailing on the merits refers to a decision by the court based strictly on the substantive law," Claire said. "Thus, if you take the position that an exchange qualifies for section 1031 nonrecognition, and a court considers that position, it would decide the case based on the merits by examining the section 1031 requirements and the facts of the transaction. Its focus would be on whether the transaction satisfied the section 1031 requirements."

"That makes sense," Earl said. "Now will you explain what substantial authority means?"

"Substantial authority is a technical term that refers to the probability of prevailing on the merits," Claire said. "A position you take on a tax return is supported by substantial authority even if you have less than a 50 percent chance of prevailing on the merits. Nonetheless, the probability has to be greater than a reasonable basis. Thus, to have substantial authority, the probability of prevailing on an issue can be 50 percent or less, but it must be greater than a reasonable basis. If your probability of prevailing on an issue is around 50 percent, the IRS would not be able to impose the substantial understatement penalty."

"It sounds like a person has to know a lot of tax law to know if a position is supported by substantial authority. How will I know if substantial authority supports a position I take on a tax return?" Earl asked.

"You will have to discuss that with me or with your tax attorney," Claire said. "Assessing the probability of prevailing requires an objective judgment based on existing legal authorities regarding the particular issue."

"You said that I would not be subject to the substantial understatement penalty if positions I take on my tax return are supported by substantial authority, but what if a position is not supported by substantial authority?" Earl asked.

"If substantial authority doesn't support a position, you can disclose relevant facts affecting the tax consequences of the position and report it if there is a reasonable basis for the position," Claire said. "The rules do not clearly establish what a reasonable basis is in terms of percentages. Instead, the rules provide that reasonable basis is significantly greater than not frivolous or patently improper but not as great as substantial authority. A position would be frivolous or patently improper if the probability of prevailing is very low. To satisfy the reasonable basis standard, the position must also be more than merely arguable or merely colorable. In percentage terms, you may be looking at something around the 30-percent range. Thus, the position must be reasonably based on some legal authority, but the predicted outcome can be fairly uncertain."

Tax Probability Continuum

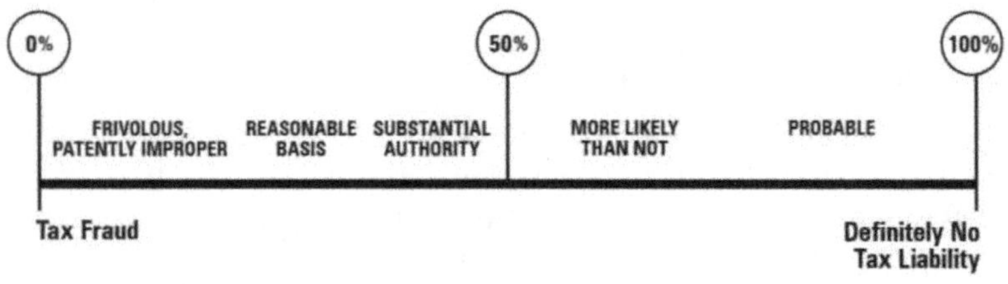

"It is interesting to know that the law doesn't provide clear answers for every question that may arise with respect to section 1031 exchanges," Earl said. "I am glad to know that a legal system that does not provide clear answers to specific questions provides leeway that does not severely punish people who make an honest effort to plan and report transactions within the law.

"What effects do IRS audit rates have on this decision?" Earl asked.

Audit Lottery Not Considered

"You are talking about what many people refer to as the 'audit lottery,' or your likelihood of being audited," Claire said. "The law specifically provides that you cannot consider your odds of being audited or the odds of the IRS raising an issue related to your reporting positions when considering whether a penalty could be imposed. Neither courts nor the IRS will consider the audit lottery when deciding whether to impose the substantial understatement penalty."

"Why is that?" Earl asked.

"The probability of being audited has nothing to do with the rule of law," Claire replied. "You should have a legal basis for any position you take on a tax return. Whether or not you will be audited does not affect the legal basis of a position you take on the return. Therefore, you shouldn't take the audit lottery into consideration when deciding whether to claim section 1031 nonrecognition on your tax return."

Loss Disallowed

Section 1031 disallows all loss realized on an exchange even if the exchanger receives boot. A property owner realizes loss on the disposition of property if the property owner's adjusted tax basis exceeds the property owner's amount realized. For example, if Earl had paid $600,000 for the property, and been allowed $95,000 of depreciation deductions, he would have had a $505,000 adjusted tax basis in the property. If he later sold it for an amount realized of $400,000, he would realize a $105,000 loss on the transaction. Section 1031 would prohibit him from recognizing that loss if he had disposed of the property as part of a section 1031 exchange. This is a very significant cost of exchanging property. Thus, taxpayers generally try to avoid coming within section 1031 if they can otherwise sell the property and recognize a loss.

Cost of Selling Compared to Cost of Exchanging

Having examined the costs of selling (i.e., the potential tax liability) and the financial and non-financial costs of exchanging, Earl must decide what to do. If Earl were to sell the Quake Building in a taxable transaction, his potential tax liability would be $41,250. If he wishes to acquire replacement property worth at least $450,000 in a routine safe harbor deferred exchange (Chapter 5), his exchange transaction costs should not exceed a few thousand dollars ($1,500 - $3,000 for qualified intermediary fees and some amount for attorney/CPA fees). If he also plans to hold the replacement property for several years, the tax savings on this transaction appear to be sufficiently greater than the transaction costs. If Earl plans to acquire other like-kind property and can satisfy all of the section 1031 requirements in a routine section 1031 exchange, the non-financial costs of exchanging are also fairly low. Assuming the transaction will probably satisfy the section 1031 requirements, the tax risk will also be low. Thus, the tax savings justify his structuring the disposition of the Quake Building as part of a section 1031 exchange.

If, on the other hand, Earl wishes to structure a more complicated exchange, such as a leasehold improvements exchange (Chapter 7), the transaction costs will likely be significant. For example, the fees, including the qualified intermediary fees, the exchange accommodation titleholder fees, and the attorney fees, could be $50,000, $75,000, or significantly more. Also, the law governing certain leasehold improvements exchanges is less developed than the law governing deferred exchanges. Therefore, the tax risk of an improvements exchange could also be higher. Because of the significant transaction costs and potential tax risk, leasehold improvements exchanges are generally only feasible if the potential tax liability is very significant. In Earl's case, his $41,250 of potential tax liability probably does not justify doing a leasehold improvements exchange.

This chapter demonstrates the benefits of doing section 1031 exchanges. The potential tax savings under section 1031 are significant. Nonetheless, exchangers must compare the potential tax savings to the costs of exchanging. If a section 1031 exchange is not too costly and does not disrupt the exchanger's business plans, it can provide a convenient way for a property owner to preserve investment net worth.

CHAPTER 4:
EXCHANGE STRUCTURES:
DIRECT AND INDIRECT EXCHANGES

Exchange structures are the lifeblood of section 1031. Without them, most property transactions would not qualify for section 1031 nonrecognition. The next few chapters discuss exchange structures, beginning with the simplest exchange structure and working up to the most complicated. To qualify for section 1031 nonrecognition, the transaction must be an exchange. Chapter 1, in discussing the history of section 1031, briefly discussed the exchange requirement. As stated in that chapter, an exchange is a reciprocal transfer of property for property. A transaction is not an exchange if the party actually or constructively receives cash as consideration for property. This does not preclude an exchanger from transferring property to one party and acquiring another property from a different party. As stated in Chapter 1, case law permits exchangers to structure multi-party, deferred, and reverse exchanges. If properly structured, each of such transactions will satisfy the exchange requirement. The chapters discussing exchange structures describe the various exchanges that may be structured to satisfy the exchange requirement. The focus in this chapter is on exchange structures generally; subsequent chapters address practical details such as the flow of money in an exchange.

DIRECT EXCHANGES

The direct exchange is the simplest exchange structure. Nonetheless, it is the least common exchange structure. The reason for the infrequent use of direct exchanges is simply that property owners who wish to do an exchange generally sell relinquished property to one party and acquire replacement property from another party. An example demonstrates how a direct exchange may be structured and reveals why such exchanges are infrequent. The examples going forward often include legal entities as parties to the exchange transaction. A basic understanding of legal entities is helpful to understanding exchange structures and property ownership.

Legal Entities

Legal entities often exchange property. In such situations, the legal entity may become the exchanger. The basic legal entities are: corporations, limited liability companies, and partnerships. Tax law recognizes two types of tax entities: (1) corporations and (2) partnerships. Legal entities come within one of these two types of tax entities.

Corporations

Business and property owners generally form corporations under state law by filing articles of incorporation within the state. The owners of a corporation are its shareholders. To put others on notice that the legal entity provides liability protection to its owners, state law generally requires the name of a corporation to include "Corp," "Inc," or "Co." Corporations are either C corporations or S corporations for tax purposes. Corporations do not have favorable tax treatment, so most property owners avoid using corporate legal entities whenever possible. Corporations prove especially problematic if the owners wish to divide and pursue different objectives as part of a disposition of property (Chapter 8).

Tax Partnerships

Two or more persons may form one of four types of partnerships: a general partnership, a limited partnership, a limited liability partnership, or a limited liability company. Each of these entities will generally be a partnership for federal tax purposes if it has at least two members.

The name of a general partnership may include only the names of the partners. State law generally requires the names of the other entities to include terms that identify them as entities that provide liability protection to some or all of the owners. States may vary on the exact terminology required, but the name of a limited partnership will often include "Ltd" or "LP," the name of a limited liability partnership will often include "LLP," the name of a limited liability company will often include "LLC."

A non-corporate entity (e.g., a limited liability company) that has a single member will generally be disregarded for federal tax purposes. Any such entity may, however, elect to be taxed as a corporation.

The shareholders of a corporation elect the corporation's board of directors. The board of directors appoints the corporation's officers, such as the CEO, president, vice presidents, secretary, and treasurer. The officers manage the corporation's day-to-day business. The members of a limited liability company may elect managers, who would be comparable to a corporation's board of directors, and the managers may elect officers. Alternatively, the members may manage the limited liability company directly, or the managers may manage the limited liability company directly, without appointing officers. General partners manage limited partnerships. The members of general partnerships and limited liability partnerships manage such entities. Legal entities make decisions through their governing bodies. Thus, when people refer to a legal entity making a decision or taking an action, they are referring to a decision or action taken by the entity through the appropriate authorized persons: officers, board members, or managers, as appropriate.

A principal reason for forming a legal entity is to provide the owners with liability protection. With the exception of the general partnership, these several legal entities should provide some or all of the owners liability protection. The form of legal entity may also affect the tax liability of the entity and its owners.

For example, corporations are subject to corporate tax, while other entities are not, unless they elect to be treated as corporations for federal tax purposes. Property owners should seek legal and tax advice in deciding whether to form a legal entity and in deciding what type of entity to form.

The following example introduces exchange structures. Excelsior LLC owns Quantum Farms, all of which is real property. Bounty Corp owns Regal Apartments, all of which is real property. The owners of Excelsior LLC decide to dispose of Quantum Farms and acquire other real property that they believe will provide a greater immediate revenue stream. Bounty Corp's board of directors decides to acquire property that will require less management and increase in value over time. They believe that Quantum Farms is such a property. Bounty Corp approaches Excelsior LLC to discuss acquiring Quantum Farms. Excelsior LLC and Bounty Corp decide that Quantum Farms and Regal Apartments are of equal value. They agree that Excelsior LLC will transfer Quantum Farms to Bounty Corp in exchange for Regal Apartments. The two entities transfer title to the two properties on the same day as part of a simultaneous exchange.

Direct Exchange

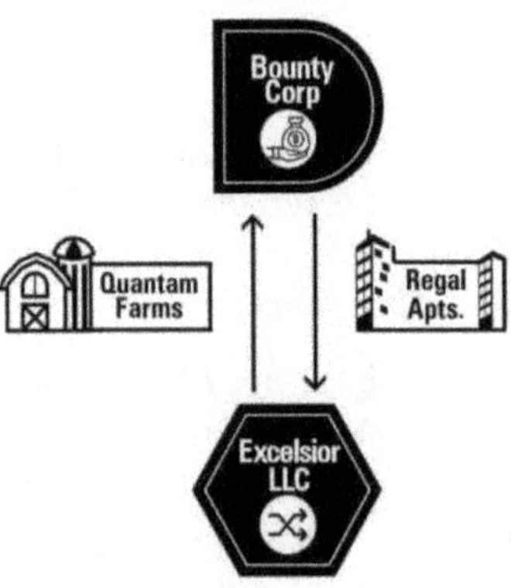

The transaction between Excelsior LLC and Bounty Corp is a section 1031 exchange. The transaction is a reciprocal transfer of property, the two properties are real property and like-kind, and both parties hold the properties and will continue to hold the properties either for productive use in a trade or business or for investment. Therefore, the transaction qualifies for section 1031 nonrecognition. In fact, the parties cannot avoid nonrecognition on this transaction.

The simple example of the Excelsior LLC-Bounty Corp exchange illustrates the two elements of the exchange requirement: (1) the property-for-property transfer and (2) the reciprocal transfer.

Property-for-Property Transfer Requirement

A transaction is an exchange only if the exchanger transfers property and acquires other property as consideration. If an exchanger transfers property and receives money, the transaction is not an exchange. In the example, Excelsior LLC transferred Quantum Farms, which is property, and received Regal Apartments, which is property. Excelsior LLC did not receive money, so the transaction was an exchange.

Reciprocal Transfer Requirement

A transaction is an exchange only if it has a reciprocal transfer of property—the reciprocal transfer requirement. This requirement provides that the party who transfers relinquished property must acquire replacement property. If we assume that Excelsior LLC transfers Quantum Farms to Bounty Corp, Excelsior LLC must acquire the replacement property (Regal Apartments) from Bounty Corp to satisfy the reciprocal requirement. If Excelsior LLC transfers Quantum Farms, and one of its members, Olivia, acquires Regal Apartments, the transaction would not satisfy the reciprocal transfer requirement. In that case, one party (Excelsior LLC) would transfer the intended relinquished property (Quantum Farms), and another party (Olivia) would acquire the intended replacement property (Regal Apartments). Because such a transaction violates the reciprocal transfer requirement, it appears to fail the exchange requirement and consequently would fail to qualify for section 1031 nonrecognition.

Violation of the Reciprocal Requirement

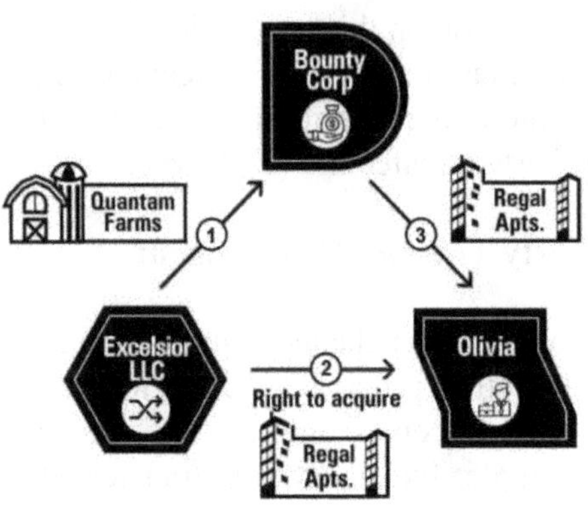

Although exchange structures have become complex, each structure must have a reciprocal transfer of property. Thus, the exchanger must transfer property to an exchange partner and acquire replacement property from that exchange partner. Notice in the multi-party exchanges discussed below that the transactions are always structured to ensure that the exchanger transfers property to and receives property from a single party.

INDIRECT EXCHANGES

Indirect exchanges are more common than direct exchanges. The relinquished property buyer and the replacement property seller are different parties. Exchangers may structure such transactions in one of several ways to satisfy the section 1031 exchange requirements. The discussion further reveals that intermediary-facilitated exchanges are the most popular structure. The reason for this is that other parties to the exchange (such as buyers and sellers) generally are not interested in facilitating an exchange.

MULTI-PARTY EXCHANGE STRUCTURES

Buyer-Facilitated Exchanges

Starker v. United States (a famous section 1031 case) provides an example of a buyer-facilitated exchange and demonstrates that such structures may qualify for section 1031 nonrecognition. A slight modification to the Excelsior LLC facts demonstrates this structure. Assume that Excelsior LLC owns Quantum Farms, that Bounty Corp wishes to acquire Quantum Farms, and that Bounty Corp has no property to transfer to Excelsior LLC. Excelsior LLC wishes to transfer Quantum Farms as part of a section 1031 exchange. To do this, Excelsior LLC must transfer Quantum Farms in exchange for like-kind property and not money. This requires a reciprocal transfer. Bounty Corp agrees to facilitate Excelsior LLC's exchange.

Excelsior LLC and Bounty Corp agree that Quantum Farms is worth $2,500,000. The two parties enter into an agreement providing that Excelsior LLC will transfer Quantum Farms to Bounty Corp in exchange for like-kind property, Excelsior LLC will identify replacement property, and Bounty Corp will acquire the replacement property if the acquisition price does not exceed $2,500,000. The agreement also provides that if Excelsior LLC is unable to identify replacement property within 180 days (the exchange period discussed below), Bounty Corp will pay Excelsior LLC $2,500,000 of cash for Quantum Farms. If Excelsior LLC identifies replacement property that costs less than $2,500,000, Bounty Corp will acquire the replacement property and transfer the replacement property and the balance of the $2,500,000 to Excelsior LLC at the time of the exchange.

Within four months after entering into the agreement with Bounty Corp, Excelsior LLC identifies as replacement property Regal Apartments, which Stan owns. Stan agrees to sell Regal Apartments to Bounty Corp for $2,100,000. Thus, Bounty Corp pays $2,100,000 for Regal Apartments, takes legal title to Regal Apartments, and transfers Regal Apartments and $400,000 of cash to Excelsior LLC in exchange for Quantum Farms. The $400,000 Excelsior LLC receives will be boot and trigger gain recognition. Excelsior LLC would, however, defer any remaining realized gain on the transaction.

Buyer-Facilitated Exchange

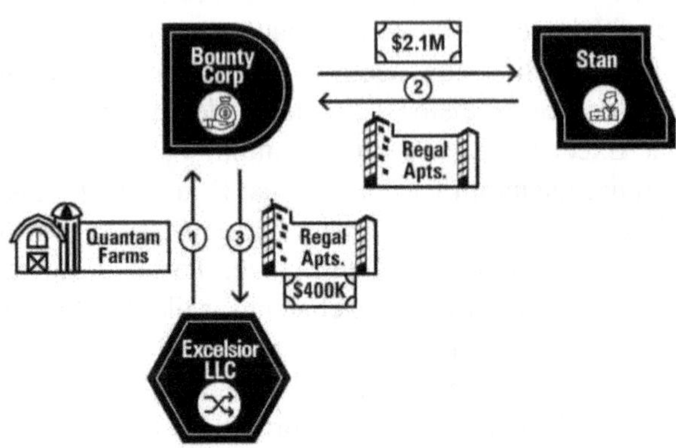

The buyer-facilitated exchange satisfies the exchange requirement because the buyer becomes the exchanger's exchange partner. The reciprocal transfer of property between Excelsior LLC and Bounty Corp is an exchange. The exchange requirement allows the buyer to acquire the replacement property and transfer it to the exchanger. The focus in determining whether the transaction is an exchange is on the exchanger and the buyer. Because the transaction is a reciprocal transfer of property, the transaction satisfies the exchange requirement. Thus, the exchange requirement in effect disregards the buyer's acquisition of the replacement property.

Seller-Facilitated Exchanges

If Bounty Corp refused to facilitate Excelsior LLC's exchange, Excelsior LLC could ask the seller of the relinquished property to facilitate the exchange. In this hypothetical, Stan is the seller, so Excelsior LLC may approach Stan to facilitate the exchange. An exchange facilitated by Stan may occur as follows. First, Excelsior LLC would enter into an agreement to sell Quantum Farms to Bounty Corp for $2,500,000. The agreement should provide that Excelsior LLC wishes the transfer to be part of a section 1031 exchange and that Bounty Corp will either pay the $2,500,000 purchase price to another party as directed by Excelsior LLC at any time prior to the end of the 180 days or pay that amount to Excelsior LLC at the end of the 180-day period.

Before the end of the 180 days, Excelsior LLC enters into an agreement to receive Regal Apartments and $400,000 from Stan in exchange for Quantum Farms. Excelsior LLC thus transfers Quantum Farms to Stan who then transfers it to Bounty Corp in exchange for $2,500,000. Stan then transfers Regal Apartments plus $400,000 of cash to Excelsior LLC to complete the exchange. As in the case of the exchange facilitated by Bounty Corp, Excelsior LLC receives like-kind property and boot. The receipt of the like-kind property satisfies the exchange requirement and the receipt of boot would trigger gain recognition.

Seller-Facilitated Exchange

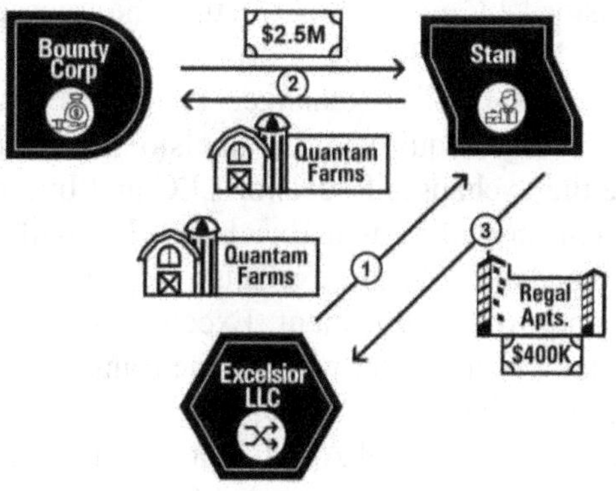

This diagram demonstrates that Excelsior LLC entered into an exchange with Stan. For federal tax purposes, Excelsior LLC transferred Quantum Farms to Stan in exchange for Regal Apartments, property like-kind to Quantum Farms, and $400,000. Because Excelsior LLC's transaction occurred with Stan, it satisfied the exchange requirement to the extent of the value of Regal Apartments. Case law supports both buyer-facilitated exchanges and seller-facilitated exchanges.

Intermediary-Facilitated Exchanges

The most common exchange structure is the intermediary-facilitated exchange. This structure is common because often neither the buyer nor the seller have any desire to facilitate an exchange. The buyer simply wants to pay money to acquire property from the exchanger and the seller simply wants to transfer property and receive money consideration. Case law provides direct authority that allows an exchanger to satisfy the exchange requirement through an intermediary-facilitated exchange.

Assume that Excelsior LLC and Bounty Corp agree that Bounty Corp will acquire Quantum Farms for $2,500,000. Before Excelsior LLC transfers Quantum Farms to Bounty Corp, Excelsior LLC enters into an agreement to acquire Regal Apartments from Stan for $2,100,000. Because Quantum Farms and Regal Apartments are like-kind real property, Excelsior LLC wishes to structure the transaction as a section 1031 exchange. Neither Bounty Corp nor Stan has any interest in facilitating Excelsior LLC's exchange. To ensure that the transaction satisfies the exchange requirement, Excelsior LLC hires Intermediary Inc to facilitate the exchange. Excelsior LLC and Intermediary Inc enter into an agreement, providing that Excelsior LLC will transfer Quantum Farms to Intermediary Inc in exchange for Regal Apartments and $400,000. Pursuant to the agreement, Excelsior LLC transfers Quantum Farms to Intermediary Inc, Intermediary Inc transfers Quantum Farms to Bounty Corp and receives $2,500,000, Intermediary Inc uses $2,100,000 of that amount to acquire Regal Apartments from Stan, and Intermediary Inc then transfers Regal Apartments and $400,000 to Excelsior LLC to complete the exchange.

Intermediary-Facilitated Exchange

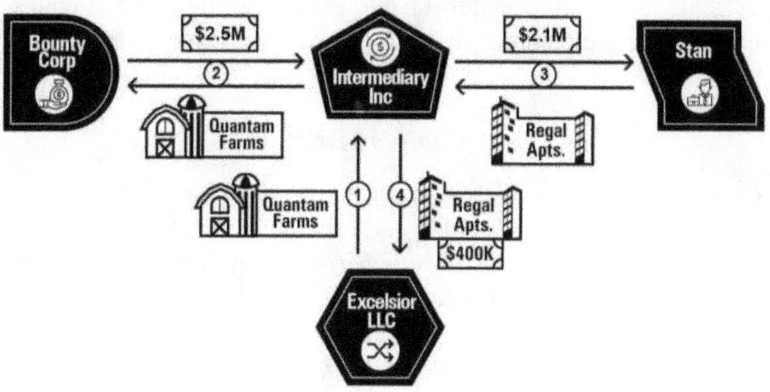

Notice in this diagram that Excelsior LLC transfers Quantum Farms to Intermediary Inc in exchange for Regal Apartments and $400,000. This creates a reciprocal transfer between Excelsior LLC and Intermediary Inc. Thus, in this exchange, Intermediary Inc is Excelsior LLC's exchange partner. The transaction satisfies the exchange requirement to the extent of the value of Regal Apartments. The $400,000 that Excelsior LLC receives is boot. Therefore, the transaction qualifies for section 1031 nonrecognition, except to the extent of boot Excelsior LLC receives. Excelsior LLC could have obtained the same result if Bounty Corp had paid Excelsior LLC $400,000 directly and paid only $2,100,000 to Intermediary Inc.

Direct Deeding

Case law also allows an exchanger to overcome one final impediment of indirect exchanges. Whether an intermediary, buyer, or seller facilitates an exchange, the party facilitating the exchange generally will want to avoid entering the properties' chain of title; the buyer may prefer that no other party enter the chain of title of the relinquished property; and the exchanger may wish that no other party enter the chain of title of the replacement property. The reason for this is that a party who enters the chain of title may be subject to liabilities that arise with respect to the property, and the liabilities of a party who enters the chain of title may attach to the property. Transfers of title may also trigger state or local transfer taxes. Prudence therefore dictates that parties not enter the chain of title unless absolutely necessary.

Chain of Title

Chain of title refers to the parties who have held legal title to property. Generally, when property is transferred, the transfer is recorded in the county of the property's situs. Thus, other parties are put on notice as to who has held legal title to the property throughout its history. Through recordation of transfers with the county, public records indicate the transfers that have occurred with respect to the property. The linkage of one owner to the next and subsequent owners forms a chain of title and property ownership.

Case law provides that if parties enter into an agreement to exchange properties but the parties directly deed the properties to the ultimate acquirer, the transaction may still satisfy the exchange requirement. For example, in the buyer-facilitated exchange discussed above, after Bounty Corp and Excelsior LLC enter into an agreement to exchange property and Bounty Corp enters into an agreement to acquire Regal Apartments from Stan, the exchange can be completed by Excelsior LLC transferring Quantum Farms to Bounty Corp, Bounty Corp paying Stan $2,100,000, Stan transferring the legal title of Regal Apartments directly to Excelsior LLC, and Bounty Corp paying $400,000 to Excelsior LLC.

Direct Deeding: Seller-Facilitated Exchange

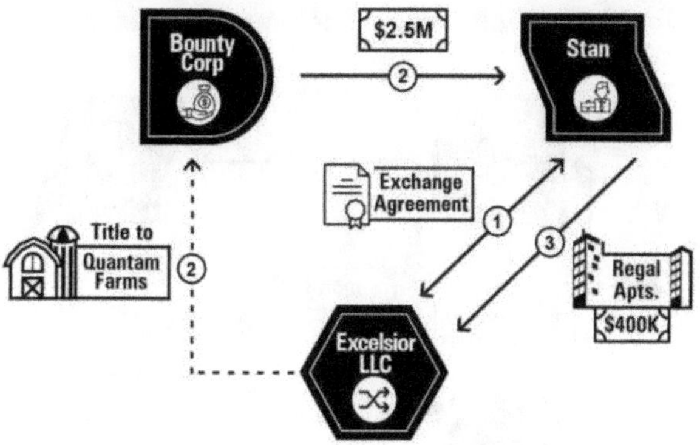

Because case law allows direct deeding, the outcome of this transaction is the same as the outcome of Excelsior LLC transferring Quantum Farms to Bounty Corp and Bounty Corp acquiring legal title to Regal Apartments and transferring legal title to Excelsior LLC. Because tax law treats Stan's deeding of Regal Apartments directly to Excelsior LLC as a transfer to Bounty Corp followed by a transfer to Excelsior LLC, the transaction satisfies the exchange requirement. Furthermore, it removes Bounty Corp from the Regal Apartments chain of title.

Exchangers may similarly structure seller-facilitated exchanges and intermediary-facilitated exchanges using direct deeding. In a seller-facilitated exchange, Stan may direct Excelsior LLC to directly deed Quantum Farms to Bounty Corp. Bounty Corp will pay Stan for Quantum Farms, even though the buyer acquires legal title to Quantum Farms directly from Excelsior LLC. Ensuring that Excelsior LLC does not receive exchange proceeds from Bounty Corp is critical. If Excelsior LLC were to receive the proceeds, the exchange would be destroyed.

Thus, in the seller-facilitated exchange described above, Stan and Excelsior LLC would agree to exchange properties. Stan would not, however, take title to Quantum Farms. Instead, Stan would direct Excelsior LLC to transfer Quantum Farms directly to Bounty Corp.

Bounty Corp would pay Stan $2,500,000 for Quantum Farms and Stan would transfer Regal Apartments and $400,000 to Excelsior LLC.

Direct Deeding: Buyer-Facilitated Exchange

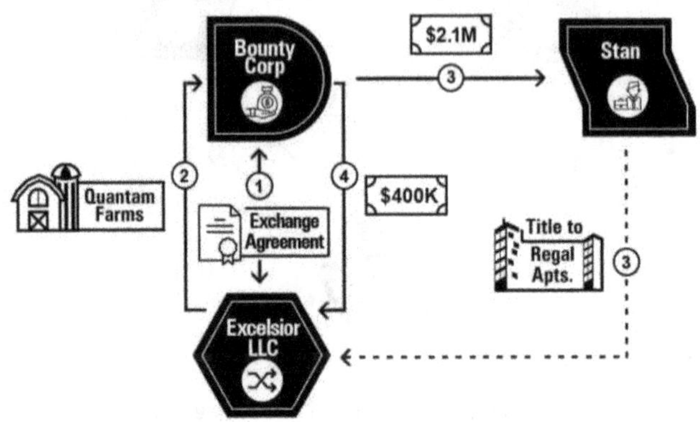

The direct transfer of legal title to Quantum Farms from Excelsior LLC to Bounty Corp is treated for federal tax purposes as a transfer to Stan followed by Stan transferring Quantum Farms to Bounty Corp. Thus, Excelsior LLC and Stan are treated as exchanging property, and Excelsior is treated as receiving $400,000 from Stan.

If an intermediary facilitates an exchange, it too may avoid entering the chain of title by directing the exchanger to transfer legal title to the relinquished property to the buyer and directing the seller to transfer legal title to the replacement property to the exchanger. The transaction will nonetheless be treated as an exchange between the exchanger and the intermediary if the exchanger and intermediary enter into an agreement providing that they will exchange properties.

Returning to the hypothetical, assume that Excelsior LLC and Intermediary Inc enter into an agreement providing that Excelsior LLC will transfer Quantum Farms to Intermediary Inc in exchange for Regal Apartments and $400,000 of cash. After entering into such an agreement, Intermediary Inc may direct Excelsior LLC to transfer legal title to Quantum Farms directly to Bounty Corp. Bounty Corp will pay the $2,500,000 consideration to Intermediary Inc. Intermediary Inc will use $2,100,000 of the consideration to acquire Regal Apartments from

Stan. Instead of taking legal title to Regal Apartments, however, Intermediary Inc will direct Stan to transfer legal title to Regal Apartments directly to Excelsior LLC. Intermediary Inc will transfer the remaining $400,000 of the proceeds received from Bounty Corp to Excelsior LLC.

Direct Deeding: Intermediary-Facilitated Exchange

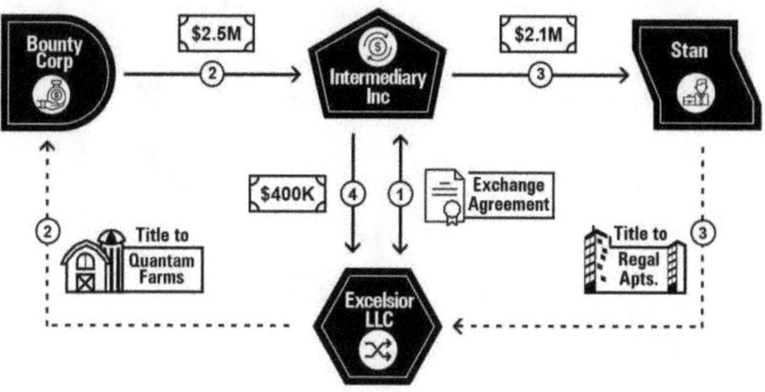

Because federal tax law treats Excelsior LLC as transferring Quantum Farms to Intermediary Inc and receiving Regal Apartments from Intermediary Inc, the transaction satisfies the exchange requirement, at least to the extent of the value of Regal Apartments. This structure allows Intermediary Inc to avoid entering the chain of title but does not disrupt the section 1031 treatment of the exchange.

This discussion presents the basic multi-party exchange structures. Case law supports each of these structures. Case law does not always provide specific rules regarding exchange structures. Congress and the IRS have created specific rules that provide guidelines for satisfying the exchange requirement with such structures. The guidance regarding these structures makes section 1031 broadly applicable.

CHAPTER 5: EXCHANGE STRUCTURES: DEFERRED EXCHANGES

Seldom does an exchanger transfer relinquished property and receive replacement property at the same time. Often the exchanger sells relinquished property and later acquires replacement property. This is common when an exchanger acts upon an offer from a buyer without arranging to acquire replacement property. Section 1031 has developed a series of rules that make these deferred exchanges possible. The following example demonstrates the alternatives for structuring deferred exchanges.

Ensign Ltd is preparing to close on the sale of Quartz Mine to Bullion Co for $25,000,000 on March 1. Ensign Ltd has a very low adjusted tax basis in Quartz Mine and wants to avoid gain recognition by using the proceeds from the sale of Quartz Mine to acquire other like-kind property in a section 1031 exchange. Ensign Ltd also wishes to diversify its portfolio by acquiring various replacement properties. As the closing date approaches, Ensign Ltd is not prepared to acquire replacement property. In fact, Ensign Ltd has not even found suitable replacement property. Nonetheless, Bullion Co wants to close on March 1. Therefore, Ensign Ltd must transfer the Quartz Mine, the relinquished property, before it acquires replacement property. Fortunately, federal tax law allows property owners to transfer relinquished property and later acquire replacement property. Because the exchanger acquires the replacement property after transferring the relinquished property, these transactions are called deferred exchanges.

STARKER V. UNITED STATES

Starker v. United States is the original authority allowing deferred exchanges. In that case, T.J. Starker transferred property to

Crown Corp., and Crown Corp. agreed to acquire replacement property as directed by Starker and transfer the replacement property to Starker. The agreement between Starker and Crown Corp. provided that Crown Corp. had five years from the date of acquiring Starker's property to acquire and transfer replacement property. To the extent the aggregate value of property Crown Corp. transferred to Starker was less than the agreed value of Starker's property, Crown Corp. would pay Starker the difference in cash at the end of the five years. Crown Corp. also agreed to pay Starker interest on the outstanding balance of its obligation to transfer replacement property.

Within two years after Crown Corp. acquired Starker's property, it had acquired and transferred replacement property to Starker. At issue in this case was whether an exchange has to be simultaneous to satisfy the exchange requirement. The court considered this issue and recognized that it was a case of first impression. Therefore, the court had to decide the issue without any precedent to provide direction. The court held that section 1031 does not require that the transfer of relinquished property and the acquisition of replacement property be simultaneous to satisfy the exchange requirement. It also held that the transaction was an exchange and that Starker could defer gain recognition to the extent it acquired like-kind property to be held for productive use in a trade or business or for investment. Thus, *Starker v. United States* provides authority for structuring buyer-facilitated indirect deferred exchanges.

TIME LIMITATIONS

Because no other legal authority had addressed whether deferred exchanges qualify for section 1031 nonrecognition, the court in *Starker v. United States* invited Congress to enact new laws if its holding was incorrect. Within a few years, Congress responded to that invitation, requiring exchangers to identify replacement property within 45 days after transferring relinquished property and to acquire replacement property within 180 days after transferring relinquished property. These time periods govern deferred exchanges.

Identification and Exchange Timelines

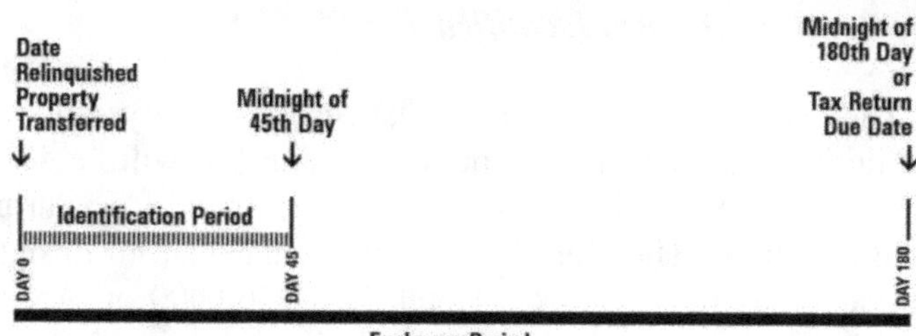

The Identification Period

The Internal Revenue Code provides that an exchanger must identify replacement property within 45 days following the transfer of the relinquished property to qualify for section 1031 nonrecognition. The 45-day period is known as the identification period. The first day of the identification period is the day following the exchange. The identification period ends at midnight on the 45th day following the transfer. The period is not extended for holidays or weekends. Congress created this rule to address its concern that deferred exchanges may appear more like a sale of property and subsequent acquisition of other property if the exchanger cannot quickly identify the property it intends to acquire.

After Congress enacted this rule, Treasury promulgated rules describing how exchangers must identify replacement property. Those rules provide that exchangers may identify multiple or alternative replacement properties, must properly describe the identified replacement property, and must appropriately deliver the identification.

Ensign Ltd plans to transfer relinquished property as part of a section 1031 deferred exchange. Therefore, it is subject to the identification rules. Because Ensign Ltd will transfer Quartz Mine on March 1, it must identify replacement property by midnight on April 15. Only property Ensign Ltd properly identifies by April 15 will qualify as replacement property for Ensign Ltd. If Ensign Ltd identifies no property by April 15, the disposition of Quartz Mine will not qualify for section 1031 nonrecognition.

Property Received Deemed Identified

The regulations deem an exchanger to identify any property received during the identification period. Ensign Ltd will be deemed to identify any property it acquires from Bullion Co during the identification period. Therefore, if Bullion Co, pursuant to Ensign Ltd's direction, acquires Royal Towers Hotel for $8,500,000 on April 5 and transfers it to Ensign Ltd that day, Ensign Ltd will receive Royal Towers Hotel within the identification period and be deemed to have identified it.

The Three-Property Rule

The identification rules also allow exchangers to identify multiple and alternative properties. As the end of the identification period approaches, Ensign Ltd may not be certain what properties it will acquire as replacement property. Nonetheless, it must identify its replacement property before the end of the identification period. The regulations provide that an exchanger may identify any three properties regardless of their values. This is known as the three-property rule.

If we assume Ensign Ltd acquired Royal Towers Hotel before the end of the identification period, it can only identify two more properties and stay within the three-property rule. Consider the impact of this rule. Assume that Ensign Ltd is considering four other properties as potential replacement properties: (1) Route 66 Warehouse worth $15,000,000, (2) Rio Grande Shopping Center worth $11,000,000, (3) Red Rock Ranch worth $6,000,000, and (4) Regal Bank Building worth $19,000,000. Under the three-property rule, Ensign Ltd can identify any two of these other properties regardless of value. Thus, it could identify Regal Bank Building and Route 66 Warehouse. If Ensign Ltd were to identify those two properties, along with Royal Towers Hotel, the aggregate value of the identified properties would be $42,500,000.

Identified Replacement Properties—Three-Property Rule	
Value of Quartz Mine	*$25,000,000*
Value of Identified Replacement Property	
Value of Royal Towers Hotel	*$ 8,500,000*
Value of Regal Bank Building	*$19,000,000*
Value of Route 66 Warehouse	*$15,000,000*
Aggregate Value of Identified Property	*$42,500,000*

Even though the aggregate value of the identified replacement properties exceeds the value of the relinquished property, Ensign Ltd satisfies the three-property rule.

The three-property rule presents somewhat of a challenge for Ensign Ltd. Ensign Ltd probably will not invest much more than the $25,000,000. Thus, if Ensign Ltd identifies Regal Bank Building and acquires it, Ensign Ltd will re-invest $27,500,000. This is $2,500,000 more than the amount of exchange proceeds it has available. Undoubtedly Ensign Ltd could borrow an additional $2,500,000 to complete the exchange. Acquiring Regal Bank Building in addition to Royal Towers Hotel would allow Ensign Ltd to defer all of its gain realized.

If, however, Ensign Ltd is not able to acquire Regal Bank Building and only acquires Route 66 Warehouse, it will not be able to completely defer gain recognition. In that scenario, Ensign Ltd would receive only $23,500,000 of replacement property. Bullion Co would also pay Ensign Ltd $1,500,000, which would be boot to Ensign Ltd. Therefore, Ensign Ltd would be required to recognize $1,500,000 of gain on the transaction. This is not a terrible outcome because Ensign Ltd was able to defer significant gain. Nonetheless, the three-property rule places Ensign Ltd in a position that may not allow it to defer all its gain realized.

The three-property rule applies on a per-exchange basis, not a per-property basis. In the case of Ensign Ltd, it transferred only one relinquished property, so the three-property rule clearly limits the number of properties it may identify to three properties. If Ensign Ltd had transferred two properties to Bullion Co instead of just the one, Ensign Ltd would nonetheless be limited to identifying three replacement properties. It could not identify six replacement properties (three for each property). If Ensign Ltd wished to be able to identify six replacement properties, it would have to divide the disposition of two properties into two separate exchanges. Then it would be able to identify three replacement properties for each exchange.

The 200% Rule

The three-property rule is not the only rule an exchanger may rely upon when identifying multiple or alternative replacement properties. If an exchanger is unable to meet the three-property rule, it will nonetheless satisfy the identification rules if it satisfies the 200% rule. The 200% rule provides that an exchanger may identify any number of replacement properties as long as the aggregate value of the properties identified does not exceed 200 percent of the value of the relinquished property. The value of the identified properties at the end of the identification period determines whether the exchange satisfies the 200% rule.

In the case of Ensign Ltd, it transferred relinquished property worth \$25,000,000. Therefore, it may identify up to \$50,000,000 worth of replacement property without violating the 200% rule. The aggregate value of Royal Towers Hotel and the four properties that Ensign Ltd wishes to identify is \$59,500,000.

Aggregate Value of all Potential Replacement Property

200% of Quartz Mine	*\$50,000,000*
Aggregate Value of Potential Replacement Property	
Value of Royal Towers Hotel	*\$ 8,500,000*
Value of Route 66 Warehouse	*\$15,000,000*
Value of Rio Grande Shopping Ctr.	*\$11,000,000*
Value of Red Rock Ranch	*\$ 6,000,000*
Value of Regal Bank Building	*\$19,000,000*

Aggregate Value of Identified Property	*$59,500,000*

Because the aggregate value of Royal Towers Hotel and the other four potential replacement properties exceeds 200 percent of the value of Quartz Mine, Ensign Ltd may not identify all four other potential replacement properties without violating the 200% rule. In fact, Ensign Ltd has to remove Route 66 Warehouse, Rio Grande Shopping Center, or Regal Bank Building from its desired list of identified properties to satisfy the 200% rule. Merely removing Red Rock Ranch will not be sufficient to satisfy the 200% rule because Red Rock Ranch is worth only $6,000,000 and Ensign Ltd must reduce the aggregate amount of identified properties to no more than $50,000,000.

If an exchanger violates both the three-property rule and the 200% rule, the regulations generally deem an exchanger to have violated the identification rules, and only property received during the identification period will be deemed to have been identified. Thus, if Ensign Ltd mistakenly identifies the four potential replacement properties after it acquires Royal Towers Hotel, the regulations will generally deem Ensign Ltd to have only identified Royal Towers Hotel, the property it acquired during the identification period. Ensign Ltd will defer gain only to the extent the value of Royal Towers Hotel exceeds the basis Ensign Ltd had in Quartz Mine; it will recognize any remaining gain realized. Thus, proper identification is critical.

The 95% Rule

Through the 95% rule, the regulations provide an out for exchangers who violate both the three-property rule and the 200% rule. Under the 95% rule, an exchanger will be deemed to have identified property if it acquires identified property having at least 95 percent of the aggregate value of the identified replacement property. Therefore, if Ensign Ltd were to identify $59,500,000 of property, it would have to acquire $56,525,000 (95 percent of all identified property) of identified replacement property to come within the 95% rule. This would require Ensign Ltd to invest another $31,525,000 in addition to the $25,000,000 from the sale of Quartz Mine to acquire the required amount of replacement property. Because the 95% rule requires such a significant additional investment by the exchanger, it is available to help exchangers only in limited situations. Generally, if an exchanger fails the three-property rule and the 200% rule, the exchanger will not satisfy the identification rule with respect to many of the potential replacement properties.

These examples demonstrate the significance of carefully considering property to be identified. Exchangers should take very seriously the identification of property. In applying the 95% rule, exchangers must consider the value of the replacement property at the earlier of the date the property is received or the end of the exchange period. Thus, fluctuating values of property following the identification may affect the amount the exchanger must invest to satisfy the 95% rule.

Identification Warning

The identification rules leave some questions unanswered. For example, they do not answer whether the value of relinquished property is the sales price before closing costs or the net amount. They also do not answer what value an exchanger should use for replacement property it does not acquire. To avoid exceeding the limits, exchangers should not come too close to the limits. Exchangers should also consider using conservative estimates (e.g., use the net sales price of the relinquished property to compute the 200% amount).

Property Description

The regulations provide that an exchanger must unambiguously describe replacement property to satisfy the identification rule. For real property this means providing a legal description, street address, or common name. Because each of the properties that Ensign Ltd is considering is real property, Ensign Ltd could describe each using its common name. To avoid possible ambiguity, Ensign Ltd may also need to state the general location of each property. For example, if Ensign Ltd simply identifies Red Rock Ranch and there is a ranch by that name in Wyoming and another one in Colorado, the identification may be ambiguous. To avoid this possibility, Ensign Ltd should also identify the state in which the ranch is located.

The law does not describe the type of identification that is an unambiguous description of a TIC interest. (Chapter 10 discusses TIC interests.) Surely, the exchanger must follow the identification rules with respect to the property in which the exchanger is acquiring the TIC interest. Thus, the exchanger must identify the underlying property by its legal description, street address, or common name. The uncertainty lies in the description of the interest in the underlying property. Exchangers wonder whether they can identify the interest with reference to a specific dollar amount (e.g., a $500,000 dollar interest in Royal Towers Hotel), or must identify a specific percentage of the property (e.g., a 6 percent interest in Royal Towers Hotel). If the percentage interest the exchanger acquires does not affect the exchanger's rights with respect to the property (e.g., its voting rights), then identifying the property with reference to a specific dollar amount should be sufficient. Unfortunately, there is no legal authority that addresses this issue.

Delivery of Identification

The IRS has not provided a form for identifying replacement property. Generally, most qualified intermediary companies have forms they have prepared. Such forms may be helpful, but they are not necessary to satisfy the identification requirement. The regulations do, however, provide rules for delivering replacement property identifications. First, the identification must be in writing signed by the exchanger. Second, the exchanger must hand deliver, mail, fax, or otherwise send the identification. Third, the exchanger must send the identification before the end of the identification period. Fourth, the exchanger must send the identification to the person obligated to transfer the replacement property or to another party involved in the exchange who is qualified to serve as a qualified intermediary. The law does not require the exchanger to send the identification form to the IRS.

Most often exchangers will send the identification to the qualified intermediaries facilitating the exchange. Professional qualified intermediaries generally are prepared to receive and date stamp identifications. This helps establish the date of receipt. The important date is the date the exchanger sends the identification, so exchangers should retain some evidence supporting the date the identification is sent. This may include a return receipt request or fax verification.

Revocation of Identification

Any time prior to the end of the identification period, an exchanger may revoke an identification. Exchangers revoke an identification in the same manner they make it. Thus, by signing a statement revoking an identification and delivering it to the person to whom the identification was delivered, the exchanger may revoke an identification.

The Exchange Period

To complete a valid section 1031 exchange, the exchanger must acquire all replacement property prior to the end of the exchange period. The exchange period begins on the day after the exchanger transfers relinquished property. The exchange period has two possible ending dates. First, the exchange period generally ends at midnight on the 180th day after the exchanger transfers the relinquished property. If, however, the due date of the exchanger's tax return for the year during which the relinquished property was transferred is before the end of the 180-day period, the due date of the tax return is the end of the exchange period. Because the due date of the return includes extensions, the exchanger (by filing an extension) can assume that the exchange period does not end prior to the end of the 180-day period.

Assume Ensign Ltd transfers Quartz Mine on December 1, Year 1. The exchange period, based on the 180-day period, would end on May 30th, Year 2 (assuming Year 2 is not a leap year). Ensign Ltd's tax return for the year it sold Quartz Mine is due on April 15, Year 2. Because that date is prior to the end of the 180-day period, it will become the end of the exchange period if Ensign Ltd does not file an extension. To ensure that the exchange period extends as long as possible, Ensign Ltd may request an automatic extension. If it does so, its tax return due date will become July 15, Year 2, and the exchange period will end on May 30, Year 2.

The exchange period is cut short by the due date of the tax return for the year during which the exchanger transferred the relinquished property. Therefore, if Ensign Ltd transferred Quartz Mine on January 1, Year 2, the 180-day period would end on May 29, Year 2, and the Year 2 return would not be due until March 15, Year 3, at the earliest. Thus, the tax return due date would not affect the exchange period. In fact, since taxpayers may request automatic extensions that extend beyond 180 days after the end of a taxable year (for example, the automatic extension for a partnership is September 15), a conscientious taxpayer should never have the exchange period cut short by a tax return due date.

Acquisition of Substantially-the-Same Property

The identification rules require an exchanger to acquire property that is substantially the same as the property identified. Thus, if Ensign Ltd identifies only Regal Bank Building, it must acquire Regal Bank Building to satisfy this requirement. This seems intuitive since the identification rules would be a nullity if the exchanger were able to acquire something other than identical property.

Satisfying this requirement may be difficult in situations where the identified property is not complete. As discussed in Chapter 7, an exchanger may identify real property improvements to be constructed as part of an improvements exchange. In such situations, the exchanger will acquire property that is substantially the same as that identified, even if the real property improvements are not completed. The only qualification is that the improvements, if they had been completed, must be substantially the same as what the exchanger identified. Furthermore, only the portion of the completed improvements at the time of acquisition will be like-kind to relinquished real property.

An exchanger may also satisfy the substantially-the-same requirement even though the identified property changes following the identification. For example, if Ensign Ltd identifies Red Rock Ranch as potential replacement property, and before Ensign Ltd acquires it the owner constructs a fence on the property, Red Rock Ranch with the fence will probably be substantially the same as Red Rock Ranch without the fence.

THE SECTION 1031 DEFERRED EXCHANGE SAFE HARBORS

If an exchanger can identify and acquire replacement property within the section 1031 time limits, the section 1031 deferred exchange safe harbors should help the exchanger satisfy the exchange requirement. Although *Starker* and other cases made indirect deferred exchanges possible, they did not make them accessible to a broad cross-section of property owners. Recall that Crown Corp, the exchange partner in *Starker*, was a large corporation. That being the case, Starker could feel fairly comfortable that Crown Corp would perform under the contract and either acquire the desired replacement property or pay Starker in cash for the relinquished property.

In some situations, a buyer's financial position may not be as stable as Crown Corp's was. In such situations, the exchanger may want security to support the buyer's obligation to acquire and transfer replacement property. For example, the exchanger may require the buyer to place in escrow an amount of money equal to the value of the relinquished property. The escrow agreement could provide that in the event the buyer does not acquire and transfer replacement property to the exchanger within the exchange period, the escrow holder will distribute the deposited funds to the exchanger.

If an escrow arrangement is not structured properly, however, the exchanger may be deemed to be in constructive receipt of the money placed in the escrow account. Constructive receipt of money destroys the possibility of obtaining section 1031 nonrecognition.

Constructive Receipt

Constructive receipt is a tax principle that treats a person as receiving something even though the person does not take possession of the thing or its legal title. Generally, to be in constructive receipt of something, a person must have control of it or otherwise receive the benefit of it. For example, an exchanger would be in constructive receipt of proceeds placed in an escrow if the exchanger could access the proceeds at any time.

Prior to the promulgation of the deferred exchange safe harbor regulations, the law regarding constructive receipt of exchange proceeds was uncertain. The safe harbors in the regulations now provide certainty and allow an exchanger to secure a buyer's or intermediary's obligation to perform under an exchange agreement without being deemed to be in constructive receipt of exchange proceeds. The Ensign Ltd hypothetical helps illustrate the several deferred exchange safe harbors.

Assume that Owen, the president of the managing partner of Ensign Ltd, manages Ensign Ltd and that Ensign Ltd engages Andre, an attorney familiar with section 1031, to advise it with respect to the Quartz Mine exchange. After Ensign Ltd has agreed to sell Quartz Mine to Bullion Co, Owen contacts Andre to discuss the exchange.

Andre responds to Owen's question about structuring, "Owen, even though Ensign Ltd has already entered into a contract to sell Quartz Mine, you have several alternatives for structuring the exchange. One of the first things you must consider is whether you want Bullion Co to help facilitate the exchange."

"How will we structure the transaction if Bullion Co agrees to facilitate the exchange?" Owen asked.

"Ensign Ltd would transfer Quartz Mine to Bullion Co and Bullion Co would agree to acquire replacement property worth $25,000,000 and transfer it to Ensign Ltd. As you know, if Ensign Ltd identifies replacement property within 45 days after Ensign Ltd transfers Quartz Mine and acquires replacement property within 180 days after the transfer of Quartz Mine, the transaction may qualify for section 1031 nonrecognition."

"So you're telling me that Ensign Ltd could transfer Quartz Mine to Bullion Co in exchange for Bullion Co's promise to acquire replacement property?" Owen asked. "That sounds easy, but I am not too familiar with Bullion Co and its financial stability. Isn't it possible that after Ensign Ltd transfers Quartz Mine to Bullion Co that Bullion Co could encounter financial troubles and not be able to perform its obligation to transfer replacement property? My partners would not be too happy with me if that happened."

"I could imagine that they wouldn't be, and you're absolutely correct that something like that could happen," answered Andre. "If you and Bullion Co decided that Bullion Co would facilitate the exchange, there are mechanisms that you can use to protect the interests of Ensign Ltd and secure Bullion Co's obligation to transfer the replacement property. The regulations provide several safe harbors that you might consider."

Security and Guarantee Arrangements

Andre continued, "The first safe harbor provides that a buyer's obligation to transfer replacement property to an exchanger may be secured by a security interest in the relinquished property, a third-party guarantee, or a standby letter of credit. The regulations refer to these arrangements as security or guarantee arrangements. If such arrangement is properly structured, the exchanger will not be deemed to be in constructive receipt of money or property that is not like-kind to the relinquished property."

Security and Guarantee Arrangements Safe Harbor

An exchanger will not be deemed to be in constructive receipt of money or other property even if the exchanger retains a security interest in the relinquished property, a third party guarantees the buyer's obligation to acquire and transfer replacement property, or a standby letter of credit secures the buyer's obligation to acquire and transfer replacement property. This is the first deferred exchange safe harbor.

"Let's take each of these security arrangements one by one," Owen requested. "You said that Ensign Ltd could transfer Quartz Mine to Bullion Co and retain a security interest in Quartz Mine. How would that work?"

"Ensign Ltd could retain a mortgage in Quartz Mine after the transfer to Bullion Co. If Bullion Co does not have to borrow to purchase Quartz Mine, Ensign Ltd will be able to take a first mortgage in the property. If Bullion Co does have to borrow to purchase Quartz Mine, the lender will probably require that Ensign Ltd take a second mortgage in Quartz Mine. Of these two alternatives, the first is obviously better for Ensign Ltd, but it still is not the best alternative."

"I can see the problem with that," Owen replied. "If Bullion Co were to default on its obligation to acquire replacement property, Ensign Ltd's recourse would be to bring a foreclosure action against Bullion Co. That could end up being time consuming and expensive. Furthermore, the partners of Ensign Ltd have decided to sell Quartz Mine. They do not want to get it back if Bullion Co does not perform under the agreement. Thus, although the security is better than nothing, if there are other alternatives, I want to talk about them."

"One other alternative is to have a third-party guarantee Bullion Co's obligation to transfer replacement property. The guarantee would provide that in the event Bullion Co does not transfer replacement property to Ensign Ltd before the end of the exchange period, the third party will pay $25,000,000 to Ensign Ltd."

"That sounds pretty good, but who is Bullion Co going to get to guarantee the payment of $25,000,000?" Owen asked. "I think if we aren't comfortable with Bullion Co performing under the agreement, it is doubtful that we will be comfortable that a third party will perform under a guarantee arrangement."

"That's probably true. If Bullion Co is owned by another company, perhaps that holding company is a third party that can provide the needed assurance through a guarantee. Otherwise, I agree with you that such a guarantee won't provide much comfort in this situation," Andre said.

"A third alternative is to have Bullion Co obtain a standby letter of credit from a bank. A standby letter of credit would provide that in the event that Bullion Co does not transfer replacement property to Ensign Ltd during the exchange period, the bank would pay $25,000,000 to Ensign Ltd. The bank would issue the standby letter of credit based on Bullion Co's credit. That would shift the risk of loss from Ensign Ltd to the bank. If the bank remains viable, then Ensign Ltd will receive its $25,000,000." Andre continued, "Those are three security or guarantee arrangements that Ensign Ltd can consider, but they are not the only alternatives. The regulations provide three other deferred exchange safe harbors. You also might consider using a qualified escrow account or a qualified trust to secure Bullion Co's obligation to transfer replacement property."

Qualified Escrow Accounts and Qualified Trusts

"The qualified escrow accounts and qualified trusts are generally more attractive," Andre continued, "because exchange proceeds are set aside to secure the buyer's obligation to acquire replacement property."

Qualified Escrow Accounts and Qualified Trusts Safe Harbor

The regulations provide that an exchanger shall not be deemed to be in constructive receipt of money held in a qualified escrow account or qualified trust to secure the buyer's obligation to transfer replacement property to the exchanger.

Money placed in a qualified escrow account or qualified trust will generally be used to acquire replacement property or will be paid to the exchanger at the end of the exchange period.

"This does sound better," Owen said. "It would be nice to know that $25,000,000 was deposited in an escrow account and out of reach of Bullion Co and its creditors."

"I thought you would prefer requiring Bullion Co to deposit the $25,000,000 into a qualified escrow account or qualified trust to secure its obligation to transfer replacement property. Such an arrangement should provide you with greater comfort because the money will be held by a third party, be available when needed, and not be subject to claims of Bullion Co's creditors," Andre explained. "Thus, you will not have to rely upon legal action to recover the price of Quartz Mine or worry about the financial strength of a third-party creditor. If Bullion Co does not acquire any replacement property by the end of the exchange period, the escrow agent or trustee may distribute the proceeds to Ensign Ltd."

Qualified Escrow Account/Qualified Trust Exchange

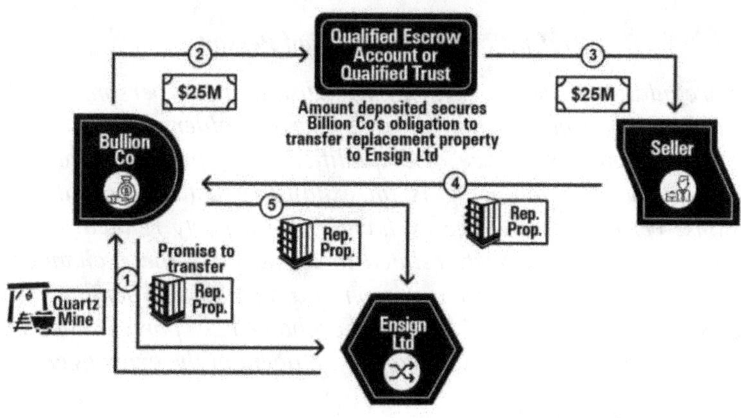

"So the benefit of this safe harbor is that it would secure Bullion Co's obligation to acquire replacement property, but Ensign Ltd would not be in constructive receipt of the money deposited in the escrow account," Owen observed.

"That's correct," Andre said. "If the arrangement is a qualified escrow, Ensign Ltd will not be deemed to be in constructive receipt of the proceeds deposited in the escrow account."

Qualified Escrow Accounts

"What makes an arrangement a qualified escrow account?" Owen asked.

Andre explained, "For an arrangement to be a qualified escrow account, the escrow holder cannot be a disqualified person, the exchanger and escrow holder must enter into a written escrow agreement, and the escrow agreement must contain the (g)(6) restrictions."

"Let's examine each of those requirements one at a time," Owen requested. "What is a disqualified person?"

Definition of Disqualified Person

The regulations define the term "disqualified person." A disqualified person may not serve as escrow holder of a qualified escrow account, as trustee of a qualified trust, or as a qualified intermediary. The following is an exhaustive list of disqualified persons: (1) an agent of the exchanger, (2) a party related to the exchanger, and (3) a party related to an agent of the exchanger. Thus, to determine whether a person is a disqualified person, one must know the definition of "agent of exchanger," "party related to the exchanger," and "party related to an agent of the exchanger."

Agent of the Exchanger

An agent of the exchanger includes any person who, within two years prior to the transfer of the relinquished property, has acted as the exchanger's employee, attorney, accountant, investment banker or broker, or real estate agent or broker. The regulations provide an exception to this rule, however. In determining whether the party has acted in one of the listed capacities, the regulations disregard services performed for the exchanger with respect to section 1031 exchanges and routine financial, title insurance, escrow, or trust services performed for the exchanger by a financial institution, title insurance company, or escrow company.

Party Related to the Exchanger

Certain family members and certain entities are related to the exchanger. The definition of related party discussed in Chapter 9 applies in determining whether a party is related to an exchanger. The definition of related party in that section uses 50 percent ownership in determining whether entities are related to the exchanger, with one modification. The definition of related party for purposes of determining whether an entity is a disqualified person uses 10 percent ownership.

Party Related to the Exchanger's Agent

The above definitions are used to determine whether a party is related to the exchanger's agent. Thus, if an attorney is the exchanger's agent, an entity wholly owned by the attorney would be a disqualified person. The regulations provide an exception to this rule that allows a party affiliated with banks to be a qualified intermediary for the bank's clients. Thus, even if a bank is an exchanger's agent, a party related to the bank may be the escrow holder of a qualified escrow account.

After sharing the definition of disqualified person, Andre explained, "Ensign Ltd agents cannot act as escrow holder. Because I provide advice to Ensign Ltd with respect to numerous matters, I cannot act as escrow holder. In the past two years, I have provided legal services with respect to many matters other than section 1031 exchanges. Therefore, I am an agent of Ensign Ltd. Similarly, Ensign Ltd's CPA, Carla, is an agent of Ensign Ltd because she has prepared Ensign Ltd's tax return for the past several years and provided other accounting services. Because we are both deemed to be Ensign Ltd's agents, we are disqualified persons and cannot act as escrow holder.

"On the other hand, although Big Title Company has provided routine title services to Ensign Ltd with respect to other acquisitions and dispositions, it is not a disqualified person. The regulations specifically provide that an escrow or title insurance company is not an agent of an exchanger if it has provided only routine title insurance or escrow services to the exchanger. Big Title Company has only provided routine title and escrow services for Ensign Ltd, so it would not be a disqualified person and could act as escrow holder."

"I wonder if Big Title Company would serve as escrow holder. Since we plan to use Big Title Company to close the transfer of Quartz Mine, if it could be the escrow holder of a qualified escrow account the arrangement would not significantly impact the closing," Owen observed.

Andre said, "From what you have told me, it sounds like Ensign Ltd can merely transfer Quartz Mine to Bullion Co and direct Bullion Co to deposit the $25,000,000 purchase price into an escrow account held by Big Title Company. In addition to containing the (g)(6) restrictions, the escrow agreement could provide that Big Title Company will use the $25,000,000 to acquire replacement property or, if Ensign Ltd is unable to find and acquire replacement property before the end of the exchange period, Big Title Company would distribute the $25,000,000 to Ensign Ltd after the exchange period."

Owen commented, "The arrangement does not seem too complicated. Now let's discuss the (g)(6) restrictions."

The (g)(6) Restrictions

The (g)(6) restrictions in the regulations limit an exchanger's access to exchange proceeds. Under those restrictions, an exchanger may not have the right to receive, pledge, borrow, or otherwise obtain the benefits of exchange proceeds or other property held in a safe harbor before the end of the exchange period. There are four exceptions to this limitation.

First, the exchanger may receive, pledge, borrow, or otherwise obtain the benefits of the exchange proceeds after the end of the identification period, if the exchanger has not identified any property.

Second, the exchanger may receive, pledge, borrow, or otherwise obtain the benefits of the exchange proceeds after the exchanger has received all of the replacement property to which it is entitled under the exchange agreement.

Third, the exchanger may receive, pledge, borrow, or otherwise obtain the benefits of the exchange proceeds after the end of the identification period if a material and substantial contingency occurs. For example, if the exchanger is unable to obtain zoning for identified replacement property, the exchanger may receive exchange proceeds after the end of the identification period, even if the exchanger has not acquired all of the identified replacement property.

Fourth, the exchanger may use exchange proceeds to acquire personal property that is incidental to real property acquired in a standard commercial real estate exchange if the aggregate fair market value of personal property acquired does not exceed 15 percent of the aggregate fair market value of the replacement properties received in the exchange.

"The (g)(6) restrictions are the crux of the safe harbors," Andre explained. "Remember that the safe harbors in the regulations provide that you will not be deemed to be in constructive receipt of exchange proceeds held under a safe harbor. The safe harbors provide certainty, but the cost of that certainty is that your access to the proceeds will be limited. The (g)(6) restrictions that the regulations require you to include in the escrow agreement will restrict Ensign Ltd's access to the exchange proceeds."

"I think I can live with Ensign Ltd's access to the exchange proceeds being restricted if no one else has access to the funds and Ensign Ltd will either acquire replacement property or receive the exchange proceeds after the end of the exchange period." Owen then asked a very common question: “How long do the (g)(6) restrictions limit Ensign Ltd’s access to the proceeds?”

Andre answered, “The escrow agreement has to restrict Ensign Ltd’s access at least until the end of the identification period. If at the end of the identification period Ensign Ltd has not identified any property, Ensign Ltd can receive the proceeds then.”

“That makes sense,” Owen said. “Ensign Ltd will not be able to do a section 1031 exchange if it does not identify any replacement property. That being the case, Ensign Ltd should be able to access the exchange proceeds after the end of the identification period. What if Ensign Ltd decides not to do an exchange before the end of the identification period? Can it receive the exchange proceeds before the end of the identification period?”

“No,” replied Andre. “If Ensign Ltd decides to use a qualified escrow account, it will not be able to receive the exchange proceeds before the end of the identification period.”

“So you’re telling me that if Ensign Ltd decides to use a qualified escrow account, the proceeds will be tied up for a minimum of 45 days, the length of the identification period?” Owen asked, just to make sure he understood the rule.

“That’s correct,” answered Andre. “The proceeds will be available for acquisition of replacement property at any time during that period, but Ensign Ltd will not be able to receive them.”

Satisfied that he understood that the exchange proceeds would be restricted during the identification period, Owen was curious about what restrictions would apply after the identification period. He asked, “What happens if Ensign Ltd identifies replacement property?”

Andre explained, “If Ensign Ltd identifies replacement property, the (g)(6) restrictions generally will limit Ensign Ltd’s access to the proceeds throughout the duration of the exchange period. One exception to this rule is that the exchanger may be able to receive exchange proceeds after the occurrence of a material and substantial contingency. Thus, if Ensign Ltd identifies replacement property at the end of the identification period and does not acquire any replacement property, it will not be able to receive the exchange proceeds until the end of the exchange period, unless a material and substantial contingency prevents Ensign Ltd from receiving replacement property.”

"What is a material and substantial contingency?" asked Owen.

"An example in the regulations is the inability to obtain desired zoning. Thus, a material and substantial contingency would occur if Ensign Ltd identified a piece of property that it will acquire only if the property is rezoned to commercial use, and before the end of the exchange period the governing body votes to not rezone the property. The failure to rezone is beyond Ensign Ltd's control and once that decision is made, Ensign Ltd will not acquire the identified replacement property. At that time, assuming the identification period has expired, the (g)(6) restrictions may permit Ensign Ltd to acquire the property. This requires, however, that the escrow agreement provides for such contingency. Thus, a material and substantial contingency will terminate the (g)(6) restrictions only if the escrow agreement identifies it."

"What if Ensign Ltd identifies a single replacement property, but realizes before the end of the exchange period that it will never reach an agreement with the owner of that property? Is that a material and substantial contingency?" asked Owen.

"The IRS doesn't believe it is," Andre answered. "According to an IRS private letter ruling, every piece of property is for sale, at the right price. Therefore, the inability to negotiate desired terms does not mean the acquisition is beyond the exchanger's control. At some point, the owner of the property will sell if the exchanger makes the right offer. Thus, the IRS believes the inability to negotiate desired terms is not a material and substantial contingency that terminates the (g)(6) restrictions."

Andre continued, "The only other way for Ensign Ltd to obtain the exchange proceeds prior to the end of the exchange period is for Ensign Ltd to acquire the identified replacement property. Thus, if Ensign Ltd identifies only Regal Bank Building and acquires it before the end of the exchange period, once it acquires Regal Bank Building the (g)(6) restrictions will lapse."

"Assume Ensign Ltd identifies Regal Bank Building worth \$19,000,000 and Route 66 Warehouse worth \$15,000,000, in addition to acquiring Royal Tours Hotel worth \$8,500,000 during the identification period," Owen said. "Would the (g)(6) restrictions terminate after Ensign

Ltd acquired Route 66 Warehouse? Could Ensign Ltd then receive the $1,500,000 remaining in the qualified escrow account?"

"Unfortunately, the regulations do not answer that question," Andre replied. "A conservative reading of the regulations would prohibit your access to the $1,500,000 until the end of the exchange period. Some practitioners may believe that you can receive the $1,500,000 following the acquisition of Route 66 Warehouse, but there is no direct authority to support that. The cost of receiving the proceeds before the termination of the (g)(6) restrictions is that you will lose the safe harbor. The result of that is that you will lose nonrecognition for the entire transaction. That's a high price to pay for receiving the $1,500,000 a few months earlier than otherwise allowed. I suggest you not attempt to draw that money down from the escrow holder before the end of the exchange period in that situation."

"That sounds like wise counsel," Owen said.

Prohibition Against Amending (g)(6) Restrictions

Owen then asked, "What if Ensign Ltd identifies replacement property, but after the identification decides not to do an exchange? Why can't we simply amend the escrow agreement to delete the (g)(6) restrictions? Or simply direct Big Title Company to distribute the proceeds? We won't get section 1031 nonrecognition, so why stay with the safe harbor?"

"An amendment would be evidence that the (g)(6) restrictions were illusory. If an exchanger could access the proceeds by simply amending the agreement, then the exchanger's access to the proceeds was never really limited. The same is true if Big Title Company disregards the language in the escrow agreement and merely distributes the exchange proceeds."

"What would be the downside of that for Ensign Ltd?" Owen asked. "If Ensign Ltd was not going to complete an exchange anyway, it wouldn't care about losing section 1031 nonrecognition."

"That may be true, but if Big Title Company is escrow holder for other exchangers and would do the same for them, then arguably the (g)(6) restrictions in all escrow agreements would be illusory, and none of the exchanges would qualify. Thus, if Big Title Company were able to amend the escrow agreement for Ensign Ltd, other exchangers that had deposits with Big Title Company would also be able to amend their escrow agreements. The ability of other exchangers to amend their escrow agreements would make all the (g)(6) restrictions illusory, and the safe harbor would not apply to any exchanges that Big Title Company facilitated. Without the safe harbor, Ensign Ltd would probably be in constructive receipt of exchange proceeds at the time it sells Quartz Mine."

"That's pretty serious," Owen realized. "I guess we have to plan to have limited access to the exchange proceeds if we decide to use a qualified escrow account."

"That is a cost of otherwise benefiting from the safe harbor," Andre said.

Qualified Trusts

"A qualified trust serves the same purpose as a qualified escrow account—it secures the buyer's obligation to acquire replacement property. The difference is that proceeds are deposited in a trust instead of an escrow account."

"Who can serve as trustee of a qualified trust?" Owen asked.

"Anyone who is not a disqualified person may serve as trustee of a qualified trust," Andre answered. "You and the trustee also must enter into a written trust agreement. That agreement must contain the (g)(6) restrictions. Therefore, it serves the same function as a qualified escrow and is subject to the same restrictions."

After thinking about this, Owen said, "It is nice to know that these options exist. If Bullion Co will agree to facilitate the exchange, either a qualified escrow account or qualified trust would seem to be a viable means of securing the exchange proceeds. The qualified escrow account may be more convenient for us because Big Title Company can serve as the escrow holder. This only works if Bullion Co will acquire replacement property. What can we do if Bullion Co is not interested in facilitating an exchange for Ensign Ltd or will only do it for an unreasonable price?"

Qualified Intermediaries

Andre suggested, "If the buyer of relinquished property and the seller of replacement property are both unwilling to facilitate an exchange, the exchanger may hire a qualified intermediary to facilitate the exchange. The qualified intermediary would acquire Quartz Mine from Ensign Ltd and transfer it to Bullion Co. Bullion Co would pay $25,000,000 to the qualified intermediary in exchange for Quartz Mine. Later, Ensign Ltd would direct the qualified intermediary to use the $25,000,000 to acquire replacement property. The qualified intermediary would then transfer the replacement property to Ensign Ltd."

Qualified Intermediary Exchange

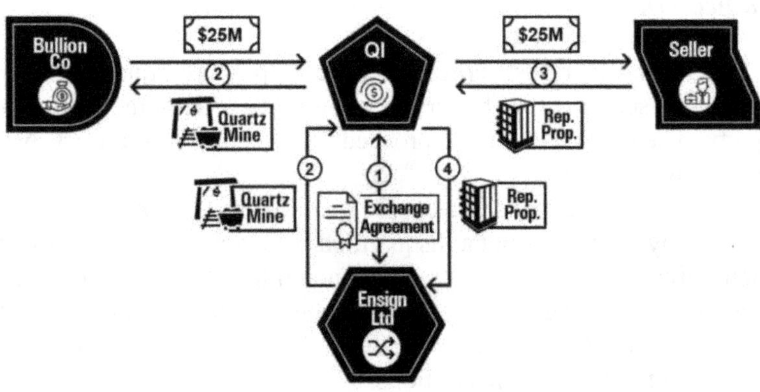

"How does the qualified intermediary help Ensign Ltd avoid constructive receipt of the $25,000,000?" Owen asked.

"The concern is generally that an intermediary would be the agent of Ensign Ltd. If the intermediary were the agent of Ensign Ltd, Ensign Ltd would be in constructive receipt of the $25,000,000. The regulations provide that a qualified intermediary will not be treated as the exchanger's agent. Because the qualified intermediary would not be Ensign Ltd's agent, Ensign Ltd would not be in constructive receipt of proceeds the qualified intermediary receives."

"That makes sense. Will you describe what a qualified intermediary is and who can serve as one?" Owen asked.

Definition of Qualified Intermediary

"Understanding who can serve as a qualified intermediary is the same as understanding what is a qualified intermediary," Andre stated. "A qualified intermediary has to be someone who is not a disqualified person. The definition of disqualified person that applies to qualified escrow account holders and qualified trust trustees applies to qualified intermediaries."

"As I recall, a disqualified person excludes three groups of people, but would allow a broad range of parties to serve as qualified intermediary," Owen said. "Do we have such leeway in choosing a qualified intermediary?"

"You do," Andre confirmed. "The regulations provide that an exchanger's agent, a party related to the exchanger, and a party related to an agent of the exchanger may not serve as qualified intermediary. Anyone else can serve as qualified intermediary."

"Because you are deemed to be my agent, I guess that means that you can't serve as qualified intermediary," Owen realized. "The definition also excludes Ensign Ltd's CPA because she prepared its tax returns and provided tax advice with respect to matters other than Ensign Ltd's section 1031 exchanges. Similarly, any person related to Ensign Ltd may not serve as qualified intermediary."

"That's correct. Our firms are also excluded because you hire the entire firm to represent Ensign Ltd," Andre said. "Not only that, our firms don't provide qualified intermediary services. It would be costly for us to create the system to act as qualified intermediary. You would, therefore, be better served finding someone else to serve as qualified intermediary."

"If Ensign Ltd transfers Quartz Mine to a qualified intermediary and the qualified intermediary transfers it to Bullion Co, what happens to the $25,000,000?" Owen asked. "Will the money be subject to any restrictions?"

"The qualified intermediary will receive the money and hold it until you are ready to acquire replacement property or until the end of the exchange period," Andre said. "The proceeds the qualified intermediary holds must be subject to the (g)(6) restrictions."

The (g)(6) Restrictions

Andre continued, "If you decide to engage a qualified intermediary, the exchange agreement includes the (g)(6) restrictions. Thus, Ensign Ltd will not be able to receive, pledge, borrow, or otherwise obtain the benefit of the proceeds until after the end of the identification period, at the earliest. Remember, however, that if Ensign Ltd identifies replacement property, it will not be able to receive, pledge, borrow, or otherwise obtain the benefit of the proceeds until it acquires the identified replacement property, a material and substantial contingency occurs (as identified in the exchange agreement), or the exchange period lapses."

Prohibition Against Amending (g)(6) Restrictions

"If we enter into the exchange agreement and the qualified intermediary receives the proceeds, could we amend the exchange agreement to eliminate the (g)(6) restrictions if we later decided not to do a section 1031 exchange?" Owen wondered.

"No," Andre said. "As with the qualified escrow account and qualified trust safe harbors, if you are able to amend the underlying document, the (g)(6) restrictions will appear illusory, and the exchange will not qualify for section 1031 nonrecognition. Moreover, an intermediary's violation of the (g)(6) restrictions may be evidence that the restrictions in all of its exchange agreements are illusory, and the intermediary may not be a qualified intermediary with respect to any of the exchanges it facilitates. This would be a disastrous result."

"We can live with limited access to the proceeds if it helps defer gain recognition," Owen said. "We will, however, want to know that the proceeds are secure and available when we need them. How can we be certain the proceeds will be safe?"

"The first step in protecting your proceeds is to choose a good qualified intermediary," Andre said.

Choosing a Qualified Intermediary

"Is it hard to find someone to serve as qualified intermediary?" Owen asked. "Do I just find someone who is not a disqualified person to serve as my qualified intermediary?"

"I generally recommend that you not use just any qualified person to serve as qualified intermediary. There are three things you should consider in choosing a qualified intermediary: (1) the competence of the qualified intermediary, (2) as you have said already, the security of the exchange proceeds, and (3) the qualified intermediary's fees."

Andre explained, "Many people believe they might be able to save money by having a friend or friendly party serve as qualified intermediary even though such person has never so served. I have found that such people don't make the best qualified intermediaries. If you ask someone who has never served as qualified intermediary to facilitate your exchange, that person will be starting from scratch in preparing or reviewing exchange documents, setting up accounts, and considering interests of their own they have to protect. Both you and the novice qualified intermediary will incur considerable fees preparing and reviewing documents and establishing exchange procedures. Even after that, the novice will have a difficult time providing the service that an experienced exchange company can provide.

"On the other hand, if you hire a professional qualified intermediary with a long history of successfully facilitating exchanges and with competent exchange specialists working for it, the process will generally go smoothly and the cost will not be significant," Andre said. "The exchange specialists will be familiar with the exchange rules and the company will have procedures in place for handling exchange proceeds and will have documents that are well drafted and satisfy the section 1031 requirements."

"How much do competent professional qualified intermediaries charge?" Owen asked.

"Interestingly, their fees are fairly nominal. Because they can spread their costs (developing a system, training exchange specialists, and preparing documents) over hundreds or even thousands of exchanges, they are able to charge fairly low fees per exchange. For example, many professional qualified intermediaries will charge around $2,500 for an exchange like the one Ensign Ltd is contemplating."

"That sounds almost too good to be true," Owen replied.

"There is more to it than that," Andre said. "Most professional qualified intermediaries that charge a flat fee also earn income off exchange proceeds they hold. Bank-affiliated qualified intermediaries make money off exchange proceeds just like they make money off other deposits. Non-bank-affiliated qualified intermediaries receive interest on exchange proceeds at a slightly higher rate because the deposits they bring to a financial institution are significant. Such qualified intermediaries then return to exchangers only the amount of interest the exchanger would have earned in a typical deposit account. This float (difference between the rate on a non-aggregated account and the rate on an aggregated account) helps qualified intermediaries make a profit."

"How will I know how much interest Ensign Ltd will receive on exchange proceeds while the qualified intermediary holds the money?" asked Owen.

"The exchange agreement might disclose what percent of the interest the qualified intermediary will keep," Andre said. "If it doesn't, we will simply discuss that with the qualified intermediary. They are successful because they focus on providing a quality service to exchangers and should be prepared to discuss all aspects of the exchange process and security of the proceeds. They focus on helping exchangers complete exchanges. This requires that they protect the proceeds."

"How do qualified intermediaries protect proceeds?" Owen asked.

"Some qualified intermediaries are bonded. They also generally carry some type of errors and omission insurance," Andre said. "That will provide some protection. If the qualified intermediary is affiliated with a large bank or title agency, the bank or title agency may guarantee the security of the proceeds."

"With the amount of money we're talking about here, it almost sounds like going with that type of qualified intermediary makes sense," Owen said.

"Not necessarily," Andre said. "Many of the private qualified intermediaries provide a great service. Some of them are very large and protect the proceeds they hold. You should talk to a few qualified intermediary companies before you hire one."

"Are there some qualified intermediary companies I should stay away from?" Owen asked.

"Probably," Andre said. "Around 2007-2008, a few high profile qualified intermediary failures occurred. In one instance, the owner stole the exchange proceeds. In the other, the qualified intermediary mismanaged the exchange proceeds. This is a reason to hire an experienced qualified intermediary with a strong record and reputation. You might also ensure that the qualified intermediary has the financial backing of a financially stable affiliate or is sufficiently bonded or insured to be able to deliver your exchange proceeds according to the exchange agreement."

Andre concluded, "In choosing a qualified intermediary, you should also find out where the qualified intermediary deposits exchange proceeds. The qualified intermediary should deposit the proceeds with a reputable financial institution and the proceeds should be deposited in segregated accounts. You should stay far from any qualified intermediary that mingles exchange proceeds in its common operating fund or with other exchange proceeds."

Direct Deeding

"So walk me through how the money and property will move," Owen requested. "I find it difficult to believe that a qualified intermediary will want to take title to Quartz Mine or any of the replacement properties."

"I can't imagine many qualified intermediaries wanting to take legal title either," Andre said. "Nor can I imagine any exchanger wanting to hire a qualified intermediary who has taken legal title to property. That could expose exchange proceeds to liability from other property."

Andre continued, "Thankfully, the regulations allow for direct deeding from Ensign Ltd to Bullion Co and from the seller of the replacement property to Ensign Ltd. Ensign Ltd will transfer legal title to Quartz Mine directly to Bullion Co. The regulations treat the qualified intermediary as acquiring Quartz Mine and transferring it to Bullion Co as long as you properly document the transaction. The seller of the replacement property can similarly directly deed the replacement property to you."

"It sounds like the documentation will be fairly extensive," Owen said.

"You will have some documentation, but not as much as you may think. The exchange agreement will be extensive, but the documents needed to transfer the property won't be that extensive," Andre explained. "For example, you will deed Quartz Mine to Bullion Co just as though the exchange had not occurred. That will not require any additional documents. You will, however, need to assign your rights to the proceeds from the sale of Quartz Mine to the qualified intermediary. A one or two-page document will assign those rights. Ensign Ltd will have to notify Bullion Co in writing of the assignment, but that won't be difficult. The assignment document that many qualified intermediaries use incorporates notice and would ask Bullion Co to sign confirming the notice. The regulations treat the assignment of rights and notice as a transfer of the property to the qualified intermediary."

"I'm not sure I understand the significance of the assignment," Owen admitted.

"The assignment helps create a fiction that is essential to section 1031 nonrecognition for exchanges facilitated by a qualified intermediary. Under the fiction, the qualified intermediary is treated as acquiring and transferring property. Thus, if Ensign Ltd assigns to the qualified intermediary its rights to receive consideration for Quartz Mine, notifies Bullion Co of the assignment, and directly deeds Quartz Mine to Bullion Co, Ensign Ltd will be treated, for tax purposes, as transferring Quartz Mine to the qualified intermediary, and the qualified intermediary will be treated as transferring Quartz Mine to Bullion Co. A similar fiction would apply to the replacement property.

Direct Deeding: Qualified Intermediary Exchange

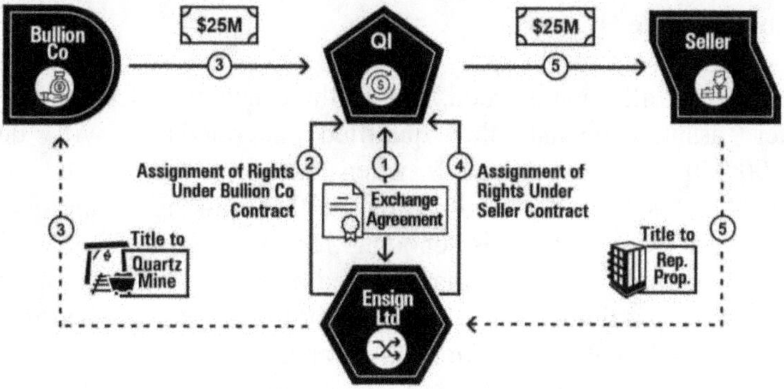

"Thus, if you correctly document the transaction, the qualified intermediary does not have to enter the chain of title. Bullion Co and the seller of the replacement property should willingly cooperate with you in structuring this transaction because it does not require anything extra of them. The assignment does not affect their rights or obligations," Andre concluded.

Interest and Growth Factors

"You said earlier that I could receive interest earned on exchange proceeds held by the qualified intermediary. What is the tax consequence of Ensign Ltd receiving the interest?" Owen asked.

"Ensign Ltd will have to report any interest it earns on the exchange proceeds," Andre answered. "Its access to the interest will be limited by the (g)(6) restrictions. Therefore, Ensign Ltd won't be able to receive the interest until it is able to receive the exchange proceeds. At that time, Ensign Ltd will have interest income."

Andre continued, "This is the final deferred exchange safe harbor. The regulations allow an exchanger to receive interest or growth factors without disrupting the safe harbor. The only stipulation is that exchanger can't receive such payments until the (g)(6) restrictions lapse."

Combining Safe Harbors

"That all sounds good, but is there any way for me to have greater assurance that the qualified intermediary will deliver $25,000,000 exchange proceeds when Ensign Ltd needs it?" Owen asked. "I guess I am not totally satisfied that banking on the qualified intermediary's reputation is enough for me. Even if we hire a professional qualified intermediary owned by a large multinational bank, there is some possibility that money will not be available when we need it. I might want to obtain additional assurance."

"The regulations provide that exchangers may combine certain safe harbors," Andre said. "For example, you could combine the qualified intermediary safe harbor with the qualified trust safe harbor."

Combining Safe Harbors

The regulations provide that exchangers may combine certain safe harbors. Thus, money deposited in a qualified trust or qualified escrow may secure a qualified intermediary's obligation to transfer replacement property to the exchanger.

"How would that work?" Owen wondered out loud.

"The exchange agreement Ensign Ltd enters into with the qualified intermediary will provide that the qualified intermediary will acquire and transfer replacement property. This makes the qualified intermediary the relinquished property buyer even if Ensign Ltd directly deeds Quartz Mine to Bullion Co," Andre said. "If the arrangement with the qualified intermediary satisfies all of the requirements in the regulations, that arrangement will be a safe harbor. You may combine that safe harbor with the qualified trust safe harbor (or the qualified escrow account safe harbor). Recall that the qualified trust safe harbor provides that an exchanger will not be deemed to be in constructive receipt of money deposited in a qualified trust. Recall further that money deposited in a qualified trust secures the relinquished property buyer's obligation to transfer replacement property. Because the regulations treat the qualified intermediary as the relinquished property buyer, Ensign Ltd will not be deemed to be in constructive receipt of the $25,000,000 if Bullion Co deposits the money in a qualified trust to secure the qualified intermediary's obligation to transfer replacement property to Ensign Ltd."

Combined Safe Harbor Exchange

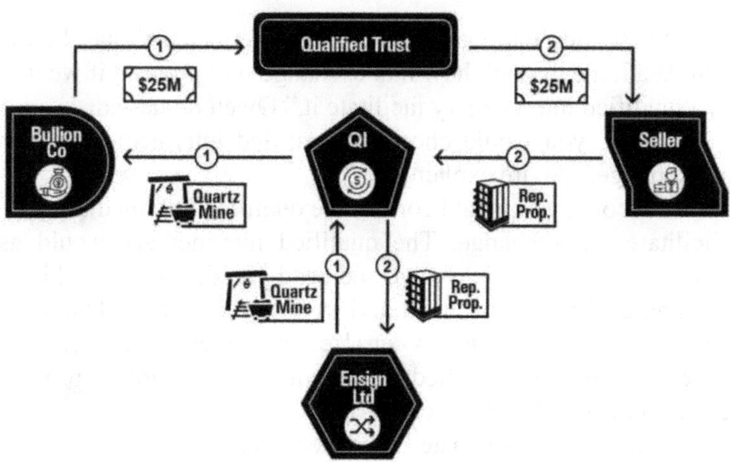

"So, if Bullion Co deposits the $25,000,000 in a qualified trust, Ensign Ltd won't be in constructive receipt of that money and the qualified intermediary won't be able to access the money except to acquire replacement property or pay Ensign Ltd when the (g)(6) restrictions lapse," Owen realized. "This will provide an extra level of security and will allow section 1031 nonrecognition. Do very many exchangers structure exchanges like this?"

"I haven't seen too many," Andre admitted. "I think part of the reason we don't see such structures very often is because exchangers don't think of it. Also, the vast majority of professional qualified intermediaries have excellent track records of delivering exchange proceeds on demand. That and the overall perceived financial strength of a qualified intermediary and its affiliates provide sufficient comfort to most exchangers. That doesn't mean you shouldn't take the extra precaution if you're so inclined. The option is there for you, if you feel you need it. Having seen the qualified intermediary failures of 2007 and 2008, I believe it's worth exploring using a qualified trust or qualified escrow account."

Steps of an Exchange with a Qualified Intermediary

"It sounds like using a qualified intermediary may be our best option. Walk me through how this exchange will proceed if we decide to have a qualified intermediary facilitate it," Owen requested.

"First, you would choose a qualified intermediary to facilitate your exchange," Andre explained.

"Second, you would contact the qualified intermediary and ask it to facilitate the exchange. The qualified intermediary would ask for information about your exchange and send you documents, which would include an exchange agreement and an assignment of rights. We would review those documents to ensure that they satisfy all of the requirements of the qualified intermediary safe harbor, protect your interests, and comply with section 1031."

"Do you anticipate the document review being a big undertaking?" Owen asked.

"Not if you choose a good qualified intermediary," Andre replied. "I have seen enough exchange documents to know what to look for. The qualified intermediary will work with us to make any reasonable modifications we request. Typically, there won't be many changes to make.

"Third, after finalizing the exchange agreement and assignment of rights, Ensign Ltd would transfer Quartz Mine. At or before closing, you would sign all of the necessary documents, including the exchange agreement and assignment of rights. You must be sure to sign the exchange documents before you transfer Quartz Mine. The wire instructions will provide that Bullion Co will transfer $25,000,000 to the qualified intermediary. Thus, at closing Ensign Ltd will transfer title of

Quartz Mine directly to Bullion Co and Bullion Co will wire $25,000,000 to the qualified intermediary or, if you prefer, to a qualified trust or qualified escrow account.

"Fourth, Ensign Ltd will identify one or more replacement properties. The qualified intermediary will have a form you can use to identify replacement properties. Remember that you have to follow the identification rules. Thus, you can identify any three properties without regard to their fair market value, or you can identify any number of properties as long as the aggregate fair market value of all of the identified properties does not exceed 200 percent of the value of Quartz Mine. Thus, under the 200% rule, you may identify up to $50,000,000 of replacement properties.

"Fifth, Ensign Ltd will enter into a contract to acquire replacement property.

"Sixth, instead of acquiring the replacement property, Ensign Ltd will assign its rights to acquire the replacement property to the qualified intermediary.

"Seventh, the qualified intermediary will wire $25,000,000 to the seller and direct the seller to directly deed the replacement property to Ensign Ltd.

"That doesn't sound too complicated," Owen said. "It's several steps, but the only significant differences between that structure and simply selling Quartz Mine and acquiring the replacement property are (1) the exchange agreement, (2) the restrictions on the exchange proceeds, (3) the assignment documents and wiring instructions, and (4) the possibility for gain deferral. Who do you recommend to serve as qualified intermediary?"

Assuming Andre has assisted others with section 1031 exchanges, he will know several qualified intermediaries that are competent and have a system in place to efficiently facilitate Ensign Ltd's exchange and safeguard the $25,000,000 of exchange proceeds. Andre will likely provide Owen with several names.

CHAPTER 6: EXCHANGE STRUCTURES: REVERSE EXCHANGES

In a reverse exchange, the exchanger acquires replacement property first and subsequently transfers relinquished property. Reverse exchanges raise a unique legal issue. Legal authority does not specifically provide that an exchanger may acquire replacement property and hold it concurrently with relinquished property. Without direct legal authority on this issue, section 1031 experts hesitate to advise exchangers to enter into such exchanges. Section 1031 experts worry that the concurrent holding of replacement property and relinquished property may not satisfy the exchange requirement and thus may prevent reverse exchanges from qualifying for section 1031 nonrecognition. Therefore, section 1031 experts recommend using title-parking reverse exchanges.

PURE REVERSE EXCHANGES

An exchanger executes a pure reverse exchange by acquiring replacement property, holding it and the relinquished property concurrently, and later transferring the relinquished property. In theory, such an exchange would be facilitated by a facilitator, perhaps a qualified intermediary. Some section 1031 commentators theorize that such transactions may qualify for section 1031 nonrecognition. Because no legal authority addresses pure reverse exchanges, however, advisors generally do not recommend them, and exchangers rarely, if ever, do them.

Pure Reverse Exchange

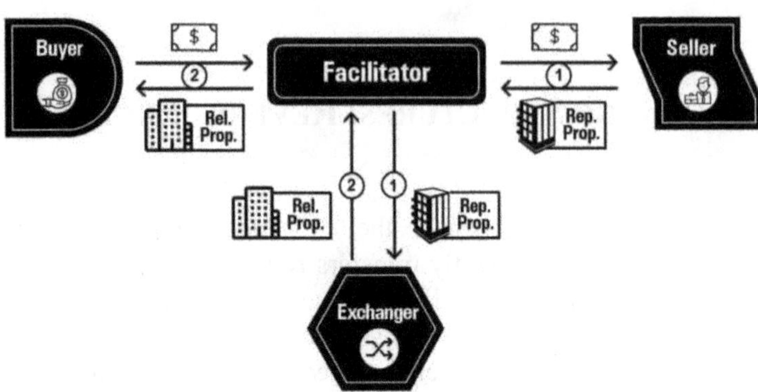

The paucity of legal authority on pure reverse exchanges may be due to a handful of cases involving botched exchanges and unsupported reporting positions by a few property owners. In those few cases, property owners acquired property and during the same year sold another piece of property. The property owner in each case was unable to demonstrate that the acquisition of one property and the disposition of the other property were interdependent. Thus, the acquisition of one property and subsequent disposition of another property were viewed as separate transactions. As such, the property owners in each case were unable to demonstrate that a reciprocal transfer of property had occurred. Because of this, the courts correctly ruled that no exchange had occurred.

Failed Attempts at Reverse Exchange

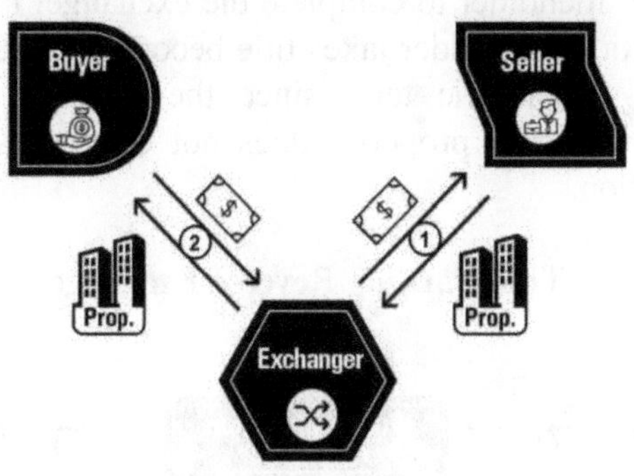

Holdings in these cases of botched reverse exchanges beg the question: would a pure reverse exchange qualify for section 1031 nonrecognition if the acquisition of the replacement property and the disposition of the relinquished property were part of an integrated plan and therefore interdependent? Based on the continued-investment purpose of section 1031 and the possibility of satisfying the technical requirements of section 1031 in such transactions, some section 1031 experts believe that such transactions could satisfy the section 1031 exchange requirement. Nonetheless, the absence of legal authority discourages experts from advising property owners to do pure reverse exchanges. Undaunted, tax planners found other methods to avoid concurrent ownership in reverse exchanges.

TITLE-PARKING REVERSE EXCHANGES

Section 1031 advisors have developed, and the IRS has sanctioned, title-parking reverse exchanges that do not require exchangers to hold replacement property and relinquished property concurrently. A typical title-parking reverse exchange structure has three steps: (1) the exchanger hires an accommodation titleholder to acquire replacement property, (2) the accommodation titleholder acquires the replacement property and holds it until the exchanger is prepared to transfer the relinquished property, and (3) the exchanger transfers the relinquished property and acquires the replacement property from the accommodation titleholder to complete the exchange. Property to which the accommodation titleholder takes title becomes parked property. This is obviously a metaphoric term since the physical location of the property, especially real property, does not change as part of a title-parking transaction.

Title-Parking Reverse Exchange

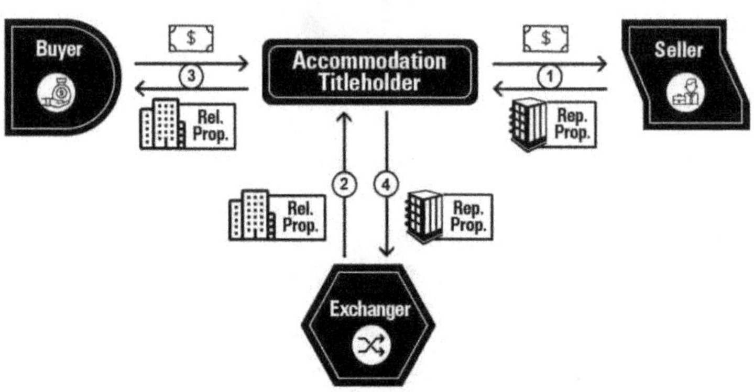

Title-parking reverse exchanges are not free from potential pitfalls. If not carefully structured, the exchanger will be treated as owning the replacement property for federal tax purposes. If the exchanger holds the relinquished property and replacement property concurrently, the exchange may not qualify for section 1031 nonrecognition. Thus, the exchanger must ensure that the exchange accommodator owns the property for tax purposes. This would generally require that the exchange accommodator not be the agent of the exchanger, and that the exchange accommodator otherwise be the owner for tax purposes.

Federal Tax Ownership

Federal tax law has its own tests for determining property ownership. Federal tax ownership does not necessarily follow state law ownership. Thus, a person may hold legal title to property but own the property for federal tax purposes. Federal tax law focuses on who enjoys the benefits and bears the burdens of the property. Under this benefits and burdens test, possession of legal title is only one indicium of tax ownership. Other indicia, as listed in Grodt and McKay v. Commissioner include: how the parties treat the transaction (e.g., who reports the ownership for tax purposes? Who takes depreciation, if the property is depreciable), whether a party has an equity interest in the property (e.g., has a party invested any of its own funds in the property?), whether the parties have a present obligation to transfer or acquire the property (e.g., have the parties entered into offsetting put and call options?), who has the right to possess the property, which party pays the property taxes, which party bears the risk of loss of the property (e.g., who would have to pay for damages or be unable to recover the loss?), and which party receives the profits from the operation and sale of the property. Courts consider these factors in determining who has the benefits and burdens of ownership.

Ensuring that the accommodation titleholder is the tax owner of parked property could be simple, but the parties' objectives complicate things. The exchanger generally wishes to maintain control over the property held by the accommodation titleholder, take possession of it, and later acquire it at a fixed price (i.e., the exchanger does not want the property to appreciate while held by the accommodation titleholder and have to pay more for the property than the accommodation titleholder paid for it). Furthermore, the accommodation titleholder generally is interested in receiving a fee for holding the property, will not finance the acquisition of the property, and does not want to be stuck with the property if its value diminishes while the accommodation titleholder is on title. Structuring the arrangement to accomplish these purposes may place the tax ownership of the parked property with the exchanger. This would nullify the attempt to structure a title-parking reverse exchange. Thankfully, the IRS provides a safe harbor for structuring title-parking reverse exchanges. The safe harbor provides that if a title-parking exchange transaction satisfies several requirements, the IRS will treat the accommodation titleholder as the tax owner of a parked property. This relieves the parties from having to ensure that the accommodation titleholder has the benefits and burdens of the parked property. Now, benefits and burdens are important only if a title-parking transaction does not satisfy the safe harbor requirements.

Safe Harbor Title-Parking Reverse Exchanges

The IRS provides the safe harbor for title-parking exchanges in Rev. Proc. 2000-37. The safe harbor provides that if the title-parking transaction satisfies several requirements, the IRS will treat the exchange accommodation titleholder (EAT) as the owner of the parked property for tax purposes. The safe harbor also allows the exchanger and EAT to enter into several agreements that effectively shift the benefits and burdens of owning parked property to the exchanger. Thus, the safe harbor provides an efficient way to structure title-parking reverse exchanges.

Title-Parking Safe Harbor

An exchange accommodation titleholder, or EAT, is a party that holds property for the exchanger as part of a title-parking reverse exchange. The reverse exchange safe harbor in Rev. Proc. 2002-22 provides that the EAT will be deemed to own property to which it holds title if several requirements are satisfied. The safe harbor helps the exchanger avoid the burdensome benefits and burdens test of tax ownership. Although established for reverse exchanges, the title-parking safe harbor applies to all title-parking exchanges, including improvements exchanges and deferred improvements exchanges.

The Safe Harbor Requirements

The IRS lists ten requirements an exchanger must satisfy to come within the title-parking safe harbor.

Requirement 1: EAT not a disqualified person. A person other than the exchanger or a disqualified person must serve as an EAT. Although the IRS does not define disqualified person for this purpose, it likely intended to adopt the definition of disqualified person used in the deferred exchange safe harbor regulations. Therefore, the EAT probably cannot be a party that is related to the exchanger, the exchanger's agent, or a party related to the exchanger's agent. (Chapter 5 discusses the definition of disqualified person.)

Requirement 2: EAT must be subject to U.S. tax. The EAT must be subject to U.S. tax. If the EAT is a tax partnership or an S corporation, its partners or shareholders must be subject to U.S. tax. This requirement becomes important because the IRS requires the exchanger and the EAT to treat the EAT as the tax owner of the property to which the EAT holds title (Requirement 6).

Requirement 3: EAT must hold qualified indicia of ownership. The EAT must acquire qualified indicia of ownership in the property. The IRS defines qualified indicia of ownership generally as legal title. Thus, if an EAT holds legal title, it will satisfy the qualified indicia of ownership requirement. The IRS also allows the EAT to form an entity disregarded for tax purposes to hold legal title. A single-member limited liability company is generally disregarded for tax purposes. Thus, the EAT may form a limited liability company, hold all of the interests in the limited liability company, and cause the limited liability company to acquire legal title to property.

Requirement 4: Bona fide intent. At the time the EAT acquires qualified indicia of ownership, the exchanger must have the bona fide intent that the parked property either be relinquished property or replacement property. The exchanger's entering into an agreement with the EAT and providing that the purpose for the arrangement is to facilitate a section 1031 exchange should demonstrate bona fide intent.

Requirement 5: Written agreement. The exchanger and EAT must enter into a written agreement within five business days after the EAT takes title to the property. Although the safe harbor provides a five-day cushion, prudence dictates that the exchanger and EAT should execute the agreement before the EAT takes title to the property. To satisfy the safe harbor, the written agreement must provide that (1) the EAT is holding property to facilitate an exchange under section 1031 and Rev. Proc. 2000-37; (2) the exchanger and EAT agree to report the acquisition, holding, and disposition of the property as required in Rev. Proc. 2000-37; and (3) the exchanger and EAT will treat the EAT as the tax owner of the property for all federal tax purposes.

Requirement 6: Tax treatment of ownership. The exchanger and EAT must treat the EAT as the owner of the property for federal tax purposes. Thus, the EAT must account for acquiring the property, holding the property, and selling the property. Because the EAT acquires the property with the intent to transfer it to the exchanger, the property will be inventory if the EAT holds it at the end of a taxable year. Generally, the exchanger and EAT will enter into permitted agreements that zero out the EAT's gain or loss from holding the property and cover any costs the EAT incurred while holding the property. Thus, the net effect of most safe harbor title-parking exchanges is that the EAT will earn a sum equal to a fee agreed upon with the exchanger. Nonetheless, the EAT must account for any income and expense realized while holding the property and account for the acquisition and disposition of the parked property.

Requirement 7: Relinquished property identification. The exchanger must identify relinquished property within 45 days after the EAT acquires the parked property. The multiple and alternative property identification rules discussed above (Chapter 5) apply to the identification of relinquished property.

Requirement 8: Replacement property holding period limitation. The EAT may hold replacement property for no longer than 180 days. As discussed below, the EAT acquires replacement property in an exchange-last transaction.

Requirement 9: Relinquished property holding period limitation. The EAT may hold relinquished property for no longer than

180 days. As discussed below, the EAT acquires relinquished property in an exchange-first transaction.

Requirement 10: Combined holding period limitation. The EAT may hold replacement property and relinquished property no longer than 180 days in the aggregate. These holding period limitations prevent exchangers from combining holding periods to extend beyond a total of 180 days.

The Permitted Arrangements

The IRS specifically allows the exchanger and the EAT to enter into several arrangements. Without the safe harbor, many of these arrangements would shift tax ownership from the EAT to the exchanger. The following permitted arrangements are key to making title-parking exchanges available to a broad cross-section of property owners. They make the transaction economically feasible by allowing parties leeway in structuring title-parking arrangements.

Permitted Arrangement 1: EAT may be a qualified intermediary. The IRS allows the EAT to also serve as qualified intermediary. Although this may be important in specific situations, a qualified intermediary should not take title to property. Doing so may expose the qualified intermediary to unnecessary liability. In some situations, however, the EAT may take possession of exchange money and need to be a qualified intermediary. (Chapter 2 and later in this chapter discuss the need to separate the EAT function from the qualified intermediary function.)

Permitted Arrangement 2: Loan guarantees. In the event the exchanger arranges third-party financing instead of lending the EAT money to acquire the property, the safe harbor allows the exchanger or a disqualified person to guarantee the loan. Thus, the burden of borrowing falls on the exchanger, not the EAT. The safe harbor also allows the exchanger to agree to indemnify the EAT for costs the EAT incurs while holding the parked property. This permitted agreement is important because most EATs are in the business of facilitating exchanges and do not plan to pay for the costs of owning the parked property.

Permitted Arrangement 3: Non-market loans. The safe harbor allows the EAT to borrow from the exchanger or a disqualified person. Furthermore, such loans do not have to reflect market terms. Thus, the exchanger or disqualified person may charge nominal interest (i.e., $1.00) without violating the safe harbor. Because the EAT's function is merely that of accommodator, the EAT will almost never put its own resources at risk to acquire property to facilitate an exchange. The exchanger generally arranges the financing for the EAT to acquire the property. This permitted arrangement alleviates the complexity of arranging financing.

Permitted Arrangement 4: Non-market leases. The safe harbor allows the exchanger or a disqualified person to lease the parked property from the EAT at other-than-market rates. Thus, the exchanger may lease the parked property from the EAT for one dollar for the entire period the EAT is on title. This allows the exchanger to take possession of the property while the EAT is on title.

Permitted Arrangement 5: Non-market management arrangements. The safe harbor allows the EAT to hire the exchanger or a disqualified person to manage the parked property, supervise improvement of the parked property, and act as contractor or otherwise provide services to the EAT with respect to the parked property. The safe harbor is once again generous and allows the EAT to pay for such services at other-than-market rates. Thus, the EAT could pay a nominal fee for the exchanger to manage a large apartment complex with hundreds of tenants while the EAT holds legal title.

Permitted Arrangement 6: Option arrangements. The safe harbor permits exchangers and EATs to enter into option arrangements. Thus, the EAT may obtain a put option from the exchanger. The put option may allow the EAT to transfer the parked property to the exchanger within 185 days after it takes title for a fixed price. To avoid any downside in the market, the EAT will generally require that the put option allow the EAT to sell the parked property for the amount it paid to acquire the property plus any costs incurred while it held the property.

The safe harbor also allows the exchanger to obtain a call option. To ensure that it retains the upside potential of the property, the exchanger will require that the call price be for the amount the EAT pays to acquire the property plus any costs the EAT incurs while holding the property.

Permitted Arrangement 7: Adjustments for economic risk. The safe harbor allows the exchanger to advance additional funds to the EAT if the value of the relinquished property diminishes while the EAT is on title. For example, if the EAT pays $100,000 to acquire relinquished property from the exchanger and receives only $80,000 on the sale of the relinquished property, the EAT may receive $20,000 from the exchanger to make up the difference. Upon the sale of the relinquished property, the safe harbor also allows the EAT to pay to the exchanger any proceeds the EAT receives that exceed its purchase price of the property. For example, if the EAT pays $100,000 to acquire relinquished property from the exchanger and later sells the property for $120,000, the EAT may pay the $20,000 excess to the exchanger. Such payments do not disrupt the title-parking safe harbor, but they will most likely be boot to the exchanger.

These are the arrangements the title-parking reverse exchange safe harbor permits. If an exchanger used all of the permitted arrangements, the benefits and burdens of holding the property would shift to the exchanger. The benefit of the safe harbor is that the IRS will treat the EAT as the owner of the property for tax purposes even if it uses these arrangements.

Although a reverse exchange is a transaction in which the exchanger receives the replacement property before it transfers the relinquished property, the safe harbor does not require the exchanger to park title to the replacement property with the EAT. Instead, the exchanger may park title to the relinquished property with the EAT. In such a transaction, the exchanger would transfer the relinquished property to the EAT before or simultaneously with the acquisition of the replacement property. Because the exchanger transfers the relinquished property before acquiring the replacement property, the transaction technically may not come within the strict definition of reverse exchange. Nonetheless, because the EAT is a facilitator who merely holds the relinquished property until the exchanger arranges for its transfer to a buyer, the structure accomplishes what a reverse exchange would accomplish.

This demonstrates that the exchanger may structure a title-parking exchange in one of two ways. First, it may structure it in such a manner that the EAT takes title to the replacement property. Under such an arrangement, the exchanger and the EAT exchange property after the EAT holds title to the replacement property. Thus, the exchange is the last part of the transaction. This type of arrangement is referred to as an exchange-last transaction. Second, the exchanger may structure a title-parking reverse exchange so that the EAT takes title to the relinquished property. Under such an arrangement, the exchanger transfers the relinquished property to the EAT in exchange for the replacement property as the first step of the transaction. The EAT then holds the relinquished property until the exchanger arranges for its ultimate disposition. This type of transaction is an exchange-first arrangement. Several factors help determine whether an exchange-first or exchange-last structure is more appropriate for the exchanger.

Structuring Title-Parking Reverse Exchanges

The following situation demonstrates the issues property owners face in structuring reverse exchanges. Evan owns a piece of raw land, Quincy Lot. It is worth $2,000,000 and Evan's basis in the property is $250,000. Evan has placed Quincy Lot on the market, and even though several people have shown an interest in purchasing it, he does not know when it will sell. In the meantime, he has entered into a contract to purchase Randolph Building, a small office building, for $2,000,000 from Stacey. Evan's CPA Charlene suggests that Evan consider structuring the acquisition of Randolph Building and the disposition of Quincy Lot as a reverse exchange. She arranges for Evan to meet with her and Isabel, an exchange specialist with an exchange company, to discuss the possibility of doing an exchange. Isabel asks Evan to discuss the transaction.

"I currently own Quincy Lot," Evan begins. "It is in a good location, with some good development happening around it, and although it is in a fairly small town, I am confident it will sell before too long. In the meantime, however, I have entered into a contract to purchase Randolph Building. As you may know, it is a small office building with a couple of tenants. I am very happy with the contract price and can get the financing to purchase it even before I sell Quincy Lot. Furthermore, I think the seller of Randolph Building was fairly generous, so I don't want to lose the contract. It is scheduled to close in three weeks, and I want to acquire it, even if I haven't sold Quincy Lot by then."

Charlene added, "Even though he wants to acquire Randolph Building before he sells Quincy Lot, he will recognize a significant taxable gain on the sale of Quincy Lot if he cannot structure this transaction as a reverse exchange. If he gets what he wants from Quincy Lot, he is looking at $1,750,000 of long-term capital gain. Even at a low 20 percent tax rate, he would owe $350,000 of tax on that gain."

"The costs will become important. The cost of the transaction ultimately depends upon how it is structured," Isabel explained. "Our exchange company has facilitated many reverse exchanges for considerably less than the amount of tax you are looking to defer, so it is very possible that the transaction costs won't make this cost prohibitive. What are you thinking as far as a structure is concerned?"

"We're just starting to think about it," Charlene said. "Evan is confident he can get the financing to acquire Randolph Building, but he hasn't spoken with the bank about how he might structure the acquisition. Have you ever run into a problem with structuring a reverse exchange because of the lender restrictions?"

"Many lenders understand reverse exchanges and will work with us in structuring the transaction as needed to accommodate the exchanger," Isabel said. "There have been times, however, when the bank has dictated the structure of the exchange. Generally, that happens when the bank insists upon the exchanger taking title to the replacement property immediately. In such a situation, Evan will have to structure the transaction as an exchange-first reverse exchange, and we will take title to the relinquished property."

"If the bank's cooperation is important, it sounds like the first thing I will have to do is speak with the bank about what I want to do," Evan said. "I have done quite a bit of business with my current bank, so I don't anticipate too much resistance on the bank's part."

"So it sounds like the options are (1) to have your company take title to Randolph Building, if the bank will allow that, or (2) to have

Evan acquire Randolph Building immediately and transfer Quincy Lot to you," Charlene summarized. "Can you tell us a little bit about how much you will charge for this so Evan can begin thinking about whether the section 1031 structure will be cost prohibitive?"

"Sure," Isabel said. "Either way we structure this transaction, Evan will use both our qualified intermediary services and our accommodation titleholder services. We generally charge a flat fee of $2,500 for qualified intermediary services and, for a transaction like this, I would anticipate that we would charge between $25,000 and $35,000 for the exchange accommodation titleholder services. Thus, based on what you've told me, you're looking at a fee of between $27,500 and $37,500."

"Why would I need to use both your qualified intermediary services and accommodation titleholder services; couldn't I just hire you to provide the accommodation titleholder services?" Evan asked. "That wouldn't be a big savings, but if I can save $2,500, I would like to. Also, why do you charge so much more for the accommodation titleholder services?"

Charlene offered, "Allow me to answer the first question. Section 1031 requires an exchange to occur between the exchanger and another party. In your situation, this would generally require that you transfer relinquished property to one person and receive replacement property from that same person. Because you are acquiring Randolph Building from Stacey and hope to sell Quincy Lot to some other party, you need an intermediary to acquire Randolph Building and transfer it to you in exchange for Quincy Lot."

"I understand that I need to transfer the property to and receive property from the same party, but couldn't the exchange accommodation titleholder act as qualified intermediary?" Evan asked. "That would seem to simplify the transaction."

Charlene answered, "We could structure the transaction to come within the safe harbor if the exchange accommodation titleholder acts as qualified intermediary. Will your company do that, Isabel?"

"I suppose we could structure the transaction that way, if you insisted. For us, however, it would complicate the transaction a little since we generally don't structure transactions in that manner. The result of the increased complexity would add costs. We might have to hire someone to modify the documents, and Evan's attorney would also have to spend time with the modified documents. In the end, the cost to you will be the same as it would be under the structure I described, perhaps more," Isabel concluded.

"More importantly," Charlene explained, "if you end up selling Quincy Lot for more than $2,000,000, you may want to use that excess to acquire other replacement property. In such a situation, you might be better off if your proceeds were deposited with the qualified intermediary, not the exchange accommodation titleholder. Having a separate legal entity hold exchange proceeds will protect them from liability arising with respect to the property."

"I guess I'm confused by what you mean when you speak of the qualified intermediary and the exchange accommodation titleholder as different legal entities," Evan confessed.

Typical Structure of an Exchange Company

"We use multiple legal entities in the exchange company to protect the assets we hold," Isabel offered. "In particular, we use separate legal entities to separate legal title to property we hold from other property and exchange proceeds. Thus, one legal entity serves solely as a qualified intermediary and another legal entity serves as exchange accommodation titleholder. Both entities are owned by the same holding company.

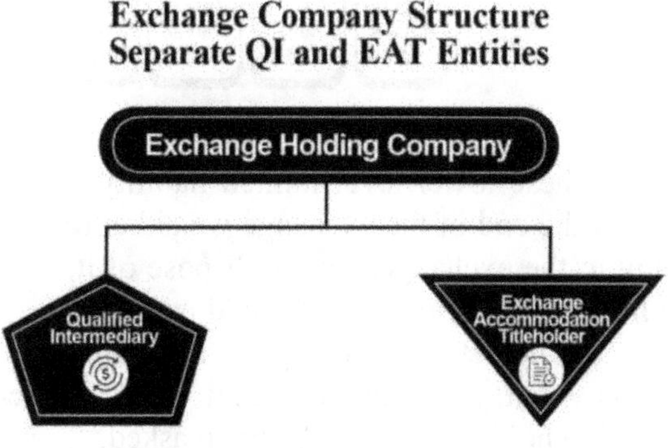

"The qualified intermediary is a legal entity separate from the exchange accommodation titleholder," Isabel explained. "We take this one step further in an attempt to protect property. We form a separate entity to acquire each piece of property to which we take legal title. Thus, at any given time, the exchange accommodation titleholder may be the sole member of several other legal entities. We almost always form limited liability companies to acquire legal title to the property we hold.

Exchange Company Structure
Separate QI and EAT Entities with Tear-Off LLCs

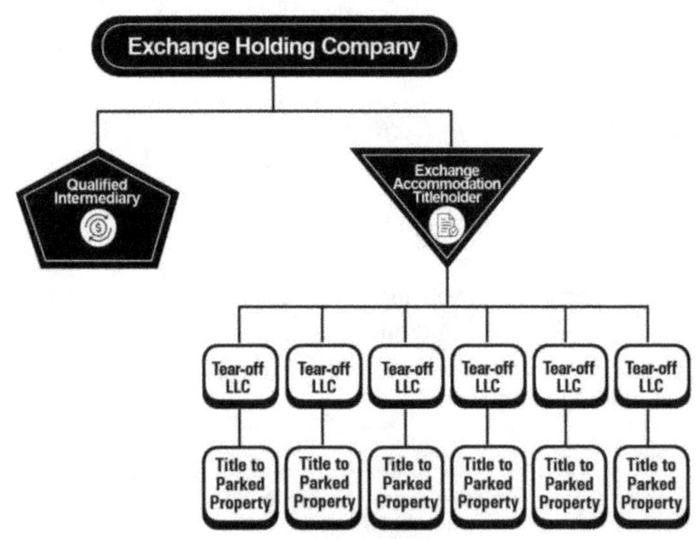

"We call these lower-level limited liability companies 'tear-off LLCs' because at the end of the exchange we either transfer the interests in the company to the exchanger, or we dispose of it. We never use the same limited liability company twice to hold property."

"I don't understand why you have to make things so complicated. Why not just use one legal entity to act as qualified intermediary and to hold the property?" Evan asked.

"We are concerned about entering the chain of title on property and the potential liability that comes from taking legal title to property," Isabel explained. "For example, it is possible that we could take legal title to property that has an environmental issue, which may result in a legal claim against the person holding legal title to the property or any person who has ever held legal title to the property. In other words, any person in the chain of title may be subject to liability from that property.

"Liability can also arise from other events. For example, it is possible that a person could be hurt on a piece of property and the titleholder could become liable for such an injury. Liability from that property could attach to other property that the titleholder owns.

"Because of this potential liability, we ensure that each piece of property we acquire is owned by a separate legal entity," Isabel continued. "We also take care to meet all of the state law requirements for forming and managing each legal entity to help ensure that it will be treated as a separate legal entity."

"How long will it take you to form a separate legal entity to facilitate an exchange for me?" Evan asked.

"Actually, because we facilitate a fairly large volume of title-parking exchanges, we form the tear-off LLCs in advance and keep them on the shelf until we need them for a specific piece of property. Therefore, we already have a legal entity ready for you."

"So you simply file the organizational documents with the Secretary of State and then complete the other entity documents, the operating agreement for example, once an exchanger needs the entity?" Evan asked. "How do you know what to name the entities?"

"The answer to your first question is yes," Isabel said. "As far as names are concerned, we use generic names. For example, the next tear-off LLC is something like 'Titleholder 2020-45 LLC.' The one we'll use after that will be 'Titleholder 2020-46 LLC.' If you have a specific name that you want to use for the tear-off LLC and we have enough time, we can form the tear-off LLC with that name, assuming it has not already been taken by someone else."

"Why would anyone want a customized name?" Evan asked.

"Some exchangers want to hold the replacement property in a separate legal entity," Isabel answered. "Instead of forming a new entity, they often prefer to take title to the interests in the tear-off LLC that we create."

"Evan can still satisfy the reciprocal requirement even if he were to acquire the tear-off LLC from you," Charlene said. "Evan holds title to Quincy Lot directly and he will transfer it. Thus, to satisfy the reciprocal requirement, he must be the party who acquires the replacement property. The tear-off LLC, as a single member limited liability company, will be disregarded for federal tax purposes. Therefore, if Evan acquires the interests in the tear-off LLC, he will be treated as acquiring the underlying property and would satisfy the reciprocal requirement."

By this time, Evan had heard enough for one day, and it was time for the discussion to end.

"That gives me a lot to think about," Evan said. "As I remember I need to talk to my banker to find out if structuring the acquisition of Randolph Building as part of a title-parking reverse exchange will be a problem for them. After that, we can talk more about the structure."

"That's correct," Isabel confirmed.

"Thank you for taking time to talk to me. Either Charlene or I will get back to you within the next few days."

With that, the discussion ended. Evan and Charlene agreed to meet later to discuss possible exchange structures. For now, Evan wanted to digest all that he had just learned about title-parking reverse exchanges and exchange companies. This was all new to him.

A few days later, Evan met with Charlene to talk about exchange structures. Charlene reminded Evan that there are two basic exchange structures to use for title-parking reverse exchanges: (1) the exchange-last structure and (2) the exchange-first structure. Charlene began by describing the exchange-last structure.

Exchange-Last Structures

"As the name implies, with an exchange-last structure, the exchange occurs as the last part of the transaction. Thus, the EAT holds title to the replacement property. The EAT would acquire replacement property and hold it while you arrange for the disposition of the relinquished property. When you dispose of the relinquished property, you would acquire the replacement property from the EAT. The transfer of the relinquished property and acquisition of the replacement property is the exchange, and it occurs as the last part of the transaction. Thus, the name exchange-last structure."

Definition of Exchange-Last Structure

A transaction is an exchange-last structure if the EAT acquires replacement property and holds it until the exchanger is prepared to dispose of the relinquished property. When the exchanger disposes of the relinquished property, it acquires the replacement property from the EAT.

Reverse Exchange: Exchange-Last Structure

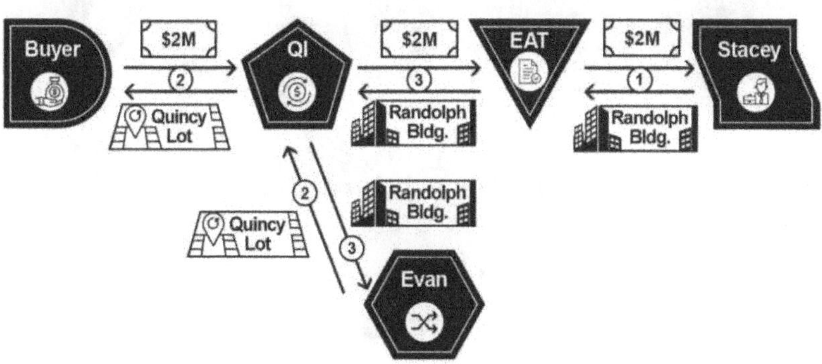

"Based on my experience, the exchange-last structure is the most common reverse exchange structure," Charlene said. "I rarely see exchange-first structures, but occasionally exchangers need to use them. If we can avoid that structure, we will. Otherwise, we will use the exchange-first structure."

"Before we talk about the exchange-first structure, explain to me why an EAT has to take title to one of the properties? This seems complicated," Evan said.

"Remember that the reason we do title-parking reverse exchanges is because we don't want you to own Randolph Building and Quincy Lot concurrently," Charlene began. "In the case of an exchange-last structure, we want to delay your acquisition of Randolph Building. The sole function of the EAT is to delay your acquisition of the property. The EAT delays your acquisition of Randolph Building by taking title to it and becoming the tax owner of it. Thus, in thinking about an exchange-last structure, remember that the EAT will become the tax owner of Randolph Building. When you dispose of Quincy Lot, you will acquire Randolph Building from the EAT just as you would from any other seller of replacement property. Thus, the EAT becomes the seller of the replacement property."

EAT as Replacement Property Seller

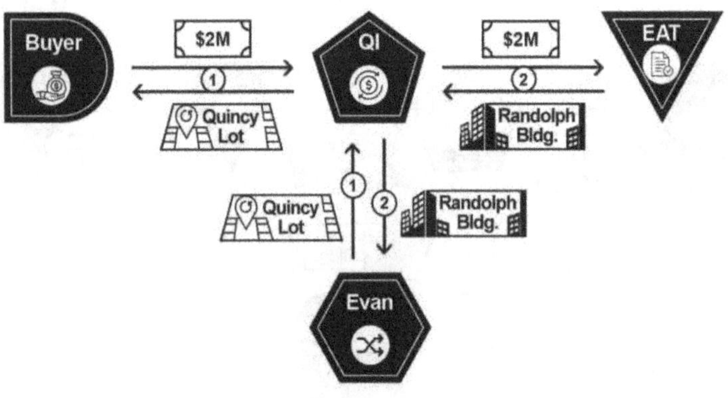

Charlene continued, "Notice that this structure looks exactly like any other multi-party simultaneous or deferred exchange (Chapters 4 and 5). That is the consequence of the title-parking safe harbor. To be certain the EAT will be treated as the owner of Randolph Building, you and the EAT will have to satisfy the requirements of the title-parking reverse exchange safe harbor."

"I'm trying to understand the significance of what you are saying," Evan confessed. "It sounds like you are telling me that the EAT will acquire the building for the simple purpose of delaying my acquisition of it. Is that correct?"

"In an exchange-last title-parking reverse exchange, that is the sole function of the EAT—it delays your acquisition of the property," Charlene said. "If for some reason you are unable to sell Quincy Lot before the end of the 180-day time period, the EAT will simply transfer the property to you. At that point, the property will no longer be eligible to be replacement property, but at least you will have title to it. You'll be in the position you would have been in had you not attempted a title-parking exchange."

"But I'll be out the fees that I pay to the EAT?" Evan asked.

"Yes, so you shouldn't plan to do a title-parking reverse exchange within the title-parking safe harbor unless you are fairly confident that you will be able to sell Quincy Lot within 180 days after the EAT takes title to Randolph Building," Charlene said.

"That makes sense. I think I am beginning to understand. If I am able to sell Quincy Lot within 180 days after the EAT takes title to Randolph Building, I can then acquire Randolph Building from the EAT. The EAT will be treated as the seller of Randolph Building, so the exchange will occur just as it would if I were to sell Quincy Lot and acquire Randolph Building from its current owner. If I am unable to sell Quincy Lot before the end of the 180-day period, the EAT will transfer Randolph Building to me, and it will no longer be eligible to be replacement property."

"That's correct," Charlene said. "Thus, the structure provides you the opportunity to do a reverse exchange. You have to commit to the structure before you know whether Quincy Lot will sell. Although you will have to pay the EAT even if you don't sell Quincy Lot, the title-parking arrangement does not have negative tax consequences.

"Furthermore, if you don't sell Quincy Lot during the 180-day period that the EAT holds title to Randolph Building, but you later sell Quincy Lot, you can still do a section 1031 exchange with Quincy Lot if you are able to purchase other like-kind property within 180 days after you transfer Quincy Lot."

"If I can do that, does it make sense for me to consider the exchange-last structure we are discussing?" Evan asked.

"It makes sense if you think you will sell Quincy Lot within 180 days after the EAT takes title to Randolph Building, don't plan to buy other like-kind property after you sell Quincy Lot, or are concerned you won't be able to acquire other property within 180 days after selling Quincy Lot." Charlene continued, "Obviously you can't see into the future, but you can think about what you want to do. If you don't plan to purchase other real property, you have to ask whether it would be prudent to structure a title-parking exchange to save the tax you would otherwise owe on the disposition of Quincy Lot. That is purely a decision you have to make. I can discuss with you the tax consequences of your decisions, but ultimately, you have to make the decision."

"That's a good point," Evan admitted. After thinking a few minutes, he asked "How does the EAT get the money it will need to purchase Randolph Building? Since its only function is to facilitate my exchange, I can't imagine it putting any of its own capital at risk to purchase Randolph Building for me."

"I don't suppose the EAT would risk its own resources. Furthermore, if it did, I am fairly certain that it would charge you considerably more for that service," Charlene said. "You will have to come up with the $2,000,000 the EAT will need to purchase Randolph Building."

"I haven't spoken to the bank yet, but I worry that it may only lend money to the party who has title to the property. They have said that they will lend the full amount of the purchase price, but I think that is because I will be personally liable for all of the debt. The bank may allow the EAT to take title to Randolph Building if it can take a mortgage in Randolph Building and if I personally guarantee that debt. Does the safe harbor allow that?"

"Yes," answered Charlene. "The safe harbor specifically allows an exchanger to guarantee debt incurred by the EAT. It also allows the exchanger to lend money to the EAT at minimal interest. Thus, if the bank would allow it, you could borrow from the bank and then lend the money to the EAT. This may be a bit difficult to arrange since the bank will require a security interest in Randolph Building."

"If the EAT borrows the money and I guarantee the loan, will I simply take the property subject to the loan after I transfer Quincy Lot?" Evan asked.

"We must carefully manage that loan and the flow of money with any title-parking exchange," Charlene said. "If you receive the exchange proceeds, you will lose section 1031 nonrecognition. If the EAT borrows the money from the bank and you take Randolph Building subject to the liability, what will happen to the proceeds from the sale of Quincy Lot? The QI will receive them initially. If it doesn't need them to acquire Randolph Building (because you are acquiring Randolph Building subject to the liability), the QI will transfer the exchange proceeds back to you. The proceeds will be boot to you and trigger gain recognition."

Charlene continued, "To prevent this, the QI will have to use the proceeds to acquire Randolph Building from the EAT and the EAT will have to use the proceeds to pay down the debt. If the EAT has borrowed from the bank, it must use the proceeds to repay the bank loan."

Flow of Funds: Direct Loan from Bank

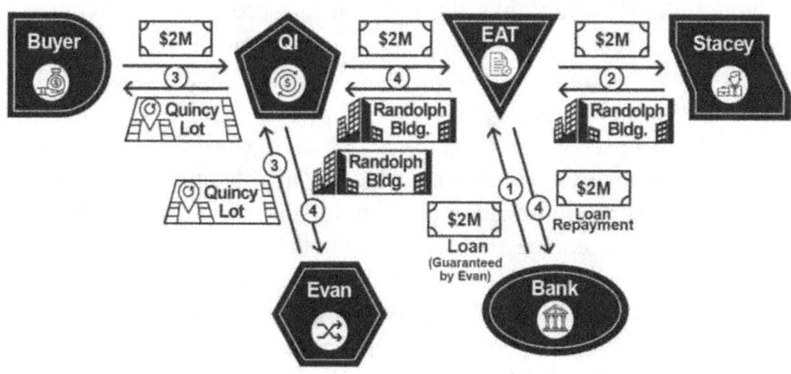

Charlene explained the diagram, "As this diagram shows, the EAT borrows money from the bank and uses that money to acquire Randolph Building. When you sell Quincy Lot through the QI, the QI receives the proceeds from the sale of Quincy Lot. Assuming you sell Quincy Lot for $2,000,000, the QI will use that entire amount to acquire

Randolph Building from the EAT. The EAT will repay the loan and you will receive Randolph Building free of any debt."

"That's interesting," Evan responded. "I'm not sure I want to pay the debt off right away. I was hoping to retain some of the borrowed money."

"If the EAT borrows from the bank, you won't be able to receive Randolph Building from the EAT subject to the loan because you will have to receive exchange proceeds from the QI, and that will trigger gain recognition." Charlene then explained that the EAT could repay the loan, Evan could acquire Randolph Building, and then Evan could borrow other funds against Randolph Building.

"If I borrow against Randolph Building after acquiring it, would I have to obtain another loan, or could I simply have the bank take the money from the EAT and then give it back to me?" Evan asked.

"The subsequent loan would have to be a separate transaction entered into after you acquired Randolph Building," Charlene answered. "If borrowing against Randolph Building is deemed to be part of the exchange, the IRS may take the position that proceeds you receive are exchange proceeds, not loan proceeds. To prevent this possibility, you must borrow against Randolph Building in a separate transaction following the exchange.

After hearing this, Evan was not as interested in an exchange-last title-parking reverse exchange. He wasn't planning to repay all of the money the bank would loan him to acquire Randolph Building. Sensing this, Charlene began to explain another possibility.

"The other possibility with the exchange-last transaction is for you to borrow the $2,000,000 directly from the bank and lend it to the EAT. If the bank will initially take Quincy Lot as collateral for the loan instead of Randolph Building, you could give the bank a mortgage on Quincy Lot and when you later receive Randolph Building, you could substitute it for Quincy Lot as collateral. As long as the loan is not part of the exchange, you should not be treated as receiving boot on the exchange."

Flow of Funds: Loan from Bank to Exchanger

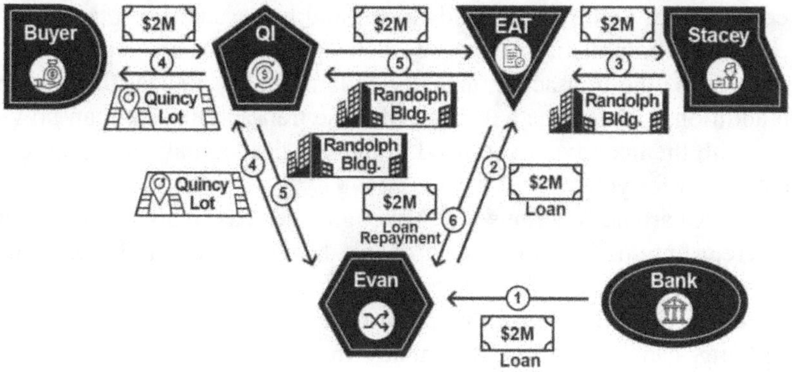

"Notice the flow of funds in this transaction," Charlene pointed out. "You borrow money from the bank personally and offer Quincy Lot as collateral. You then lend the $2,000,000 loan proceeds to the EAT. The EAT uses the proceeds to acquire Randolph Building. Later, when you sell Quincy Lot, the QI will receive the exchange proceeds and use them to acquire Randolph Building from the EAT. The EAT will use the proceeds it receives for Randolph Building to repay the loan from you. Because the proceeds, when received from the EAT, will be deemed to be loan proceeds and not exchange proceeds, you will not be deemed to receive boot at that time.

"As you know," Charlene continued, "to avoid being treated as receiving boot when relinquished property is subject to debt, replacement property must be acquired subject to an equal or greater amount of debt, or you must invest additional funds in the transaction. If the exchange is structured as we have discussed, you will transfer Quincy Lot subject to debt but acquire Randolph Building subject to the same amount of debt. Thus, you won't come under the debt-boot rules."

"It's amazing how many hoops I have to jump through to structure this reverse exchange," Evan said.

"These transactions have many steps to accomplish an exchange," Charlene responded, "but remember that section 1031 is a very formalistic provision of tax law. To structure transactions to come within section 1031, you have to meet its technical requirements. Although the transaction is complicated, a good exchange company has seen many of them, understands them, and has systems in place to deal with their complexity. Because their systems absorb much of the complexity, the transaction actually ends up being manageable for you. In addition, I have done a number of these transactions, so I can provide you with the tax advice you need to make a decision about the structure that is best for you."

Charlene continued, "Although we have discussed several different options for you, if you decide to do a title-parking exchange, you only have to consider a couple of things. First, how will you finance the transaction? If the bank will allow the EAT to take title to Randolph Building, can you borrow the money from the bank and lend it to the EAT or will the bank require the EAT to borrow the money directly? Second, if the bank will allow you to borrow the money directly, do you plan to pay down the loan from the bank immediately after the exchange?

"If the bank requires the EAT to borrow the money directly, the flow of exchange proceeds will require that you pay down the debt immediately. Otherwise, any money you receive from the QI or EAT will be boot. If the bank does not require the EAT to borrow the money, you can borrow from the bank and lend to the EAT and then have some leeway, under the tax law at least, as to when you repay loan."

Decisions Regarding Financing

If an exchanger uses an exchange-last title-parking structure, a third party finances the acquisition of the replacement property, and the third party allows the exchanger to take title to the replacement property, the exchanger must determine whether the lender will require the EAT to borrow the money directly from the lender. If so, exchange proceeds will have to pay down the EAT's debt to the lender. If the lender does not require the EAT to borrow directly from the lender, then the exchanger may choose a structure that will provide it leeway in negotiating the timing of the loan repayment.

Evan reviewed to make sure he understood. "For me to use the exchange-last structure, the bank must allow the EAT to take title to Randolph Building. I will have the most leeway if I can borrow from the bank and lend the proceeds to the EAT to finance the acquisition of the replacement property."

"That's correct." Charlene said.

"I don't know if my bank has ever seen this type of transaction," Evan said. "Do you think it would lend the money to the EAT or to me?"

"I have never had a client finance this type of exchange through your bank," Charlene said, "so I can only speculate. Having said that, if we explain how the transaction can be structured to protect the bank's interest, including providing it with a security interest in Randolph Building and your personal guarantee, it shouldn't be too hostile to the arrangement. It may make the loan, albeit probably at a higher interest rate."

"What if, after explaining all of that, the bank still requires me to take title to Randolph Building?" Evan asked.

"Then you might consider using an exchange-first structure," Charlene recommended.

Evan speculated, "The name, exchange-first transaction implies that the exchange of property is the first part of the transaction. That must mean that I would exchange into Randolph Building immediately and transfer Quincy Lot to the EAT."

"That's correct," Charlene commented.

Exchange-First Structures

"Does this transaction also require a QI and an EAT?" Evan asked.

"Yes," Charlene answered. "You will receive Randolph Building through the QI and transfer Quincy Lot to the EAT through the QI."

Definition of Exchange-First Exchange

A transaction is an exchange-first exchange if the exchanger transfers relinquished property to the EAT and immediately receives replacement property from the seller. Under the exchange-first structure, the EAT holds the relinquished property until the exchanger arranges for its disposition to a buyer.

Reverse Exchange: Exchange-First Structure

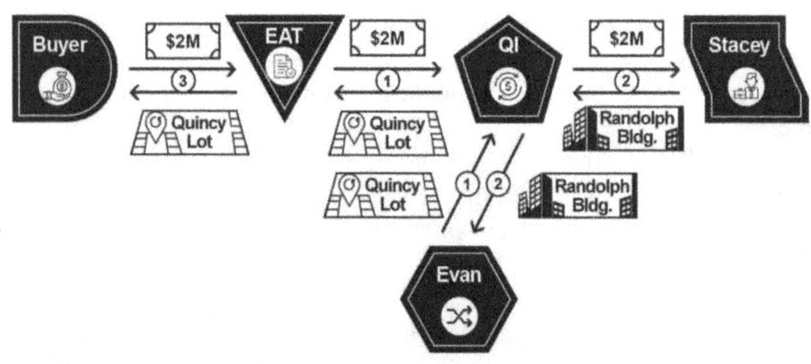

"I can only imagine that somehow I will have to arrange the financing for the EAT to acquire Quincy Lot from me," Evan said.

"That's exactly what you will have to do," Charlene stated. "As with the exchange-last structure, this structure requires that you carefully direct the flow of funds. It is a bit more complicated, however, because you have to estimate its ultimate sales price at the time you transfer Quincy Lot to the EAT."

Flow of Funds

The EAT needs funds to acquire the relinquished property. Generally, it borrows such funds from the exchanger or a third-party lender and the exchanger guarantees the loan. The EAT may not, however, pay those funds to the exchanger. If it does, the funds will be boot to the exchanger and the section 1031 nonrecognition will be lost. The interposition of a qualified intermediary shields the exchanger from receiving the exchange proceeds. The EAT borrows the relinquished property purchase price, the EAT pays the qualified intermediary for the relinquished property, and the qualified intermediary uses the funds to acquire the replacement property and transfer it to the exchanger. Later, when the EAT disposes of the relinquished property, it uses the proceeds to pay down any debt it incurred to obtain funds originally.

Charlene explained to Evan how the funds would flow in an exchange-first transaction. "To structure the transaction as an exchange-first transaction, you will borrow money from the bank and lend it to the EAT. The EAT will pay that money to the QI to acquire the relinquished property; you will directly deed the relinquished property to the EAT just as you would transfer it to any other purchaser as part of a deferred exchange. The QI will use the funds to acquire replacement property for you, and you will take the replacement property subject to the loan from the bank. Later, when the EAT sells Quincy Lot, it will use the sale proceeds to repay the loan from you.

Flow of Funds: Exchange-First Structure

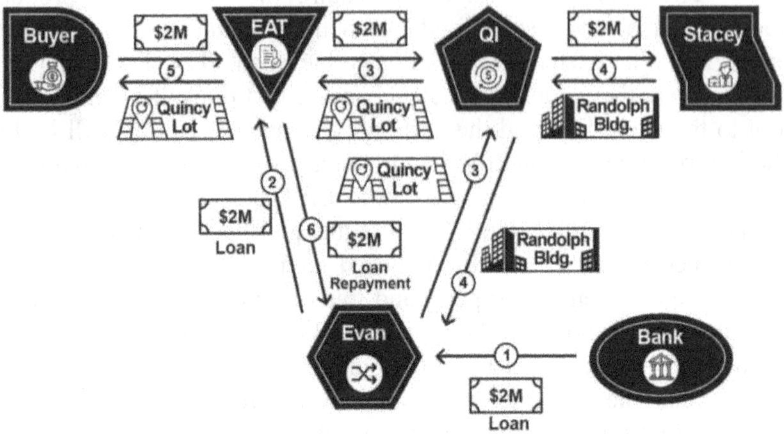

"Notice that this transaction looks like a deferred exchange, except the EAT is the buyer and you acquire Randolph Building immediately," Charlene said. "The exchange is done at that time."

"I have two questions," Evan stated. "First, why do the debt-boot rules not apply? Second, if the EAT uses the Quincy Lot sale proceeds to repay my loan, how is that not boot?"

"A few general concepts help provide the answers to both of your questions," Charlene said. "First, the purpose of section 1031 is to defer gain recognition if a property owner continues an investment in like-kind property. Second, remember that section 1031 is very formalistic. Third, the title-parking safe harbor in effect transforms what would otherwise be exchange proceeds into loan repayment proceeds. Without that transformation, the reverse exchange would be impossible. Fourth, borrowing money is not a taxable event."

"I understand the purpose of section 1031 and I realize that it is formalistic and rule-based," Evan said. "Explain to me how exchange proceeds can be converted to loan proceeds. Why does it matter that I receive proceeds from the EAT instead of the QI?"

"The EAT needs financing to acquire the relinquished property," Charlene said. "It will borrow $2,000,000 from you to acquire Quincy

Lot. That lending transaction will not be taxable. After the EAT sells Quincy Lot, it will have proceeds to repay your loan. Because lending transactions are not taxable events, the loan repayment won't be boot."

"But we know that the money is coming from the sale of Quincy Lot," Evan said. "The IRS could easily trace it to its source."

"Indeed they can," Charlene said, "but remember that the IRS gave us the safe harbor. For it to work, the payment from the Buyer to the EAT and from the EAT to you must transform the exchange proceeds into loan proceeds."

"I can see how the safe harbor would be meaningless otherwise," Evan said. "The IRS had to realize that the source of loan repayment would be exchange proceeds."

"From a policy standpoint, it also makes sense," Charlene said. "Your receiving the proceeds as a loan repayment would return you to the position you were in prior to the exchange. You would not have taken cash out of the transaction, and you would have continued your real property investment. Therefore, the transaction should qualify for section 1031 nonrecognition."

"Do I have to worry about the debt-boot rules?" Evan asked.

"We do have to pay attention to the debt-boot rules," Charlene said, "but you shouldn't have any debt relief for boot as part of the transaction. You will have to borrow against the replacement property, but borrowing against the replacement property is not a taxable event. Similarly, receiving repayment of a loan is not a taxable event. Therefore, you should not be taxed when you borrow against the replacement property or receive repayment of the loan from the EAT. If this interpretation of the title-parking safe harbor is not correct, the safe harbor is a mere ruse; it would have no effect because it would be useless. It can't be that—it has to have some significance, so this interpretation can't be meritless."

"But there does appear to be some tax risk with financing the transaction in this manner," Evan said.

"The safe harbor is designed to minimize tax risk by providing certainty for those who satisfy its requirements," Charlene said. "It allows the exchanger to lend money to the EAT. The only way that you will be able to get the money you need to lend to the EAT is to borrow from the bank and secure the loan with Randolph Building. The safe harbor does not specifically provide that you can do this, but for it to have effect, it must allow this sort of financing."

"Will I have to repay the loan from the bank after the transaction?" Evan asked.

"The safe harbor doesn't speak to that issue either, and I'm not aware of any other legal authority that does," Charlene said. "There should be no reason for the law to require you to repay the loan. You can borrow against the replacement property once you receive it, so you should be able to retain loan proceeds obtained when you acquire replacement property in an exchange first transaction."

"You have a good answer for all my questions. I appreciate that," Evan said. "I hope that Quincy Lot will sell for at least $2,000,000, but it may sell for more or less than that. How would any variation in sales price affect the transaction?"

Deficient or Excess Relinquished Property Proceeds

The exchange-first structure requires the exchanger to transfer relinquished property to the EAT. At the time of the transfer, the exchanger must establish what the relinquished property will ultimately sell for. Because the exchanger does not know for sure what the relinquished property will ultimately sell for, the exchanger may not receive repayment from the EAT for the entire amount of the loan, or the EAT may receive an amount from the ultimate sale that exceeds the amount of the loan. If the amount of the relinquished property proceeds are less than the amount of the loan, the exchanger may merely forgive any balance outstanding following the payment of the proceeds from the EAT to the exchanger. This should not produce adverse tax consequences to either the EAT or the exchanger.

The EAT should have income from the loan forgiveness, but it should be offset by the loss the EAT would recognize from selling the property for less than it paid for it. For example, if Evan lends $2,000,000 to the EAT and the EAT uses that to acquire Quincy Lot, the EAT will take a $2,000,000 basis in Quincy Lot (this will most likely not be adjusted because the EAT will not be allowed depreciation deductions and the EAT will not improve the lot). If the EAT later sells

Quincy Lot for $1,800,000, the EAT will recognize $200,000 of loss on the sale (the excess of adjusted tax basis over the amount realized). The EAT will use the $1,800,000 to pay down the loan from Evan. Evan will forgive the $200,000 that the EAT does not pay. That amount will be cancellation of indebtedness income to the EAT. The $200,000 loss will offset that income, giving the EAT no taxable income or loss on the transaction.

The exchanger should have a bad debt loss equal to the amount of debt forgiven, but the amount of debt forgiveness is reflected in the value of the replacement property and the exchanger will eventually offset the bad debt loss with gain realized on the future sale of the replacement property (i.e., the exchanger's lower basis in the replacement property will give it more gain on a subsequent sale). The loss and the gain will offset each other, but time may pass between the recognition of loss and the recognition of gain. Thus, due to the time value of money, the offset will not be perfect.

Evan will acquire Randolph Building for $2,000,000. He will take an adjusted tax basis in Randolph Building equal to the adjusted tax basis he had in Quincy Lot. Therefore, Evan will take a $250,000 basis in Randolph Building. If Evan had transferred Quincy Lot for $1,800,000 and used those proceeds plus an additional $200,000 to acquire Randolph Building, he would have taken a $450,000 basis in Randolph Building (the exchanged basis of Quincy Lot plus the additional $200,000 investment). If he were to sell Randolph Building immediately for its fair market value with that basis, he would recognize a $1,550,000 gain ($2,000,000 amount realized minus $450,000 adjusted tax basis).

Tax Consequences of Exchange-Last Transaction

Adjusted tax basis in Quincy Lot	*$250,000*
Additional investment	*$200,000*
Basis in Randolph Building	*$450,000*

Amount realized on FMV sale	*$2,000,000*
Adjusted tax basis in Randolph Building	*($450,000)*
Gain on hypothetical sale	*$1,550,000*

That is $200,000 less of gain than Evan would recognize doing the exchange-first transaction. Under the exchange-first structure, Evan's basis in Randolph Building would be $250,000, and his gain on a hypothetical sale would be $1,750,000. That additional potential gain is offset by the loss Evan would recognize by canceling $200,000 of the EAT's outstanding liability.

Tax Consequences of Exchange-First Transaction

Adjusted tax basis in Quincy Lot	*$250,000*
Additional investment	*$ 0*
Basis in Randolph Building	*$250,000*
Amount realized on FMV sale	*$2,000,000*
Adjusted tax basis in Randolph Building	*($250,000)*
Gain on hypothetical sale	*$1,750,000*
Loss on cancellation of debt	*($200,000)*
Net gain	*$1,550,000*

If the EAT sells the relinquished property for more than the amount of the loan, the EAT may merely pay the excess to the exchanger. That excess will be boot to the exchanger, but it will not damage the safe harbor. Or the EAT may pay the excess to the QI, and the QI may use it to acquire additional replacement property for the exchanger if, (1) 180 days have not lapsed since the day the exchanger transferred the relinquished property, (2) the exchanger has properly identified other replacement property, and (3) the documents provide for the possibility of the excess being used to acquire replacement property.

Hearing that he might be able to use excess proceeds to acquire additional replacement property, Evan asks Charlene to explain how he might structure the arrangement with the EAT and the QI to leave open that possibility.

"What would happen if I were able to sell Quincy Lot for $2,500,000 instead of $2,000,000?" Evan asks.

Charlene begins, "Let's consider a few different scenarios. First, let's assume you don't identify any replacement property and the identification period has expired. When the EAT sells Quincy Lot, you will simply receive the extra $500,000 and it will be boot. Therefore, you will recognize gain.

"Second, if you set the transaction up correctly with the exchange company, properly identify other replacement property, and the EAT sells Quincy Lot before the expiration of the exchange period, you can use the $500,000 to acquire other replacement property. Of course, you will have to acquire the replacement property before the end of the exchange period which will lapse no later than 180 days after you transfer Quincy Lot."

Exchange-First with Excess Exchange Proceeds

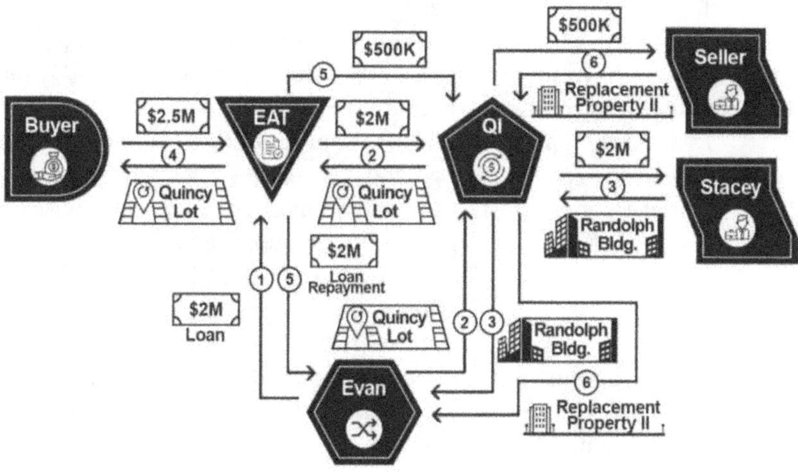

"What do I have to do to set the transaction up correctly?" Evan asked.

Charlene said, "You will have to put a provision in the exchange accommodation agreement—the agreement with the EAT—that provides that the EAT will pay you, as part of the Quincy Lot purchase price, any proceeds that exceed the amount it borrows from you. Under that provision, if the EAT borrows $2,000,000 from you and later sells Quincy Lot for $2,500,000, it will owe you $500,000."

"Won't that be boot to me?" Evan asked.

"If you receive the $500,000 excess, it will be boot to you," Charlene said. "To prevent this, you will assign your rights in the exchange accommodation agreement to the QI. Thus, the EAT will pay the $2,000,000 loan proceeds to the QI when you transfer Quincy Lot to it. Later, it will pay the $500,000 excess proceeds to the QI in complete satisfaction of the Quincy Lot purchase price in the exchange accommodation agreement."

Charlene continued, "There will also be an agreement between you and the QI. You will transfer Quincy Lot to the QI in exchange for Randolph Building. That starts the identification period and the exchange period. The EAT's holding Quincy Lot does not affect your relationship with the QI. The EAT is treated as the purchaser of Quincy Lot from the perspective of your relationship with the QI and with respect to the identification period and exchange period. If the QI receives additional funds from the EAT before the end of the exchange period and you have identified other replacement property, the QI may use those funds to acquire the other property."

Evan said, "That's interesting. I never would have thought that I could combine a reverse exchange and a deferred exchange. Because the EAT is a titleholder, it substitutes for the buyer or seller. Otherwise, the exchange with the QI is the same as any other deferred exchange."

"That's the way I look at it," Charlene said. "The only difference between the EAT and other traditional buyers or sellers is that you have to ensure that the EAT is the tax owner of the parked property. If you satisfy the title-parking safe harbor, you will do that. The main focus with that is the 180-day period because that can often be the most difficult requirement to satisfy."

Choosing Between Exchange-Last and Exchange-First Structures

This discussion of the exchange-last and exchange-first structures provides a basis for determining which structure is right for a particular transaction. As discussed, if the exchanger is borrowing from a third party to acquire the replacement property and the lender requires the exchanger to take title to the replacement property immediately, the exchanger has no choice but to structure the transaction as an exchange-first arrangement. The exchanger may also be forced to use the exchange-first structure if the exchanger has to take title to the property because of some type of specific management issue that require the exchanger to be on title to the property right away. These transactions present two disadvantages: (1) the identification and exchange periods begin running at the beginning of the exchange transaction and (2) the exchanger may not be able to predict the ultimate sales price of the relinquished property.

Although there are reasons for using an exchange-first structure, absent those reasons, the exchange-last structure generally is preferable. If an exchanger uses an exchange-last structure, the exchanger will know the relinquished property's sales price. Therefore, prior to transferring the relinquished property, it will know whether it will have to acquire additional replacement property to defer all of the gain from the disposition of the relinquished property. Furthermore, the exchanger will know whether it has to acquire additional replacement property on the date it transfers the relinquished property. Thus, before the EAT has held the replacement property for 180 days, the exchanger can transfer the relinquished property in exchange for the replacement property and still have an additional 180 days to acquire other replacement property. The combination of the deferred exchange safe harbor's 180-day exchanger period and the title-parking safe harbor's 180-day period provides the exchanger a combined 360 days to complete the exchange within the safe harbors.

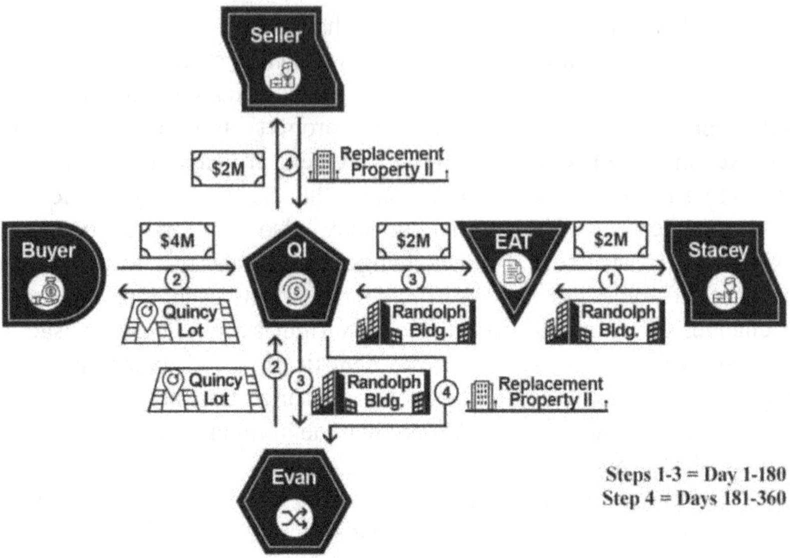

This example demonstrates that the exchange-last structure provides the exchanger considerable leeway in structuring a transaction. The exchanger has more time to identify and acquire other replacement property, allowing the exchanger to use any excess exchange proceeds to acquire replacement property. Therefore, when the exchange-last option is available, exchangers will almost always choose it. The primary reason an exchanger would use the exchange-first structure would be to satisfy a lender's requirement that the exchanger take possession of the replacement property immediately.

Non-Safe Harbor Reverse Exchanges

Having examined the opportunities that are available within the title-parking safe harbor, Evan was curious if there would be opportunities to structure an exchange if he thought he would not be able to sell Quincy Lot within 180 days after the EAT took title to Randolph

Building. Charlene told Evan that he was asking about a non-safe harbor reverse exchange.

Non-Safe Harbor Reverse Exchanges

A non-safe harbor reverse exchange is a title-parking reverse exchange that requires the accommodation titleholder to hold title to property for more than the 180 days allowed in the safe harbor. The IRS specifically provided that reverse exchanges that cannot be structured within the safe harbor are not necessarily excluded from section 1031 nonrecognition. This left open the possibility of doing non-safe harbor reverse exchanges. To successfully structure a non-safe harbor title-parking reverse exchange, the accommodation titleholder should typically hold the benefits and burdens of owning the property. But the U.S. Tax Court sanctioned a non-safe harbor reverse exchange, even when the benefits and burdens of the parked replacement property transferred to the exchanger while the accommodation titleholder held title.

Charlene explained to Evan that a non-safe harbor does provide opportunities to do reverse exchanges that require parking title for more than 180 days. If structured correctly, such a transaction should allow Evan to complete a section 1031 exchange. Because the accommodation titleholder has to be the tax owner however, the transaction is more complicated and costs more than a safe harbor. Charlene explained to Evan that because non-safe harbor reverse exchanges do not qualify for the title-parking safe harbor, they will create some tax risk. A case from the U.S. Tax Court has, however, provided a road map to follow in structuring these types of transactions. Also, because the costs of structuring such transactions can be significant, Evan would have to weigh this increased cost against the potential tax cost. Evan would have to consider all of these factors in making a decision.

A title-parking safe harbor exchange probably cannot be converted to a non-safe harbor exchange. The reason for this is that an exchanger generally takes advantage of the title-parking safe harbor's permitted arrangements. Without the title-parking safe harbor, the exchanger will most likely be the tax owner of the parked property and could not later acquire it as replacement property in the case of an exchange-last transaction (and would not have transferred it, in the case of an intended exchange-first transaction). Thus, Evan would have to choose to do a safe harbor or non-safe harbor exchange before he begins the exchange.

All told, reverse exchanges provide significant planning opportunities. They allow exchangers to park title to property with an accommodation titleholder to facilitate reverse exchanges. If such an exchange comes within the title-parking safe harbor, it will be relatively routine and the tax outcome will be certain. If the exchanger cannot sell the relinquished property within 180 days after the replacement property acquisition, a non-safe harbor reverse exchange may be a viable alternative. Because non-safe harbor reverse exchanges cost more and have more tax risk, the potential tax must be significant.

CHAPTER 7: EXCHANGE STRUCTURES: IMPROVEMENTS EXCHANGES

Improvements exchanges (also referred to as build-to-suit exchanges and construction exchanges) are perhaps the most complicated section 1031 exchange structures, but they continue to grow in popularity and provide significant exchange opportunities. A properly structured improvements exchange allows an exchanger to reinvest exchange proceeds in improvements on replacement property. For the improvements to qualify as replacement property, however, the improvements must be constructed before the exchanger acquires the property.

Improvements Exchange

A transaction is an improvements exchange if the exchanger invests exchange proceeds in improvements constructed on the replacement property prior to the exchanger's acquisition of the property. An improvements exchange can be structured using one of several different structures. The structures include: seller-facilitated improvements exchange, accommodator-facilitated improvements exchange, and leasehold improvements exchange.

HIGHLIGHTED REQUIREMENTS

Improvements exchanges generally have all of the complexity of a title-parking reverse exchange with the additional complexity that constructing improvements creates. Even with the added complexity, the goals of an improvements exchange are the same as the goals of a reverse exchange. Those goals are: (1) ensure that the exchanger does not constructively receive exchange proceeds and (2) ensure that the exchanger does not receive replacement property prematurely. Avoiding premature receipt of replacement property requires that a party other than the exchanger own the property being improved and the improvements being constructed. If an improvements exchange satisfies these goals and the other section 1031 requirements, it should qualify for section 1031 nonrecognition. Improvements exchanges raise unique issues with respect to three section 1031 requirements—the like-kind property requirement, the real property requirement, and the exchange requirement.

The Like-Kind and Real Property Requirements

The like-kind property requirement is one of the basic requirements of section 1031. It deserves special attention in this section on improvements exchanges because constructing improvements raises specific issues related to the like-kind requirement. Improvements exchanges have been the subject of several cases and rulings. That body of law provides that an exchange does not satisfy the like-kind requirement if an exchanger transfers real property and receives building materials and construction services in exchange. Thus, if the exchanger owns the improvements as they are being constructed, the exchanger will acquire building materials or construction services, which will not be real property or like-kind to other real property. This is almost intuitive since building materials and construction services delivered piecemeal are not real property.

To satisfy the like-kind and real property requirements in an improvements exchange, a party other than the exchanger must own the property being improved and the improvements as they are constructed. If another party receives the building materials and the construction services, and constructs the improvements, the materials and construction services become real property before the exchanger acquires them. The exchanger acquires the improvements after they become real property. Because the exchanger acquires improvements that are real property, the improved property could satisfy the like-kind requirement.

The Significance of the Like-Kind Property Requirement

Materials and construction services are not like-kind to real property. They can, however, be used to construct improvements. Once affixed to real property, improvements become real property. For an improvements exchange to qualify for section 1031 nonrecognition, a party other than the exchanger must own the property being improved and the improvements being constructed. This ensures that the exchanger does not receive the non-like-kind materials or services. Instead, the exchanger receives improvements that are like-kind to other real property. The property will be like-kind to other real property only to the extent of improvements that are constructed and affixed to other real property. Prepaid services do not satisfy the like-kind requirement, nor do pre-purchased materials that are not affixed to real property.

The Exchange Requirement

The exchange requirement is relevant with all exchanges. It receives increased attention in the improvements exchange context with certain structures. Recall that the exchange requirement provides that the exchanger must transfer property to another party and receive property from that same party. With many of the improvements exchange structures, this is not difficult because the exchanger will acquire new property with newly-constructed improvements from a third party. In some situations, however, the exchanger may wish to construct improvements on property it already owns. In such situations, even if the exchanger could satisfy the like-kind property requirement, at least with respect to the improvements, any property the exchanger does not acquire as part of the transaction cannot be part of the exchange. To successfully structure an improvements exchange with property the exchanger already owns, first the exchanger must transfer the property to another party. The other party must construct the improvements and then transfer the property and improvements back to the exchanger. To be successful, this transaction must transfer tax ownership to the other party.

Significance of the Exchange Requirement

The exchange requirement becomes significant when considering improving property the exchanger already owns. Because the exchanger must receive replacement property as part of the exchange, property the exchanger already owns generally will not qualify as replacement property. Thus, the exchanger must either construct improvements on property owned by another party or transfer property it owns and re-acquire it after the construction of the improvements. The transfer from the exchanger to the other party must be respected for tax purposes for the property to qualify as replacement property.

IMPROVEMENTS EXCHANGE STRUCTURES

The several improvements exchange structures provide several options for exchangers to choose from when planning an improvements exchange. Generally, the nature of the transaction will determine the structure an exchanger selects. The following example illustrates a typical improvements exchange and alternative improvements exchange structures.

Epic Corp owns Quarles Factory, which it built several years ago for $85,000,000 and currently uses as an important part of its manufacturing operations. Epic Corp's adjusted basis in Quarles Factory is $60,000,000. Quarles Factory no longer meets Epic Corp's needs, and it is looking to sell it and build a new factory in Richmond, the Richmond Factory. Epic Corp anticipates that it will sell Quarles Factory for $170,000,000 to Big Co and pay roughly $250,000,000 to acquire property and construct Richmond Factory. If possible, Epic Corp would like to defer the significant gain it will realize on the disposition of Quarles Factory. It hires Atlas & Leviathan LLP, a large international law firm, to help it consider how to minimize tax on the disposition of Quarles Factory and the construction of Richmond Factory. Arnold, an attorney with Atlas & Leviathan LLP, meets with Erin, Epic Corp's VP of tax, to discuss the possibilities.

"Before we talk too much about the structure, let's first discuss where you are in the process," Arnold requested.

Erin began, "We have just decided to sell Quarles Factory and we are looking for property on which to build Richmond Factory. We are talking with three property owners (Sara, Sufi, and Saul) about a few pieces of property (Reach Ranch, Raw Land, and Rueben Sandlot) that will suit our needs. We anticipate the land will cost roughly $2,000,000 and Richmond Factory will cost $248,000,000 to construct. There is an outside possibility that we will build on property we already own, but that is a last resort."

Erin continued, "We can't sell Quarles Factory until Richmond Factory is operational because we can't afford to lose production capacity. We anticipate that we will sell Quarles Factory for $170,000,000 to Big Co. Because the adjusted basis in Quarles Factory is only $60,000,000, we want to find a way to defer recognition of the $110,000,000 of gain that we will be looking at."

"Because you are so early in the process, we can discuss several alternatives that may be available to you in structuring this transaction," Arnold said. "What percent of Quarles Factory sales price will be real property and what percent will be personal property for section 1031 purposes?"

"We anticipate that 90 percent of the sales price be for real property, and the remainder for personal property," Erin answered. "The value of the replacement real property will exceed the value of the relinquished real property and the value of the personal property associated with the replacement property will exceed the value of the relinquished personal property. Thus, we will reinvest more than the sales price of the relinquished property."

"That will make things easier," Arnold said. "We just have to make sure that if you acquire Richmond Factory before it is completed that you acquire enough real property to cover the value of the real property you are transferring in Quarles Factory. If you don't reinvest the value of Quarles Factory, you will receive cash, which will be boot and trigger gain recognition. Any gain you realize on the sale of the personal property will not qualify for section 1031 nonrecognition, so you should receive the proceeds from the sale of the personal property at the close of Quarles Factory—there's no reason for those proceeds to go to the qualified intermediary. As we discuss the possible structures, we will assume that you will satisfy the like-kind property requirement, even though that can be a complicated question with the types of assets involved. We will focus for now on how to structure the improvements exchange."

"There are five basic improvements exchange structures," Arnold continued. "They are: (1) the seller-facilitated improvements exchange, (2) the accommodator-facilitated improvements exchange, (3) the leasehold improvements exchange, (4) improvements exchange on exchanger-owned property, and (5) the deferred improvements exchange. Let's discuss each in turn."

Arnold explains generally that a qualified intermediary will facilitate each of these structures, and an accommodation titleholder will facilitate some of them. Erin is familiar with the deferred exchange and title-parking safe harbors and the general structure of each. Therefore, Arnold explains the transactions and talks more specifically about the unique aspects of improvements exchanges. To properly structure the exchanges, Arnold and Erin would have to ensure that all of the safe harbor requirements are satisfied. They also must ensure that the flow of funds does not trigger the boot rules. Meeting these objectives will require significant documentation. Because Erin understands the safe harbor requirements, Arnold and Erin talk of property being transferred through a qualified intermediary instead of discussing the details of assignment of rights and direct deeding. This makes the discussion a bit more manageable. The qualified intermediary would not, of course, take title to the property. Instead, as discussed above, Epic Corp would directly deed property to the buyer and directly acquire legal title from the seller or accommodator. Erin also understands the exchange must be completed within the safe harbor time limitation, when applicable. Arnold and Erin realize the significance of these details and leave them out of the following discussion.

Seller-Facilitated Improvements Exchange

"An improvements exchange is seller-facilitated if, as the name implies, the seller of the replacement property constructs the improvements before Epic Corp acquires the replacement property. This is definitely the simplest improvements exchange structure," Arnold said.

Seller-Facilitated Improvements Exchange

An improvements exchange is a seller-facilitated improvements exchange if the seller of the replacement property constructs improvements for the exchanger before transferring the property to the exchanger.

"In *Coastal Terminals v. United States*, a federal circuit court of appeals approved a seller-facilitated improvements exchange. That case provides authority that such an exchange, if properly structured, will qualify for section 1031 nonrecognition," Arnold explained. "In fact, the court allowed the exchanger to require the seller to construct specific improvements. Nonetheless, the seller remained the owner of both the land and the improvements as they were being constructed."

"You said that the exchanger required the construction of specific improvements. What kind of control would the case allow us to have over the construction of the improvements that a seller might construct?" Erin asked.

"You can have considerable control but remember, you can't become the owner of the property for tax purposes," Arnold explained. "In *Coastal Terminals*, the seller financed the construction of the improvements and then transferred them to the exchanger in exchange for property the exchanger held. In that situation, the exchanger was able to influence the construction by making the proper completion of the improvements a condition of the acquisition of the property."

"We probably won't have that luxury," Erin observed. "All of our sellers are individuals, or entities owned by individuals. None of them will be interested in acquiring Quarles Factory, and none of them will be able to finance the construction of Richmond Factory. If we were to attempt such an exchange, we would have to arrange the financing. If we do that, we will want to secure our interests in the property. Also, we will want to manage the construction of Richmond Factory. Do you think we can do all of that without becoming the tax owner of the property and improvements?"

"The threshold for transferring benefits and burdens is fairly high, so you could probably do most of what you want to do, but there will be risk that you will own the replacement property and improvements with such a structure," Arnold explained. "Some tax advisors would require the seller to take an equity interest in the improvements. That probably won't be possible with any of your potential sellers. For example, let's consider how the transaction would work if you were to acquire Reach Ranch from Sara and ask her to construct the improvements on the property.

"First, Epic Corp would contract with Sara to purchase Reach Ranch for $2,000,000. Second, you would lend $248,000,000 to Sara to construct the improvements, and Sara would hire you to manage the construction of the improvements. Third, when you had completed the improvements, you would transfer Quarles Factory to Big Co. Fourth, the QI would use the $170,000,000 sale proceeds to acquire Richmond Factory from Sara subject to an $80,000,000 liability (the difference between the sales price of Quarles Factory and the acquisition price of Richmond Factory, including the land) and transfer it to Epic Corp to complete the exchange. Fifth, Sara would repay the $168,000,000 (the $170,000,000 proceeds from the QI minus the $2,000,000 for Reach Ranch) loan from you. Using a qualified intermediary to facilitate the exchange, the structure would look something like this."

Seller-Facilitated Improvements Exchange

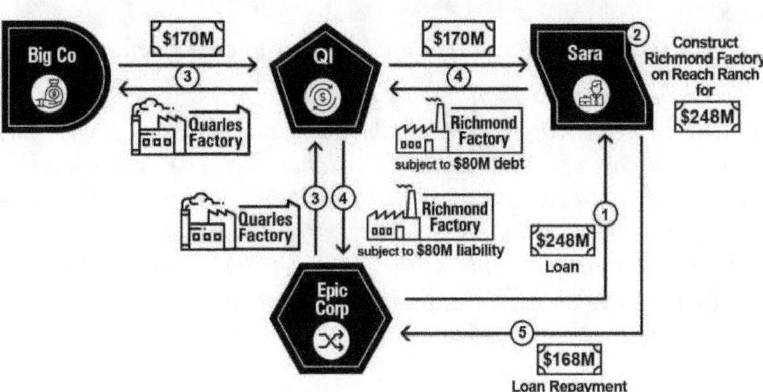

Arnold continued, "The $80,000,000 liability is the loan from Epic Corp to Sara. That will disappear when Epic Corp acquires Richmond Factory. Of course, this assumes that you complete Richmond Factory before the acquisition. Section 1031 does require that improvements be completed before acquisition. Thus, Epic Corp could lend Sara $168,000,000 and acquire Richmond Factory improvements that are worth $168,000,000."

"That transaction isn't too difficult if we can ensure that Epic Corp does not become the tax owner before sufficient improvements are constructed," Erin said. "The problem of course is that this is way beyond something that Sara will want to do or should be involved with."

"I agree," Arnold said. "You will probably want to have the EAT acquire Reach Ranch and construct the improvements."

Accommodator-Facilitated Improvements Exchange

Arnold explained the accommodator-facilitated improvements exchange: "If an accommodator facilitates the improvements exchange, the accommodator would acquire Reach Ranch from Sara and construct Richmond Factory. Using a qualified intermediary, you would transfer

Quarles Factory to Big Co and in exchange acquire Richmond Factory from the accommodator."

Accommodator-Facilitated Improvements Exchange

An accommodator-facilitated improvements exchange is the following transaction: An accommodator acquires raw land from a party who is not related to the exchanger. The accommodator constructs improvements on the raw land. The exchanger later transfers the relinquished property through a qualified intermediary and acquires the replacement property from the accommodator through the qualified intermediary.

"Is there legal authority that says an accommodator-facilitated improvements exchange will qualify for section 1031 nonrecognition?" Erin asked.

"Yes," Arnold answered. "There are a couple of cases that have held that such a transaction may qualify for section 1031 nonrecognition. Also, if the accommodator can complete the improvements within 180 days after acquiring Reach Ranch, the transaction can be structured using the title-parking safe harbor.

"If you can come within the title-parking safe harbor, the transaction will be much easier to structure," Arnold continued. "Remember, even if an accommodator facilitates the transaction, you will have to finance the acquisition of Reach Ranch and the construction of Richmond Factory. Also, the accommodator will most likely hire you to manage the construction. All of this you can do with confidence that the accommodator will be the owner of the property for tax purposes if the transaction comes within the title-parking safe harbor."

Accommodator-Facilitated Improvements Exchange

"Because Rev. Proc. 2000-37 only allows a 180-day holding period, does anyone ever do a safe harbor accommodator-facilitated improvements exchange?" Erin asked. "I can't imagine acquiring property and completing any significant improvements before the end of the 180-day period. It will take us at least that long to get all of the necessary permits, approvals, and zoning completed. We probably won't be able to begin construction within 180 days."

"I have seen people complete a significant amount of improvements using a safe harbor accommodator-facilitated improvements exchange," Arnold responded. "To do so, however, the exchanger generally must obtain all permits, approvals, and zoning before the accommodator takes title to the property. If Sara were willing to hold the property while you worked with her to prepare the property for construction, you might be able to use the title-parking safe harbor."

"If we can't come within the safe harbor because of the 180-day time period, can we structure the transaction outside the safe harbor?" Erin asked. "I understand that will complicate things, but there are enough potential tax dollars at stake that I think we will want to consider that alternative, if available."

"You can structure the transaction outside the safe harbor, but you will have to ensure that the accommodator is treated as the tax owner of the property," Arnold said. "That will make the transaction more complicated and more expensive. As you said, however, the potential tax liability would justify more effort and higher transaction costs.

"Those are the two basic structures for constructing improvements on property owned by a party that is not related to Epic Corp," Arnold said. "If you decide to construct improvements on property owned by a party related to Epic Corp, then you might consider using a leasehold improvements exchange."

Leasehold Improvements Exchange

"If you choose to build on property owned by a party related to Epic Corp, you will cause the related party to lease the property to an accommodator, the accommodator will construct Richmond Factory, Epic Corp will transfer Quarles Factory, and Epic Corp will use the proceeds from the sale of Quarles Factory to acquire Richmond Factory and the lease from the accommodator to complete the exchange."

Leasehold Improvements Exchange

The following transaction is a leasehold improvements exchange: A party related to the exchanger leases property to an accommodator (the lease must be for more than thirty years). The accommodator constructs improvements on the leased property. The exchanger transfers the relinquished property and acquires the leasehold interest and the improvements from the accommodator to complete the exchange. After the transaction, the exchanger owns the improvements and leases the underlying property from a related party. For the lease to be like-kind to the relinquished property, it must have at least thirty years remaining when the exchanger acquires it.

"That's a very general explanation of leasehold improvements exchanges," Arnold said. "They are actually fairly complicated, and you must satisfy several requirements to obtain section 1031 nonrecognition. In addition to satisfying the requirements of deferred and title-parking reverse exchanges, you must avoid the pitfalls of related-party exchanges and ensure the lease and improvements are like-kind to Quarles Factory."

Related-Party Exchanges

"Without going into too much detail at this point about related-party exchanges, I would like to discuss a few issues that you must consider," Arnold said. (Chapter 9 discusses related-party exchanges in detail.) "Generally, section 1031 prohibits an exchanger from acquiring replacement property from a related party in a multiple-party exchange. This area of the law is not as developed as other areas of section 1031, so we can only anticipate what might happen if certain issues were litigated. Thankfully, we can structure leasehold improvements exchanges to avoid some of the unresolved issues the related-party rules present.

"Stated simply, section 1031 prohibits exchangers from acquiring replacement property from a related party if the related party has high basis property and will not recognize gain (or recognize only a small gain) on the disposition of the replacement property. If the related party transfers high-basis property to the exchanger and recognizes little or no gain upon receiving proceeds for the sale of that property, the overall transaction results in a tax-free cash out. As I'll explain in a few minutes, the use of leases helps the parties avoid this potentiality in a leasehold improvements exchange."

Related-Party Exchanges

Section 1031 generally prohibits exchangers from acquiring high-basis property from a related party because such exchanges offer the potential for basis shifting and cashing out tax free (Chapter 9).

The use of the lease helps exchangers and related parties avoid this because a lessor is not deemed to transfer property when entering into a lease, the lessor has no basis in the lease, the lease has no value, and rental payments the related party receives will be ordinary income to the related party.

Arnold continued, "Tax law does not treat a lessor's entering into a lease as a transfer of property. Therefore, the lease, in lieu of the related party's transfer of property to the accommodator, helps avoid the pitfalls of related-party exchanges. Because the related party is not deemed to transfer property, there is no possibility that the related party had a high basis in the property the accommodator takes. Also, because the lease will require fair market rent, it will have zero value. In other words, the present value of the accommodator's right to use the property will be offset by the present value of the accommodator's obligation to pay rent. The absence of basis and the lack of value in the lease make it impossible for the related party to take any cash out of the transaction tax free. The related party will receive rental payments and will include those payments in its gross income. Because the related party will be liable for tax on those rental payments, it does not take cash out of the transaction tax free. Thus, the use of the lease in a leasehold improvements exchange helps exchangers avoid the pitfalls of the related- party exchange rules."

Like-Kind Leases

Having discussed the issues that related-party exchanges raise and how a lease helps to avoid them, Arnold described why leases must be more than thirty years to be like-kind to the exchanger's relinquished real property. The regulations provide that a lease in real property of thirty years or more is like-kind to a fee in real property. (Chapter 3 discusses the like-kind property requirement.) To satisfy this requirement, the lease from the related party to the accommodator must be a bit more than a thirty-year lease. The lease term must account for the time that the accommodator will lease the property so that when the exchanger acquires the lease from the accommodator, it will have more than thirty years to run. If an exchanger plans to do a safe harbor leasehold improvements exchange, the common practice is to have the related party enter into a thirty-two-year lease, which provides some cushion to ensure that the exchanger acquires a lease with more than thirty years remaining.

The lease of more than thirty years in real property should be like-kind to a fee in real property, and the improvements constructed on leased property should be like-kind to other real property, especially if acquired with an interest in the underlying property. For the improvements to be like-kind, however, they must be real property. This does not require that the improvements be completed before the exchanger acquires the replacement property. Remember, however, that only the portion of improvements that are constructed at the time the exchanger acquires the lease and the improvements will qualify as section 1031 replacement property.

Leasehold Improvements Exchange Structure

After Arnold explained the purpose of the lease and how the lease and the improvements can be like-kind to the relinquished property, Erin asked Arnold to explain the leasehold improvements exchange structure. Epic Corp has several affiliated entities, all of which are related to Epic Corp under the section 1031 definition of related party. One of those entities, Dynamic Subsidiary, has a piece of property, Rectangle Lot, that would be suitable for Richmond Factory. Erin asked Arnold to assume that Epic Corp would construct Richmond Factory on Rectangle Lot if they decided not to construct on property currently owned by a third party.

Arnold began, "The leasehold improvements exchange has several steps. First, Dynamic Subsidiary will lease Rectangle Lot to the EAT. Second, using funds provided by Epic Corp, the accommodator will construct Richmond Factory. Third, Epic Corp will transfer Quarles Factory to Big Co through a QI. The QI will receive the proceeds from the sale of Quarles Factory. Fourth, the qualified intermediary will acquire Richmond Factory from the EAT and transfer it to Epic Corp. At the end of the exchange, Epic Corp will own Richmond Factory and lease Rectangle Lot from Dynamic Subsidiary."

Leasehold Improvements Exchange

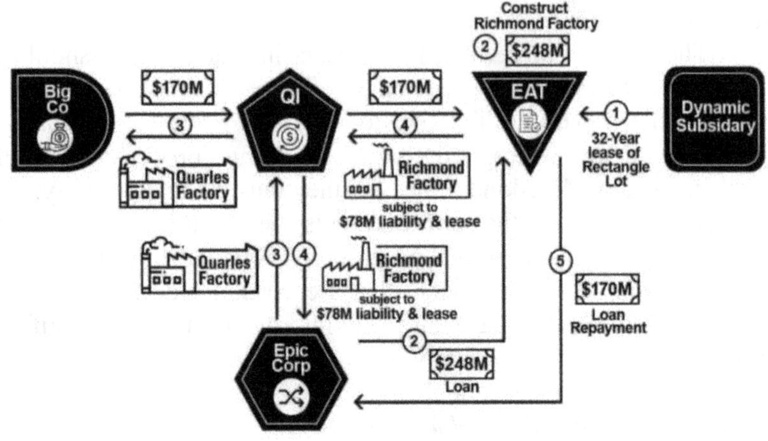

"So is the replacement property the improvements or the lease?" Erin asked.

"Both the improvements and the lease are part of the replacement property," Arnold answered. "The value of the property is the right to use Rectangle Lot for a rental amount based on its unimproved value. Because Richmond Factory will be on Rectangle Lot, the lease has significant value. The amount spent to construct Richmond Factory should equal that value."

"The leasehold improvements exchange might be the best alternative so far," Erin observed. "If we build on property we already own, we can prepare the property for construction and be prepared to move on to the property and begin building improvements as soon as Dynamic Subsidiary leases Rectangle Lot to the EAT. If everything is ready to go, we can definitely spend the entire $170,000,000 of exchange proceeds on improvements in 180 days. We might even be able to complete the entire factory in that period."

"As you intimate, however, the EAT doesn't have to complete Richmond Factory before you acquire it. Any part of Richmond Factory that is considered real property when you acquire it can qualify as replacement real property, if you properly identify Richmond Factory."

"I just thought of something else," Erin said. "Could we have Dynamic Subsidiary acquire Reach Ranch from Sara, prepare it for the construction of Richmond Factory, and then have Dynamic Subsidiary lease the property to an EAT?"

"There is no reason why you shouldn't be able to do that," Arnold said. "If you structure the transaction as an improvements exchange, the improvements should still qualify for section 1031 exchange treatment. Remember, however, that Dynamic Subsidiary couldn't transfer Reach Ranch as part of the exchange. Epic Corp's replacement property would have to be a long-term lease in Reach Ranch, Richmond Factory."

"It will be easy enough to use the lease structure, so that shouldn't be a problem," Erin said. "We'll have to keep that in mind as another possible alternative. What else can we do?"

"Didn't you also mention that Epic Corp owns some property that you would consider using for Richmond Factory if you can under section 1031?" Arnold asked.

"We do," Erin said. "I'm pretty sure that we would use it only if things didn't work out with any of the other properties we are considering. Can you spend just a few minutes describing how we might use property Epic Corp already owns in an improvement exchange? We call that property Reference Square."

Improvements Exchange on Exchanger-Owned Property

"I'm happy to hear that you most likely won't need to use property that Epic Corp owns right now," Arnold said. "We call such exchanges improvements exchanges on exchanger-owned property. Although such exchanges can qualify for section 1031 nonrecognition, they are the most complicated exchange structure, and they don't come within the title-parking safe harbor. Thus, Epic Corp must transfer tax ownership of Reference Square to an accommodator."

Improvements Exchange on Exchanger-Owned Property

An improvements exchange on exchanger-owned property requires that the exchanger dispossess itself of the property on which the improvements will be constructed. Thus, an accommodator acquires the property and constructs improvements on it. The exchanger transfers relinquished property and re-acquires the property and the improvements. The IRS has stated that the title-parking safe harbor does not apply to improvements exchanges on exchanger-owned property. Therefore, all such exchanges must be structured outside the safe harbor. This requires that the exchanger transfer the benefits and burdens of ownership of the land on which improvements will be constructed to the accommodator.

"I already don't like the sound of these exchanges," Erin said. "If we can't rely upon the title-parking safe harbor, we will have to transfer the benefits and burdens of Reference Square to an accommodator, either by transferring legal title or entering into an arm's length lease with the accommodator. That will complicate the transaction significantly. Other than requiring the transfer of tax ownership to the accommodator, the transaction sounds basically the same as the other structures we have talked about. Does it have as much legal support as the others do?"

"It's hard to say," Arnold said. "Case law approves both the seller-facilitated and the accommodator-facilitated structures. Furthermore, if the accommodator can construct sufficient improvements within the 180-day safe harbor period, you can use the safe harbor for the accommodator-facilitated exchanges. Within the last several years, the IRS has also privately ruled that leasehold improvements exchanges can qualify for section 1031 nonrecognition. Thus, we have some support for each of the first three structures we discussed. The only indication that an improvements exchange on exchanger-owned property will work is a couple of old private rulings. Recent case law has disallowed exchange treatment to such an exchange, but it was poorly structured and the exchanger was treated as having never transferred the property on which the improvements were constructed. Thus, the exchanger owned the property and improvements while they were being constructed. As stated above, such a transaction fails both the exchange requirement and the like-kind requirement."

Improvements Exchange on Exchanger-Owned Property

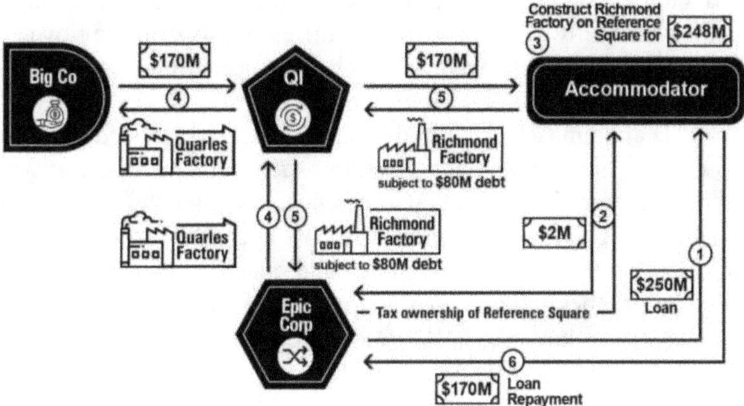

"You aren't doing a very good job of selling this idea," Erin said.

"I'm not trying to sell the idea," Arnold replied. "If you need to use the structure and the potential tax savings justify its costs, you might consider an improvements exchange on property owned by Epic Corp. Otherwise, it shouldn't be your first choice. In fact, if you think you may need to use Reference Square for Richmond Factory, you may consider transferring it to a related party immediately. If you can then wait at least 180 days to begin construction, you will be able to use a leasehold improvements exchange that should qualify for the title-parking safe harbor."

"That's interesting," Erin said. "We'll have to think about that. In fact, because constructing improvements on property owned by Epic Corp is so difficult, perhaps we should transfer other property from Epic

Corp to related parties. That way the other property will be available for future leasehold improvements exchanges. We intend to construct enough new improvements that it would make sense to have property available for one of the easier structures if needed."

"I have noticed more and more clients do the same thing," Arnold replied. "If they have a significant construction program and sell property from time to time, they like to ensure that they have raw land in related entities so they can do leasehold improvements exchanges if needed. A lot of my clients ensure that different properties are owned by different related entities, each of which is respected as a separate entity for tax purposes."

"That sounds like a good planning idea," Erin said. "It sounds like our best choice is an accommodator-facilitated exchange if we can complete enough construction within 180 days after the EAT acquires Reach Ranch. The leasehold improvements exchange would be the first choice if we have to take Reach Ranch and obtain zoning or construction permits before beginning construction. If we can't complete enough improvements within 180 days, we'll have to do something outside the title-parking safe harbor. Is that correct?"

"That's a good summary," Arnold said. "You have some decisions to make, but the transaction will influence your choice of exchange structure."

"We'll see what we learn as we find out more about where we will build Richmond Factory," Erin said. "You have been a great help. I have at least one more question."

Deferred Improvements Exchanges

"As long as we're talking about improvements exchanges, there is one other thing I would like to ask about," Erin said. "From time to time, we sell property and want to use the proceeds to acquire replacement property and construct improvements on that property. Is it possible to do an improvements exchange if we transfer the relinquished property first?"

Deferred Improvements Exchange

A deferred improvements exchange is a transfer of relinquished property with the exchange proceeds going to a qualified intermediary. The qualified intermediary advances the exchange proceeds to an exchange accommodation titleholder who uses the proceeds to acquire property and construct improvements. Within 180 days after the exchanger transfers the relinquished property, it acquires the newly-constructed improvements as replacement property.

"We call those transactions deferred improvements exchanges," Arnold said. "Let's assume that Quarles Factory is the relinquished property and you want to sell it and use the proceeds to construct improvements on the property owned by Dynamic Subsidiary using a title-parking safe harbor.

"We could structure the deferred exchange like this: First, Epic Corp could transfer Quarles Factory to Big Co. A QI would receive the proceeds from the sale of Quarles Factory. Second, an EAT would lease Rectangle Lot from Dynamic Subsidiary. Third, the EAT would construct Richmond Factory. Fourth, the QI would acquire Richmond Factory and the lease from the EAT and transfer it to Epic Corp to complete the exchange."

Deferred Improvements Exchange

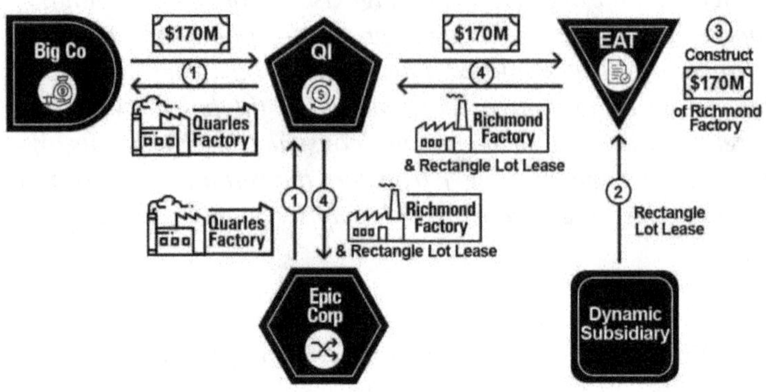

"How does the EAT obtain funds to construct the improvements?" Erin asked. "Can the QI advance exchange proceeds to the EAT to fund the construction of the improvements?"

"The section 1031 rules do not prohibit the QI from advancing funds to finance the construction of the improvements," Arnold answered. "The EAT must, however, use the proceeds exclusively to pay for the materials and construction services. A gratuitous payment of the funds to Epic Corp would put Epic Corp in receipt of exchange proceeds. Any payment from the EAT to Epic Corp or any disqualified person must be in exchange for construction services, construction materials, or rent.

"Perhaps more important than the tax consequences, you and the QI should give attention to the security of the exchange proceeds," Arnold continued. "The QI will be under an obligation to transfer replacement property or exchange proceeds to Epic Corp. If it advances the proceeds to the EAT to fund the construction of improvements and for some reason Richmond Factory is not constructed and the money is no longer available (perhaps because the lien of another creditor attached to the property), the QI would still be liable to deliver replacement property or exchange proceeds. To protect itself from this contingency, the QI should take a security interest in the replacement property, the improvements being constructed, and the ownership interest of the tear-off LLC that will lease Rectangle Lot from Dynamic Subsidiary. The QI should also amend the exchange agreement to provide that it may advance the exchange proceeds to the EAT."

"It sounds like a deferred improvements exchange will require significant documentation," Erin observed.

"It will, just like the other improvements exchanges will," Arnold said. "As with all improvements exchanges, the concepts are complicated, and documenting the transaction properly requires significant effort. Thus, the transaction generally has to be fairly large to justify using an improvements exchange structure. It doesn't have to be as large as the Quarles Factory exchange, but the economics would not justify such complexity for a relatively small transaction. Improvements exchanges present tremendous tax-planning opportunities, but they are complex."

INCOMPLETE IMPROVEMENTS AS REPLACEMENT PROPERTY

Often either the exchange period or the Rev. Proc. 2000-37 holding period expires before the EAT can complete all of the improvements. Incomplete improvements may, however, qualify as like-kind replacement property, so this should not prevent section 1031 nonrecognition. Two things determine whether incomplete improvements will qualify for section 1031 nonrecognition.

First, if the exchanger transferred real property, only the portion of the improvements that are constructed and have become real property will qualify as replacement property. Thus, prepaid construction costs will not qualify, nor will materials that have not been affixed to real property.

Second, the exchanger must acquire property that is substantially the same as the property the exchanger identified. An exchanger may satisfy this requirement even though it identifies a completed building but only acquires a partially completed building. The rule provides that if the building had been the same as the identified building had it been completed, it will be treated as substantially the same as the identified building, even if it is not completed.

An improvements exchange should also allow an exchanger to continue the construction of improvements begun by a related party. For example, an exchange accommodation titleholder should be able to lease a partially completed building from a party related to an exchanger and continue to construct the improvements. Although only the improvements the accommodation titleholder constructs will count towards the expenditure of the exchange proceeds, an exchanger could invest a substantial amount of exchange proceeds in continued construction. The general rules of identification should apply to such transactions.

Finally, an exchanger who structures a leasehold improvements exchange should identify the improvements and the leasehold interest as replacement property. Although the value of the replacement property will derive from the improvements, the leasehold interest is part of the replacement property, and the exchanger should identify it as such. This helps avoid the ambiguity of whether the exchanger must acquire an interest in the underlying property to satisfy the like-kind requirement.

CONSTRUCTION MANAGER

The accommodation titleholder most likely will not manage construction of improvements built on property it owns. Instead, it will hire the exchanger or a party related to the exchanger to manage the construction. The IRS permits such an arrangement in the title-parking safe harbor. Therefore, the accommodation titleholder may hire the exchanger or a party related to the exchanger to manage the construction, and that party will in turn most likely hire a contractor to construct the improvements.

Although Rev. Proc. 2000-37 allows the exchange accommodation titleholder to hire the exchanger or a party related to the exchanger to manage the construction of the improvements, any amounts paid to either party must be for materials or construction services. Otherwise, the amounts may be boot to the exchanger. Also, the exchanger or the party related to the exchanger who acts as construction manager must include in gross income any amount received in exchange for construction services. The amount paid for construction will be included in the cost of the replacement property, which will help reduce the amount realized if the exchanger needs to invest additional proceeds in replacement property. The trade-off for deferring that additional gain, however, is that the party managing the construction of the improvements will have ordinary income equal to the amount paid for construction services.

The various improvements exchange structures make section 1031 available to a larger cross section of property owners. The transactions can become quite complex, but they provide unique tax-saving opportunities. They also reflect the purpose of section 1031 because property owners, by satisfying the technical requirements of section 1031, are able to continue an investment in like-kind property.

CHAPTER 8:
EXCHANGES AND PROXIMATE BUSINESS TRANSACTIONS

Frequently exchanges occur in proximity to other business transactions. For example, an individual may exchange property and then contribute the replacement property to a limited liability company (this would be an exchange followed by a contribution). Or, a partnership may distribute property to one or more of its members who would then transfer the distributed property in exchange for other property (this would be a distribution followed by an exchange). Or, a corporation may transfer property as the first leg of an intended exchange and then distribute the right to receive intended replacement property to a shareholder who acquires the property (this would be a midstream distribution). A proximate business transaction may destroy an intended section 1031 exchange. In particular, a midstream business transaction may prevent the intended exchange from satisfying the reciprocal requirement (Chapter 4 discusses the reciprocal requirement). An exchange before or after a proximate business transaction could fail the holding and use requirements (Chapter 3 discusses the holding and use requirements). The colloquial terms for these transactions are "drop-and-swap" and "swap-and-drop."

Proximate Business Restructuring

A proximate business transaction alters a business structure and occurs shortly before, shortly after, or during an intended section 1031 exchange. Business transactions include contributions to businesses, distributions from businesses, mergers, acquisitions, divisions, conversions, and any other event that alters a business structure.

EXCHANGES FOLLOWED BY CONTRIBUTION (SWAP-AND-DROP)

An example demonstrates the issues that arise with exchanges followed by contributions. Beonce recently offered to purchase Quaff Vineyard from Ella. Ella was happy to receive the offer and interested in selling Quaff Vineyard because she is tired of maintaining the property and wants to diversify her holdings (Quaff Vineyard represents the vast majority of her wealth). For several months now, Ella's friend Yvonne has been talking to Ella about joining Eclectic Ltd, a partnership that Yvonne manages. Eclectic Ltd holds several pieces of rental real property and is always in the market to buy other property. Ella offered to contribute Quaff Vineyard to Eclectic Ltd, but Yvonne said that it wouldn't generate enough consistent rental income to satisfy Eclectic Ltd's investors. Instead, Yvonne recommended that Ella sell Quaff Vineyard and contribute the proceeds to Eclectic Ltd for a limited partnership interest. Eclectic Ltd would then buy one of the several properties it was considering. Ella didn't like this plan because she had a very low basis in Quaff Vineyard and didn't want to lose investment net worth by paying tax on the disposition.

Yvonne told Ella about another way to avoid tax on the disposition of Quaff Vineyard that would still allow Ella to join Eclectic Ltd. Yvonne recommended that Ella transfer Quaff Vineyard as part of a section 1031 exchange; acquire Ruddock Hotel, one of the properties that Eclectic Ltd was interested in holding; and transfer Ruddock Hotel to Eclectic Ltd in exchange for a limited partnership interest in Eclectic Ltd. When Ella questioned whether the exchange would qualify for section 1031 nonrecognition if she immediately contributed it to Eclectic Ltd, Yvonne informed her that other members of Eclectic Ltd entered the same way.

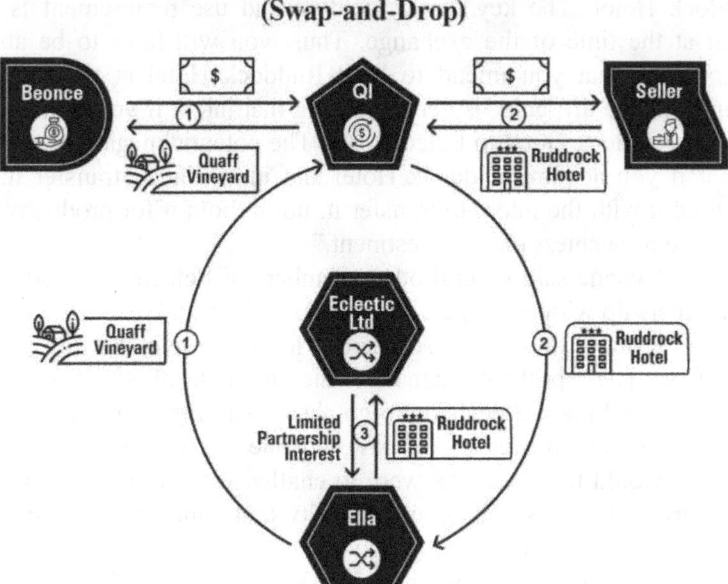

Ella decided to talk to Ali, her attorney, about this structure. Ali had assisted other clients with several exchanges, so when Ella began to explain the structure, Ali was able to predict what she planned to do. That being said, Ali also understood that such transactions are somewhat complicated and the law governing them not fully developed. He told Ella that she could not be 100 percent confident that she would prevail if the IRS challenged the section 1031 nonrecognition and the case proceeded to trial. This, of course, got Ella's attention and she asked Ali to explain.

Ali began, "Section 1031 requires that you hold Quaff Vineyard for productive use in a trade or business or for investment and that you acquire Ruddock Hotel to hold for productive use in a trade or business or for investment. We call this the holding and use requirement." (Chapter 3 describes the holding and use requirement.)

"You have held Quaff Vineyard to produce grapes that you sell. That satisfies the holding and use requirement. I can't be as certain about Ruddock Hotel. The key to the holding and use requirement is your intent at the time of the exchange. Thus, you will have to be able to demonstrate that you intend to hold Ruddock Hotel at the time you acquire it. The difficulty is demonstrating that intent if you immediately transfer Ruddock Hotel to Eclectic Ltd. The potential negative argument is that if you acquire Ruddock Hotel and immediately transfer it, you acquired it with the intent to transfer it, not to hold it for productive use in a trade or business or for investment."

"Yvonne said several other members of Eclectic Ltd had joined the partnership with this type of transaction," Ella said.

"I don't doubt it," Ali said. "Many people do this type of exchange. They probably consider the tax risk of structuring their exchanges and make a decision to go ahead with the exchange. Because this is an unsettled area of the law, no one knows for sure what the outcome would be if the IRS were to challenge the transaction you are considering. There is analogous authority that supports a section 1031 nonrecognition position."

"What do you mean when you say analogous authority supports a section 1031 nonrecognition position?" Ella asked.

"In a famous case, *Magneson v. Commissioner*, the court granted section 1031 nonrecognition to an exchange followed by a contribution of replacement property—an undivided interest in real property, all of which became the asset of the limited partnership—to a limited partnership for a general partner interest," Ali said. "The transaction you are contemplating is similar to the transaction in *Magneson*, but different in a potentially important way. It is similar in that you intend to acquire replacement property and contribute it to an entity taxed as a partnership. It is different, however, in that you are not acquiring an undivided interest in the property and you will not receive a general partner interest. The type of partnership interest you receive may be important."

"How significant is the difference?" Ella asked.

"No one knows," Ali replied. "That is why the transaction has some tax risk. The court in *Magneson* considered two things in ruling in the exchanger's favor. First, it considered the contribution to the limited partnership to be a mere change in the form of ownership but a continuation of investment. Second, it recognized that the exchanger, as a general partner, retained management control of the contributed property. Arguably, your contribution of Ruddock Hotel to Eclectic Ltd would be a mere change in the form of ownership that is a continuation of your investment. You will, however, give up management control of Ruddock Hotel when you contribute it to a limited partnership in exchange for a limited partner interest. In this respect, your transaction is different from the *Magneson* transaction.

"Just because your transaction is different from the *Magneson* transaction," Ali continued, "doesn't mean that it won't qualify for section 1031 nonrecognition. It just means that there is some uncertainty regarding what the outcome will be if the issue is litigated. Whether you will be able to satisfy the holding and use requirement is an open issue. Some people don't like any uncertainty, so they wouldn't do the transaction or, if they did, wouldn't report the exchange as a section 1031 exchange. Others would consider the consequences that would result from a court ruling that *Magneson* does not apply to their transaction and decide, despite that risk, to do the transaction and report it as a section 1031 exchange."

After thinking for a few minutes, Ella said, "I can live with some uncertainty, depending upon the consequences that would result if a court ruled that the exchange did not qualify for section 1031 nonrecognition. Because this is an uncertain area, I can't imagine that I would be liable for any type of fraud. Would a court impose any penalties?"

"I agree with you that reporting nonrecognition under section 1031 would not be fraud. The most serious penalty that you would have to worry about is the substantial understatement penalty. That penalty will not apply, however, if 'substantial authority' supports the position you take on your tax return. Thus, the question is whether *Magneson* provides substantial authority for section 1031 nonrecognition on the transaction you are considering. Substantial authority means that you have slightly less than a 50 percent chance of prevailing on the merits of the case." (Chapter 3 discusses tax probability.)

Ali continued, "As I said earlier, no one can know for certain what a court would hold if it considered the transaction you are contemplating. Nonetheless, many tax practitioners would agree that *Magneson* is substantial authority for claiming nonrecognition on the transaction you are contemplating. Even if it is substantial authority, a court could hold that you owe tax on the transaction. Therefore, you may have to pay tax later, plus interest."

"Tax plus interest on the tax would put me in the same position I would be in if I paid tax right now," Ella observed. "If I won't be subject to a penalty in the event the issue is challenged and the IRS prevails, it makes sense for me to do the exchange and take a nonrecognition position. Has the IRS expressed a position regarding this type of transaction?"

Ali said, "Several years ago, prior to the *Magneson* decision, the IRS ruled that an exchange followed by a contribution to a corporation does not qualify for section 1031 nonrecognition. Since *Magneson*, the IRS has been silent on this issue. Unfortunately, their silence and inaction in this area doesn't provide much insight. You can't rely upon that silence. Instead, the law must dictate the position you will take on your tax return."

"That's a lot to think about," Ella said. "It sounds like I can't be certain that a court will uphold the nonrecognition position I want to report. On the other hand, it probably won't be able to impose penalties."

"That's a good summary of the tax situation," Ali said. "You also need to remember that this will not be a simple transaction. It will require detailed documentation. The documentation must be prepared to ensure that you are treated as acquiring Ruddock Hotel for tax purposes and that you transfer it to Eclectic Ltd. If Eclectic Ltd. is treated as acquiring Ruddock Hotel directly from the seller, you won't be able to use it to complete the exchange. Ensuring you acquire the property for tax purposes will require some effort. Therefore, the transaction will involve some legal fees, for both the document preparation and tax advice."

"Will I need to hold the replacement property for any period of time before contributing it to Eclectic Ltd?" Ella asked.

"There is no explicit holding period requirement in the section 1031 holding and use requirement," Ali replied. "What you ask implicitly is whether holding the property for some time before contributing it will help you establish that you acquired the property with the intent to hold it for productive use in a trade or business or for investment. Informed section 1031 practitioners may dispute this, but I don't think holding Ruddock Hotel for a specific time period will strengthen your argument that you acquired it for productive use in a trade or business or for investment. Your intent for acquiring property is measured at the time you acquire the property. Intent is a factual question. The holding period would become important if your intent was uncertain. In such a situation, a fairly short holding period may indicate that, at the time you acquired the property, you intended to contribute it to Eclectic Ltd. A longer holding period would tend to show that your intent was not to contribute the property."

Ali continued, "We know your intent is to acquire Ruddock Hotel and contribute it to Eclectic Ltd. Knowing that makes the holding period irrelevant. Thus, the only way you can prevail if the holding and use requirement becomes an issue is to rely upon the rationale and holding in *Magneson*."

Although the tax treatment of exchanges followed by contributions to certain entities is uncertain, many exchangers choose to enter into such transactions. They rely upon *Magneson* to support section 1031 nonrecognition, understanding that they could lose if the position is litigated. Nonetheless, believing that *Magneson* is substantial authority, many tax advisors will counsel their clients accordingly. Most informed section 1031 practitioners would, however, agree that an exchange followed by a contribution qualifies for section 1031 nonrecognition only if the contribution is tax free, as it was in *Magneson*.

CONTRIBUTION FOLLOWED BY EXCHANGE (DROP-AND-SWAP)

Ali then suggested, "Perhaps we should ask Yvonne if you can do a contribution followed by an exchange. Under this structure, you would contribute Quaff Vineyard to Eclectic Ltd, and Eclectic Ltd would exchange it for Ruddock Hotel. The structure is fairly straightforward."

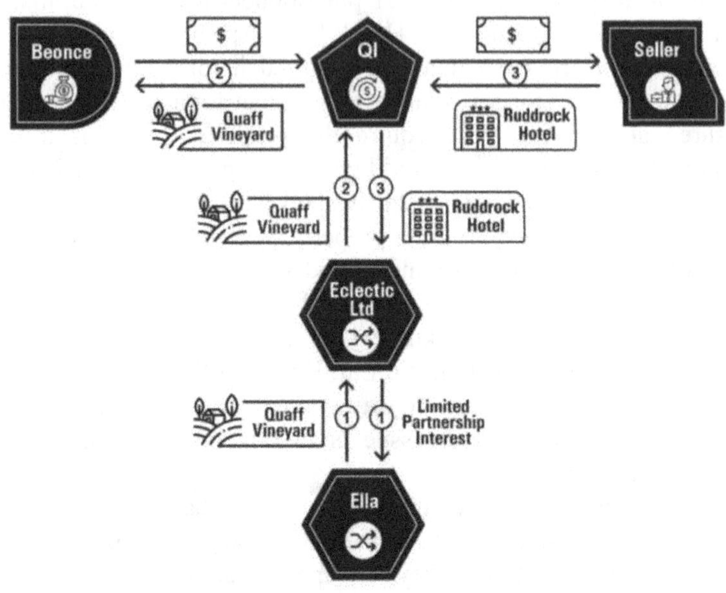

"It does seem fairly straightforward," Ella said. "Why wouldn't we simply use that structure?"

"From a practical standpoint, Yvonne may not allow Eclectic Ltd to take title to Quaff Vineyard," Ali said. "She may be concerned about Eclectic Ltd entering the chain of title. If, however, we offer to contribute Quaff Vineyard to a single-member limited liability company controlled by you and then contribute the single-member limited liability company to Eclectic Ltd, perhaps we can allay her concerns about liability exposure."

"Would this structure provide any tax advantages?" Ella asked.

"It would reduce your tax risk without exposing Eclectic Ltd to tax risk," Ali said. "The tax advantage to you is that a court has provided that an exchange following a tax-free distribution qualifies for section 1031 nonrecognition. The court reasoned that an exchanger can satisfy the holding and use requirement with respect to recently acquired property if the exchanger transfers it in exchange for other like-kind property it will hold for productive use in a trade or business or for investment. The same rationale should apply to an exchange following a tax-free contribution. Thus, there is support for section 1031 nonrecognition if Eclectic Ltd were to acquire and exchange Quaff Vineyard. In fact, the support for nonrecognition is stronger with this structure than with an exchange followed by contribution.

"Eclectic Ltd should not be concerned about the tax consequences of such a transaction," Ali continued. "If the exchange did not qualify for section 1031 nonrecognition, the partnership tax allocation rules would allocate the gain recognized by Eclectic Ltd to you. Thus, Eclectic Ltd's tax risk would be nominal."

"That should be attractive to Eclectic Ltd," Ella said. "If Yvonne can get comfortable taking title to Quaff Vineyard, either directly or indirectly, Eclectic Ltd should have no reason to object to this structure."

"I agree," Ali said. "I look forward to talking to Yvonne and seeing what she says. I think I prefer this structure over the exchange followed by the contribution."

PROXIMATE PARTNERSHIP DISTRIBUTIONS

The following situation is common. Esther and Elvira, two individuals, are the sole members of Elated LLC, an entity taxed as a partnership for tax purposes. Brady offered to purchase Elated LLC's only asset Quirky Lot, a piece of raw land, for $1,500,000. This offer far exceeds what Esther and Elvira thought the property was worth. Consequently, they decided to accept the offer. In discussing what to do with the proceeds from the sale of the property, the two realized that they will likely have different investment objectives. Esther wants to reinvest the proceeds in other land. Elvira would like to either invest the proceeds in income-producing property or receive the proceeds and recognize gain on the transaction. Either way, they understand that continuing the partnership for an extended period after the exchange would not make sense. Esther contacted Alex, her attorney, to discuss any options that might help her and Elvira reach their separate goals on this transaction.

After learning about the situation, Alex tells Esther that she and Elvira could consider one of three possible alternatives: (1) an exchange followed by a distribution, (2) a distribution followed by exchanges, or (3) an installment note transaction. Alex explained that choosing the appropriate alternative could depend in large part upon what Elvira decides to do. If Elvira is undecided on the Quirky Lot sales date, that will limit the available alternatives.

"As we discuss the three alternatives, you will notice that the suitability of each depends upon Elvira's and your objectives," Alex described. "We will also discuss the tax risk of each alternative. Some of the alternatives have greater support in the law than others.

"Before we talk about this, remember that these alternatives only apply if Elated LLC is taxed as a partnership," Alex said. "Often, owners of corporations, even S corporations, ask whether they can do a section 1031 exchange in proximity to an S corporation liquidation. Because distributions from S corporations are taxable, doing section 1031 exchanges in proximity to an S corporation liquidation does not make sense. The distribution will trigger gain and defeat the benefits of doing a nonrecognition transaction. Thus, the entity that is liquidating must be taxed as a partnership for the exchange to have any value. S corporations may consider doing tax-free divisions if the shareholders each plan to acquire like-kind replacement property as part of the separation"

Esther confirmed that Elated LLC is definitely taxed as a partnership and that it files a Form 1065 (partnership return) each year. Having established that, Alex continued.

Exchange Followed by Distributions (Swap-and-Drop)

Alex explained, "An exchange followed by distributions would be appropriate if both you and Elvira intend to do section 1031 exchanges but want to dissolve Elated LLC. For example, if you wish to use your share of exchange proceeds to acquire Ruddy Building and Elvira wishes to use her share of exchange proceeds to acquire Red Lot, the exchange followed by distributions may help you accomplish these goals. The transaction would occur as follows: Elated LLC would transfer Quirky Lot and acquire Ruddy Building and Red Lot. Elated LLC would then distribute Ruddy Building to you and Red Lot to Elvira."

Exchange Followed by Distributions (Swap-and-Drop)

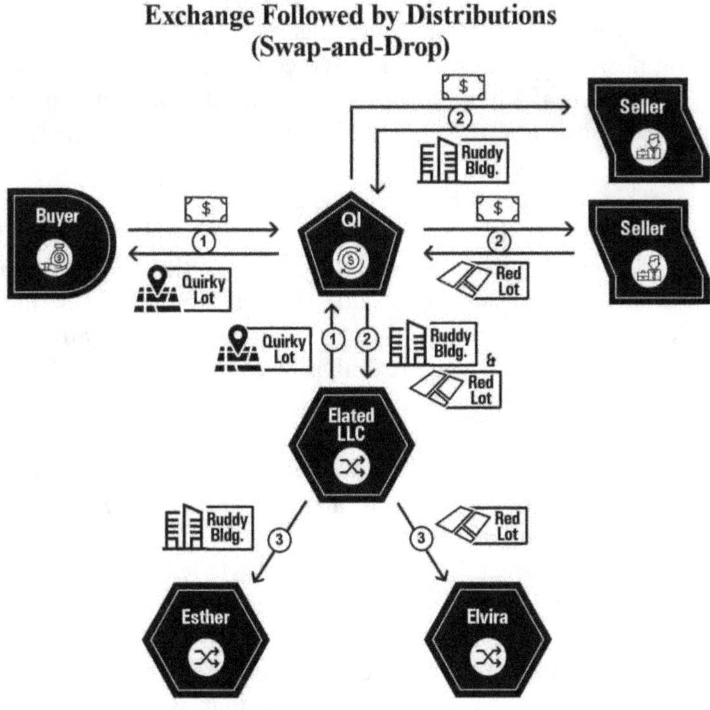

"What type of authority supports this type of transaction?" Esther asked.

"The Tax Court allowed section 1031 nonrecognition to an exchange followed by a tax-free distribution," Alex said. "The case was *Maloney v Commissioner* and the court stated that an exchange before or after a tax-free business transaction should qualify for section 1031 nonrecognition because the proximate tax-free business transaction is a continuation of an investment. The distribution from Elated LLC following the exchange should be tax-free, so the *Maloney* rationale provides support for section 1031 nonrecognition on the exchange. *Maloney* appears to support a claim that Elated LLC would acquire the replacement properties to hold for productive use in a trade or business or for investment. This reduces your tax risk with respect to that issue."

"It's always good to know that there is some authority for a reporting position we wish to take. We could probably get comfortable with the structure if Elvira decides to do an exchange, but could we use this type of transaction if Elvira decides not to do an exchange?" Esther asked.

"This transaction helps you obtain section 1031 nonrecognition only if both you and Elvira wish to do a section 1031 exchange and if Elated LLC can acquire both replacement properties within the section 1031 time limitations," Alex said. (Chapter 5 discusses the time limitations.) "If you choose to do an exchange followed by distributions and Elated LLC does not acquire both replacement properties but instead receives exchange proceeds, Elated LLC will recognize gain. Elated LLC will allocate that gain to both partners."

"Does that mean that even though Elated LLC is able to acquire Ruddy Building and distribute it to me, I would recognize gain if it did not also acquire Red Lot?" asked Esther.

"That's correct," Alex said. "A failed exchange at the partnership level will result in partnership level gain, and the partnership will most likely allocate that gain to both you and Elvira."

"So this structure would be beneficial only if we both want to do section 1031 exchanges and if we think that we can acquire both replacements within the section 1031 time limitations," Esther mused.

“That’s the baseline issue you have to consider with this type of transaction,” Alex said. “If Elated LLC will not acquire both replacement properties, then this structure won’t work for you. Some practitioners believe that Elated LLC could allocate all of the gain to Elvira if Elated LLC were unable to acquire Red Lot. In most situations, however, the substantial economic effect test will prohibit allocating all of the gain to one partner.”

“I don’t know what you meant by the substantial economic effect test,” Esther confessed, “but I will rely upon your knowledge of this issue. If we decide to go forward with this transaction, we can explore further whether this transaction might be one of the few that would allow Elated LLC to allocate all of the gain to Elvira. Are there other non-tax issues that this structure would raise?”

“Even if you are confident that Elated LLC will acquire both replacement properties within the section 1031 time limitations, other factors may convince you to use a different structure,” Alex said. “For example, you must consider your relationship with Elvira. Your intent is to use your share of the proceeds from the sale of Quirky Lot to acquire Ruddy Building. Do you feel comfortable acquiring Ruddy Building in an entity in which you share control with Elvira? Is it possible that Elated LLC could acquire Ruddy Building and then be unable to distribute it to you because Elvira would oppose the distribution for some reason?”

“I trust Elvira,” Esther stated, “but, as you said, I want to own Ruddy Building individually. I don’t think Elvira would hold up the distribution of Ruddy Building to me. Thus, that isn’t a significant concern. If I had a different partner, I would worry more about that. I would, however, be concerned about Elated LLC holding both properties at the same time because of potential liability.”

“That’s a legitimate concern,” Alex said. “Both properties have the potential of creating liability. You could minimize liability exposure by causing Elated LLC to form two limited liability companies, each of which would acquire one of the replacement properties. This will help contain the liability of each property within the respective limited liability company.”

Alex continued, "Don't blow off the other issue too quickly. Even though you enjoy working with Elvira and have had no problems working with her, things could change. For example, as much as I hate to think about this, she could die or become incapacitated. I hope the Elated LLC operating agreement addresses such contingencies, but if not, things could get messier than you would like. We will need to look at the operating agreement, at a minimum, if we decide to do the exchange followed by distributions."

"It sounds like the exchange followed by distributions raises three issues," Esther said. "First, although the tax risk appears to be low, the IRS could argue that Elated LLC did not acquire the replacement property with the intent to hold it for productive use in a trade or business or for investment because of the proximate distribution of the intended replacement property. Because *Maloney* addresses this type of exchange, that wouldn't be the most significant concern. Second, if Elated does not acquire all of the replacement property before the end of the section 1031 time limitations, the partnership will recognize gain and will allocate that gain to both partners. This is a significant concern because it could destroy my goal of nonrecognition. Third, the partnership will acquire the replacement properties, even though the intent is for the partners to respectively own the separate properties individually. This will create a problem for me if Elvira tries to block the distribution of Ruddy Building. I'm not too concerned about that because of the relationship I have with Elvira. We will, however, want to verify the terms of the operating agreement and be certain that no one can take Elvira's interest in Elated LLC and block the distribution."

Disadvantages of Exchange Followed by Distributions

An exchange followed by distributions has the following disadvantages:

(1) The immediate distribution could be evidence that the partnership did not acquire the property to hold for productive use in a trade or business or for investment;

(2) If the partnership cannot acquire all the replacement property prior to the end of the section 1031 time limitations, the partnership will recognize gain, and it will most likely allocate some of that gain to each partner;
(3) The partnership will own the replacement property for a period of time, even though the partners wish to hold the separate properties individually; and
(4) The law does not clearly establish that the partnership acquires replacement property to hold for productive use in a trade or business or for investment.

"That's a good summary of the disadvantages of an exchange followed by distributions," Alex said. "The advantage is that it is relatively simple."

"What's the next alternative structure?" Esther asked.

Distribution Followed by Exchanges (Drop-and-Swap)

"The next alternative is a distribution followed by exchanges," Alex said. "Elated LLC could distribute undivided interests in Quirky Lot to you and Elvira, and the two of you could exchange your respective interests in Quirky Lot."

Distribution Followed by Exchanges (Drop-and-Swap)

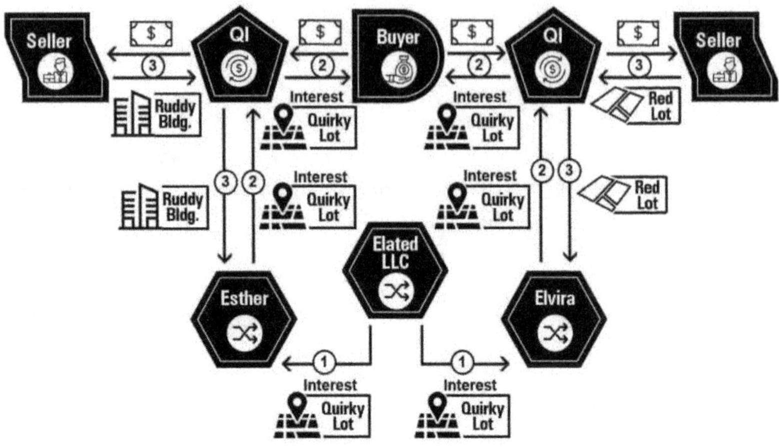

"I can see one advantage of this structure right away," Esther said. "It won't matter to me what Elvira does with her interest. If she is unable to acquire Red Lot or decides to cash out, she will recognize all of the gain from the sale of her interest in Quirky Lot, and I will be able to acquire Ruddy Building in an exchange. This structure also allows me to acquire Ruddy Building directly. Because I wouldn't have to worry about Elated LLC acquiring Ruddy Building and it getting stuck there for some reason, this structure provides considerably more freedom."

Advantages and Disadvantages of Distribution Followed by Exchanges

Advantages

Structuring a transaction as a distribution followed by exchanges provides the partners greater leeway. First, the partners may individually transfer their interests in the distributed property and separately do exchanges. If one of the partners is unable to complete an exchange, this inability will not affect the tax consequences of the other partner. Second, the partners will receive replacement property directly. Thus, they will not have to worry about the partnership acquiring the property and they can prevent partner gridlock, which could delay the distribution of the property.

Disadvantages

Distribution followed by exchanges raise tax issues. First, because the exchanger immediately transfers the distributed property, some practitioners express concern about whether the transaction satisfies the holding and use requirement. Second, the exchanger must acquire tax ownership in the property. Third, if the distributed property is an undivided interest in property, you must ensure that it is not a partnership interest for tax purposes.

"Those are the advantages of doing a distribution followed by exchanges," Alex confirmed. "Tax issues become the primary concern with this structure.

"Case law provides support for the distribution followed by exchanges. In *Bolker v Commissioner*, the court held that if (1) an exchanger acquires property in a tax-free distribution, (2) exchanges that property for other property in a transaction that otherwise qualifies for section 1031 nonrecognition, and (3) acquires the replacement property to hold for productive use in a trade or business or for investment, then the exchange satisfies the holding and use requirement with respect to the distributed property. Thus, the court treated the exchanger as holding the distributed property for productive use in a trade or investment, even though the exchanger acquired it with the intent to exchange it for other property. This case should provide support for a nonrecognition position if you choose to do a distribution followed by exchanges."

"It sounds like the tax issues are pretty straightforward and this transaction has little tax risk," Esther said.

"With respect to the holding and use requirement, I agree, but we must consider a couple of other tax issues," Alex said. "Prior to

Bolker, the IRS ruled that a similar transaction would not qualify for section 1031 nonrecognition. Because the IRS has not revoked that ruling, we don't know what position it would take if a similar case arose. Thus, although *Bolker* supports a nonrecognition position, the IRS could challenge the position and, in theory, could prevail. I am not extremely worried about this possibility, however, since the IRS has not litigated this issue since *Bolker*. In fact, in a subsequent challenge of exchanges following a distribution the IRS did not raise this issue. Other tax issues raise greater concern.

Proximate Transaction Caveats

"The ownership of Quirky Lot after the distribution cannot be a tax partnership," Alex continued. "If I understand correctly, Quirky Lot is vacant land that Elated LLC does not lease; it is merely holding the lot to recognize appreciation in its value."

"That's correct," Esther confirmed.

"That being the case, the ownership of Quirky Lot by you and Elvira as tenants in common following the distribution should not be a tax partnership. Tenants-in-common may be partners if they co-own income-producing property such as rental property that requires management. You and Elvira, however, should not be partners because Quirky Lot is not income-producing property. Fortunately, we do not have to worry about that tax issue in this situation."

Alex continued, "Although Elated LLC will transfer legal title to Quirky Lot to you and Elvira, we must ensure that the transaction is a transfer for tax purposes. In *Chase v. Commissioner*, the Tax Court held that even though a partner held legal title to an interest in a partnership, the partnership held tax ownership of the interest. Thus, the partnership, not the partner, was deemed to transfer the interest for tax purposes. That being the case, the partner was not able to do a section 1031 exchange. Thus, you must acquire the interest in Quirky Lot for tax purposes. To do this, you will have to acquire the benefits and burdens of owning the property and you, Elated LLC, and Elvira must treat you as the owner of that interest for tax purposes. Because the lot is vacant and not generating income, this should not be too difficult.

"Finally, if the contract to sell your interest in Quirky Lot is in your name and you negotiate the terms of the contract on your own behalf, your position that you own the property will be even stronger. We must consider the *Court Holding* doctrine with this type of transaction. Under *Commissioner v. Court Holding,* a corporation that negotiated the sale of property was treated as selling it, even though it distributed the property to its shareholders, the shareholders entered into the sales contract, and the shareholders sold the corporation's property. Because the corporation clearly negotiated the sale of the property, the court ignored the form of the transfer. To help ensure that you will be treated as selling the property, you should negotiate the sale of your interest if you decide to use the distribution followed by exchanges form."

Alex continued, "Parties may have a difficult time establishing tax ownership after a distribution if all of the sales documents are in the partnership's name, the purchaser understood the partnership was selling the property, and the partnership continued to account for the ownership of the property until the date of disposition. You should be able to avoid each of these pitfalls in your transaction."

"Based on what you're telling me, the distribution followed by exchanges sounds like a better transaction for me," Esther observed. "It will require re-titling the property before the sale, but we will have less tax risk and I will not have to worry about what Elvira does with the proceeds from the sale of her interest in Quirky Lot."

"I agree with you. The distribution followed by exchanges removes some of the difficulties that an exchange followed by distributions raises," Alex said. "Don't forget, however, that there is one other alternative that may be better, if Elvira decides not to do an exchange before Elated LLC transfers Quirky Lot."

Installment Note Distribution (Partnership Installment Note—"PIN")

"The other alternative that you may consider is the installment note distribution," Alex said. "This transaction would be appropriate only if Elvira is not interested in doing a section 1031 exchange. The installment note provides her an opportunity to leave the partnership and receive cash without disrupting the exchange. The transaction is complicated a bit because Elated LLC is a two-member entity, but the transaction may still be attractive."

"Of course, we would like to keep the transaction as simple as possible, but we can absorb some complexity if it will help us obtain our objectives," Esther said. "Please explain the installment note distribution."

Alex explained, "As the name implies, the installment note distribution requires Elated LLC to receive an installment note in part payment for Quirky Lot. Elated LLC then distributes the note to Elvira. After Elvira receives the note, she receives payment on the note."

Installment Note Distribution

The installment note distribution is appropriate if one member of a partnership wants to cash out and the others want to continue together. The installment note distribution requires that the partnership receive an installment note as part of the consideration for the relinquished property. The partnership distributes the note to the partner cashing out and acquires replacement property with exchange proceeds equal to the balance of the relinquished property sale proceeds. The partner cashing out receives payments on the installment note and recognizes gain as payments are received. For the installment note distribution to be effective, the note must qualify for installment sale treatment.

"I'm surprised that transaction will work," Esther said. "I thought that if an exchanger, who I understand Elated LLC would be in this case, receives anything other than like-kind property, the exchange would not qualify for section 1031 nonrecognition. Wouldn't the note be non-like-kind property that would be boot and trigger gain recognition?"

The Installment Sale Method

"The note will be boot, but it will not trigger gain recognition to Elated LLC," Alex stated. "If properly structured, the sale for the note will qualify under the installment sale method of accounting. Under the installment sale method, the holder of an installment note recognizes gain as payments are made on the note. Elated LLC will receive no payments on the note and will not recognize gain on the transaction. Instead, Elvira will receive payments on the note and she will recognize gain as she receives the payments."

"It sounds like the key to making this transaction work is to ensure that the transfer qualifies for the installment method," Esther said.

Installment Sale Method

The installment sale method provides that if a property owner receives an installment note in exchange for property, the property owner will recognize gain from the sale as payments are made on the note. Thus, the installment sale method defers gain recognition until the maker of the note makes payments. For a transaction to qualify for the installment sale treatment, the note must provide that at least one payment will be made in a taxable year following the taxable year of the property sale.

"That's correct," Alex said. "For this transaction to accomplish your goals, the note must qualify for the installment sale method. This requires that the note provide that at least one payment will be made in a subsequent year."

"I don't think Elvira will be interested in the installment note distribution if she has to wait to receive her share of the exchange proceeds," Esther said. "If she can't receive almost all of her share of the proceeds at the time of the sale, or shortly after it, she won't agree to this structure. How large does the subsequent-year payment have to be?"

"The law does not establish a minimum requirement for the subsequent-year payment, so apparently the amount can be fairly small,"

Alex said. "Tax experts probably wouldn't agree on what is a safe minimum amount—either in terms of absolute dollars or as a percentage of the total amount of the note—and neither the courts nor the IRS have addressed this question. Therefore, we are left with no guidance on this issue."

"If there's no guidance," Esther said, "we should make the subsequent-year payment small."

"You will bear the tax risk of this transaction," Alex said. "If for some reason the installment note does not qualify for installment sale treatment, Elated LLC will recognize gain on the receipt of the note and allocate that gain to you and Elvira. Elvira would plan to recognize gain anyway, so gain at the partnership level will not negatively affect her expected tax treatment. Because you want to defer gain, however, gain at the partnership level will most likely mean that you have to recognize gain on the transaction. That being the case, you may want the payment to be more than nominal."

"Because I would bear the tax risk of this transaction, Elvira will most likely insist that the subsequent year payment be nominal," Esther predicted.

"That means that the availability of the installment note distribution structure will depend upon the decision you make regarding the amount of the subsequent-year payment," Alex said. "If you require that the amount be greater than Elvira is willing to accept, she probably won't do this transaction using the installment note distribution structure."

"How will I determine the minimum amount of subsequent-year payment that I can be comfortable with?" Esther asked.

"I can help you with that," Alex said. "I think the law is clear enough to allow the subsequent-year payment to be a very small percentage of the amount of the note. Before we do too much more with that, however, let's see what Elvira wants to do and what she will require. Only then will we be in a position to make a decision about how much of a subsequent-year payment we will be comfortable with."

"That sounds good," Esther said. "We don't need to spend more time on that if Elvira may want to do an exchange. If that is the case, it sounds like this transaction is out of the question, because Elated LLC will receive the note at the time of the Quirky Lot disposition."

"You're right," Alex said. "The installment note distribution is a good structure only if you know up front that Elvira wants to cash out of her interest. If Elated LLC receives the installment note, the exchange is over with respect to the amount of the note."

"That's good to know. Is there anything else about the installment note distribution structure that I need to know?" Esther asked.

Avoiding Partnership Termination

"There is," Alex said. "Because you and Elvira are the sole members of Elated LLC, distributing the note to her in complete liquidation of her interest in Elated LLC will terminate its tax partnership status. To be a tax partnership, an entity must have two members. A liquidating distribution to Elvira would reduce Elated LLC's membership to just you, terminating the tax partnership. After the tax partnership terminates, for tax purposes you would be deemed to own all of Elated LLC's property. Thus, if Elated LLC acquired Ruddy Building, you would be deemed to acquire Ruddy Building."

Partnership Terminations

A partnership terminates if it ceases doing business as a partnership. This can happen in one of two ways. First, the partnership may sell all its assets and thereby cease business operations. Second, the interests of all but one member of a partnership are liquidated, leaving only one person to conduct business. Since a partnership requires at least two members, the resulting one-person operation would not be a partnership.

"Couldn't I just complete the exchange after the partnership terminates?" Esther asked. "What's wrong with Elated LLC acquiring Ruddy Building if I am its sole member?"

"You couldn't complete the exchange Elated LLC begins," Alex replied. "To have an exchange, the person who transfers relinquished property must acquire replacement property. If Elated LLC transfers Quirky Lot, it must also acquire the replacement property. If Elated LLC terminates while the intended exchange is pending, it won't be in existence to acquire Ruddy Building to complete the exchange."

"Does this mean that we have no hope of using the installment note distribution structure?" Esther asked.

"No, but to use it you will have to add another member to Elated LLC to ensure that it does not terminate when Elvira leaves," Alex said.

"Can just anyone become a member of Elated LLC?" Esther asked.

"Just about," Alex said. "You just need another taxpayer to be a partner."

"That shouldn't be too difficult; my husband Happy and I own almost everything together anyway. I can simply transfer some Elated LLC membership interests to him to ensure that Elated LLC does not terminate," Esther said.

Installment Note Distribution

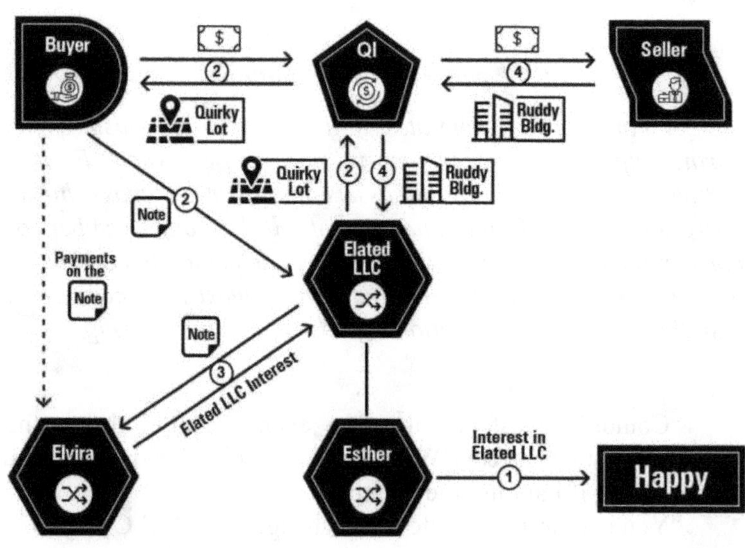

"Admitting Happy as a member of Elated LLC will help prevent

Elated LLC from terminating," Alex said. "Just be sure you admit him before Elvira leaves. Why don't we talk to Elvira and see what she wants to do and then try to make a decision about the appropriate structure for you all."

The installment note distribution appears to be a good choice for Esther. These structures can, however, be difficult to do. In particular, if the relinquished property is subject to liability, the installment note distribution may not be viable. Recall that the exchanger must replace liabilities that encumbered relinquished property (Chapter 3). If the amount of the note represents a significant portion of the relinquished property's equity, then the debt-equity ratio of the replacement property may become very high after the distribution of the note. Lenders may not be willing to provide financing with such numbers. Thus, the installment note may not be viable if the relinquished property is subject to liability.

MIDSTREAM CONTRIBUTIONS AND DISTRIBUTIONS

Midstream contributions and distributions are the most dangerous proximate business restructurings. With a few rare exceptions in the corporate context and partnership merger and division rules, an intended section 1031 exchange cannot survive a midstream contribution or distribution. A contribution is a midstream contribution if a person transfers intended relinquished property, contributes the right to acquire the intended replacement property to a separate tax entity, and causes the separate tax entity to acquire the intended replacement property. A distribution is a midstream distribution if a tax entity transfers intended relinquished property, the tax entity distributes the rights to acquire the intended replacement property to at least one of the entity owners, and the owner acquires replacement property.

Midstream Contributions and Distributions

A midstream contribution is a contribution to a separate tax entity of the right to receive intended replacement property while an intended exchange is pending.

A midstream distribution is a distribution by a tax entity of the right to receive intended replacement property while an intended exchange is pending.

Recall that section 1031 reciprocal requirement provides that the party who transfers relinquished property must acquire replacement property (Chapter 4). In every midstream contribution or distribution, one party transfers intended relinquished property and another party acquires intended replacement property. These transactions therefore foil the reciprocal requirement and cannot qualify for section 1031 nonrecognition (but, as discussed below, certain corporate reorganizations carry over the tax attributes of one party to another, allowing the transaction to satisfy the reciprocal requirement).

A simple example demonstrates a midstream contribution. Erik owns Quick-Go, a small gas station. He decides to exchange it for Raw Land as part of a section 1031 exchange. He hires QI, a qualified intermediary, to facilitate his exchange. The exchange agreement Erik enters into with QI provides that in exchange for Quick-Go, QI will acquire Raw Land and transfer it to Erik. Erik transfers Quick-Go to Bobby through QI, and QI receives the Quick-Go sale proceeds from Bobby. Before QI acquires Raw Land, Erik decides to join Enchantment Ltd, a partnership that owns several investment properties. Erik contributes his right under the exchange agreement to acquire Raw Land to Enchantment Ltd in exchange for a limited partnership interest. Enchantment Ltd acquires Raw Land.

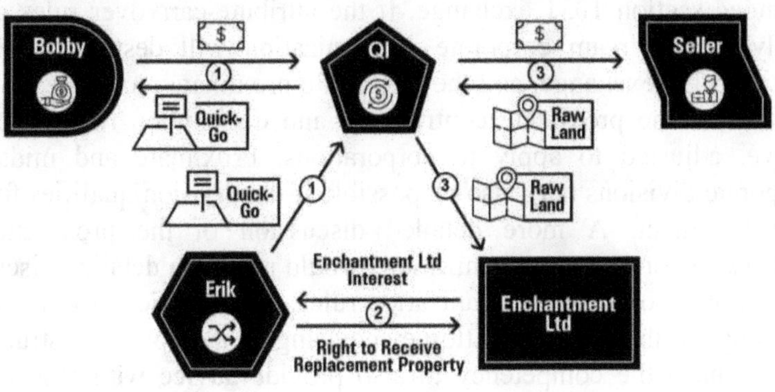

As the diagram shows, Erik transferred Quick-Go, the intended relinquished property, and Enchantment Ltd acquired Raw Land, the intended replacement property. Splitting the transaction like this prevents a reciprocal transfer of property, so the transaction does not satisfy the reciprocal requirement and will not qualify for section 1031 nonrecognition. The transaction would similarly fail to satisfy the reciprocal requirement if Enchantment Ltd owned Quick-Go, it transferred Quick-Go as part of an intended exchange, distributed the rights to receive intended replacement property to Erik, and Erik acquired Raw Land. Both types of transactions destroy section 1031 nonrecognition. Thus, to preserve section 1031 nonrecognition, exchangers must ensure that they avoid most midstream contributions and distributions.

PROXIMATE AND MIDSTREAM CORPORATE REORGANIZATIONS

Midstream contributions and distributions in the corporate reorganization context will not destroy a pending section 1031 exchange if the reorganization qualifies for tax-free treatment. The corporate merger rules provide that certain tax attributes carry over to the corporation that survives the merger. The IRS has privately ruled that if these attribute-carryover rules apply to a corporate reorganization, that reorganization, whether proximate or midstream, will not affect an intended section 1031 exchange. If the attribute-carryover rules do not apply, a midstream corporate reorganization will destroy a pending section 1031 exchange, and the effect of a proximate reorganization will depend on the proximate contribution and distribution rules discussed above, adjusted to apply to corporations. Proximate and midstream corporate divisions may also be possible if the division qualifies for tax-free treatment. A more detailed discussion of the proximate and midstream corporate reorganizations would require a detailed discussion of complex corporate reorganization rules. Such a discussion is beyond the scope of this book. An attorney advising on a corporate restructuring should have the competency to also provide advice with respect to a proximate or pending section 1031 exchange.

PROXIMATE AND MIDSTREAM PARTNERSHIP MERGERS

For tax purposes, a partnership merger may include any of a variety of partnership transactions. The various transactions have one thing in common, however: with every partnership merger, at least one partnership terminates and only one partnership continues. Any partnership that terminates is a terminated partnership. The partnership that continues is the resulting partnership. With every partnership merger, a terminated partnership either contributes or distributes its assets as part of the merger. This may affect a proximate or pending section 1031 exchange.

Partnership Mergers

All partnership mergers take one of two forms—either an assets-over merger or an assets-up merger.

Assets-Over Merger

Under the assets-over form of merger, the terminated partnerships contribute all of their assets and liabilities to the resulting partnership in exchange for interests in the resulting partnership. The terminated partnership then distributes the resulting partnership interests to its members in complete liquidation.

Assets-Up Merger

Under the assets-up form of merger, the terminated partnerships distribute their assets and liabilities to their members in complete liquidation. The members then contribute the assets and liabilities to the resulting partnership in exchange for interests in the resulting partnership.

Tax law generally respects the form used for partnership mergers. Thus, the law respects mergers structured as assets-up mergers. All mergers not structured as assets-up mergers, however, will be assets-over mergers. The terminated partnerships cease to exist for tax purposes. The resulting partnership continues from an existence prior to the merger. It therefore retains the tax identification number it had prior to the merger. Some mergers may have no resulting partnership. In such a situation, all merging partnerships will terminate and a new partnership will result.

A proximate or midstream partnership merger should not affect a section 1031 exchange of the *resulting* partnership. The *resulting* partnership retains the tax identification number of the continuing partnership and receives property from the terminated partnerships. Thus, a merger does not affect the tax status of the *resulting* partnership and does not disrupt a pending section 1031 exchange of the *resulting* partnership.

Because terminated partnerships either contribute or distribute their assets as part of a partnership merger, a midstream partnership merger will destroy a pending section 1031 exchange of a *terminated* partnership. In a midstream merger, the *terminated* partnership will transfer the intended relinquished property and the *resulting* partnership will acquire the intended replacement property. Because these are two different parties, the intended exchange cannot satisfy the reciprocal requirement.

The following example demonstrates how a midstream partnership merger can destroy an intended section 1031 exchange. Extinct LLC is a tax partnership. It owns Quail Farms. As part of an intended section 1031 exchange, Extinct LLC transfers Quail Farms to Benson. The qualified intermediary facilitating the exchange receives the proceeds from the sale. Before Extinct LLC acquires replacement property, it merges with Acquire LLC, another tax partnership. As part of the merger, Extinct LLC contributes all of its assets to Acquire LLC in exchange for Acquire LLC membership interests. Extinct LLC then distributes those interests to its members in complete liquidation. This is an assets-over merger. Extinct LLC is the terminated partnership, and Acquire LLC is the resulting partnership. Acquire LLC acquires Randolph Shopping Center under the exchange agreement Extinct LLC entered into before the merger.

Midstream Partnership Merger

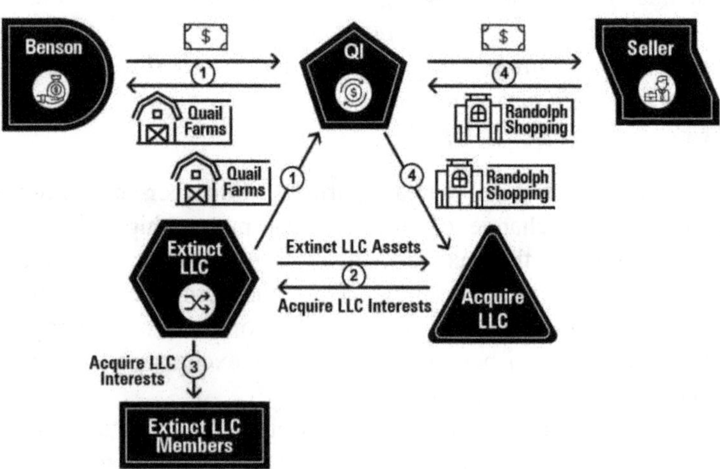

The transaction Extinct LLC intended to be a section 1031 exchange will not qualify for section 1031 nonrecognition because it was not an exchange. As part of the merger, Extinct LLC terminated and Acquire LLC acquired the intended replacement property. Thus, one party transferred the intended relinquished property and another party acquired the intended replacement property. As stated earlier, such transactions do not satisfy the reciprocal requirement. If, instead, Acquire LLC had started the section 1031 exchange, it could have completed it following the merger since Acquire LLC was the resulting partnership.

A partnership merger that occurs after an exchange by a terminated partnership should be subject to the same rules that apply to an exchange followed by a contribution or a distribution, depending upon the form of the partnership merger. If a partnership merger occurs before an exchange, the rules governing contributions or distributions followed by an exchange should apply, depending upon the form of the partnership merger.

PROXIMATE AND MIDSTREAM PARTNERSHIP DIVISIONS

A partnership division is a transaction that divides one partnership and creates at least one new partnership from the assets of the original partnership. In considering the impact a proximate or midstream partnership division may have on an intended section 1031 exchange, the important question is whether the divided partnership or a continuing partnership is attempting the exchange. Only the divided partnership in a partnership division retains the EIN of the prior partnership. All other partnerships are new partnerships with new EINs, but they can be continuations of the prior partnership.

Partnership Divisions

Partnership divisions take one of two forms—either an assets-over form or an assets-up form.

Assets-Over Division

Under the assets-over division, the prior partnership (or divided partnership if at least one resulting partnership is a continuation of the prior partnership) contributes certain assets and liabilities to a recipient partnership in exchange for interests in the recipient partnership. The prior partnership then distributes the interests in the recipient partnership to its members.

Assets-Up Division

Under the assets-up division, the prior partnership (or divided partnership if at least one resulting partnership is a continuation of the prior partnership) distributes certain assets and liabilities to its members. The members then contribute the interests to a new partnership.

Because the divided partnership continues after a partnership division, the division should not affect any exchange it has pending at the time of the division, completes before the division, or enters into following the division. If a partnership begins an intended exchange prior to a division and a new partnership completes the intended exchange following the division, the transaction would appear to violate the reciprocal requirement and not qualify for section 1031 nonrecognition. Nonetheless, several practitioners take the position that any continuing partnership can complete an exchange started by the prior partnership. With no authority directly addressing this issue, one cannot know how the IRS and courts would treat such transactions.

The new partnerships obtain assets in a partnership division through contributions. Thus, an exchange by a new partnership would appear to be subject to the rules governing contributions followed by an exchange. A partnership that divides either distributes or contributes assets. An exchange immediately before a division would, therefore, appear to be subject to the rules that govern exchanges followed by distributions or contributions.

PROXIMATE CONVERSIONS AND TERMINATIONS

A conversion is a transaction that transforms a tax entity into a different form. For example, transformations from a tax partnership to a tax corporation and from a tax corporation to a tax partnership are conversions. For tax purposes, conversions involve contributions or distributions of assets. Therefore, a midstream conversion will prevent a pending intended section 1031 exchange from satisfying the reciprocal requirements because one party will transfer the intended relinquished property and another party will acquire the intended replacement property.

For tax purposes, a conversion will require a contribution of assets to the resulting entity. Thus, an exchange following a conversion will be subject to the rules governing an exchange following a contribution. An exchange preceding a conversion will be subject to the rules governing exchanges followed by contributions or distributions, depending upon the structure of the conversion.

A termination results from any event that terminates an entity. As part of any termination, the assets of the terminated entity will transfer to another party. Thus, a midstream termination should destroy pending intended section 1031 exchanges. Proximate terminations are governed by the proximate contribution and distribution rules, depending upon the form of the termination.

TRANSACTIONS WITH DISREGARDED ENTITIES

Federal tax law disregards certain single-member entities that are not corporations (Chapter 4). For example, federal tax law will generally disregard a single-member limited liability company. Such an entity may elect under the check-the-box regulations to be taxed as a corporation. The entity will be disregarded by default, however, if it does not make an election to be taxed as a corporation. The consequence of being disregarded is that federal tax law will treat the single member of the limited liability company as owning the assets and operating the business of the limited liability company. Understanding the significance of this is often important in the section 1031 exchange context. The following example demonstrates this significance.

Ebony owns Quaint Warehouse, real property in California, indirectly through Elian LLC, a California limited liability company that is disregarded for federal tax purposes. Ebony causes Elian LLC to sell Quaint Warehouse to Benedict as part of an intended section 1031 exchange. The qualified intermediary facilitating the exchange receives the sale proceeds from Benedict. Because Elian LLC is disregarded for tax purposes, Ebony is treated as transferring Quaint Warehouse. Ebony identifies Rowdy Casino, Nevada real property, as replacement property. The lender for Rowdy Casino requires Ebony to acquire Rowdy Casino in a new limited liability company, so Ebony terminates Elian LLC and forms Evergreen LLC, a Nevada limited liability company, to acquire Rowdy Casino. Ebony will be the sole member of Evergreen LLC and it will be disregarded for federal tax purposes. Ebony's attorney drafts the necessary documents to transfer all of Elian LLC's assets (which consist almost exclusively of the right to receive replacement property from the qualified intermediary) to Evergreen LLC. Evergreen LLC then acquires Rowdy Casino from Sven.

Valid Exchange with Disregarded Entities

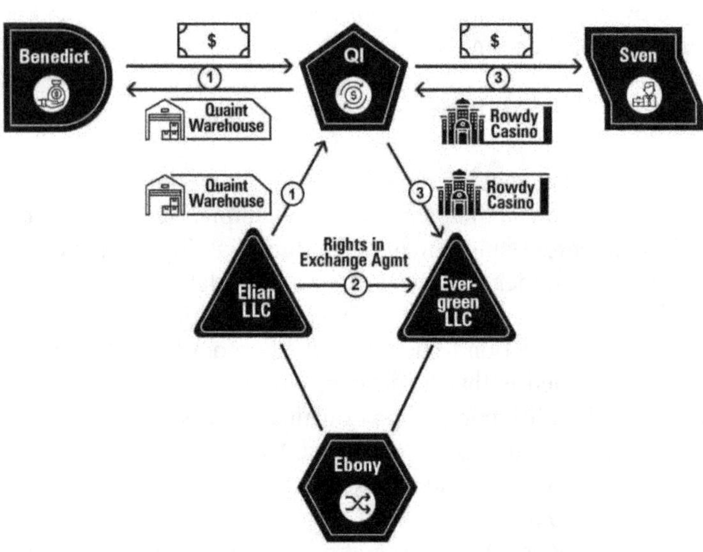

Although Elian LLC transfers its assets to Evergreen LLC while the intended section 1031 exchange is pending, the transfer does not destroy the intended section 1031 exchange. Both Elian LLC and Evergreen LLC are disregarded entities, so federal tax law treats Ebony as transferring Quaint Warehouse and acquiring Rowdy Casino. This transaction can satisfy the section 1031 exchange requirement, so the midstream transfer of rights between the two disregarded entities should not adversely affect the intended section 1031 exchange.

The most common type of disregarded entity is the single-member limited liability company, but federal tax law may also disregard certain limited partnerships. For example, Oscar is the sole member of General LLC, a limited liability company that is the general partner of Limited Ltd, a limited partnership. Oscar also is the sole limited partner of Limited Ltd. Assuming General LLC has made no election to be a tax corporation, federal tax law will disregard it. In that case, Oscar will be Limited Ltd's general partner and sole limited partner for federal tax purposes. Thus, Oscar will be Limited Ltd's sole member for tax purposes. Because Oscar is the sole member of Limited Ltd, federal tax law will disregard Limited Ltd.

Disregarded Limited Partnership

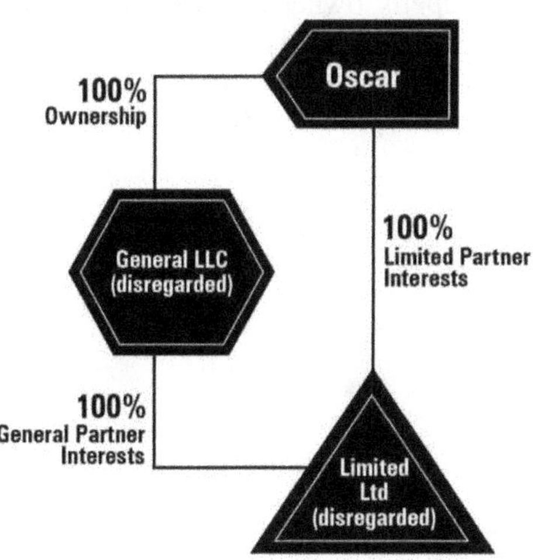

If an exchanger wishes to own replacement property in a limited partnership, but the entity must be disregarded, the disregarded limited partnership provides the exchanger that opportunity. Because federal tax law would treat Oscar as the owner of Limited Ltd's property, Oscar could dispose of relinquished property in his individual capacity, form Limited Ltd, and cause Limited Ltd to acquire replacement property.

If federal tax law disregards an entity, the transfer of all of the interests in the disregarded entity will be a transfer of the underlying assets for federal tax purposes. Thus, if Limited Ltd owned Quitclaim Lot, Oscar's transfer of all of his interests in General LLC and Limited Ltd would be a transfer of Quitclaim Lot. Exchangers may prefer transferring interests in disregarded entities instead of transferring the underlying property to avoid state transfer taxes or other title transfer expenses. This is often the case with reverse exchanges. Many exchangers prefer to receive all the interests of a tear-off limited liability company as opposed to receiving title to the parked property.

Because most property is owned by legal entities, exchangers and tax advisors must be aware of the rules governing exchanges and proximate business transactions. Failure to do so may bring disastrous results to intended section 1031 exchanges. Paying attention to the rules may also enable a property owner to accomplish non-tax goals without disrupting an intended section 1031 exchange. Finally, property owners frequently use disregarded entities to hold property. Such entities provide liability protection with no adverse federal tax consequences.

CHAPTER 9: RELATED-PARTY EXCHANGES

Section 1031 allows exchangers to exchange property with related parties, but only under certain conditions. The related-party exchange rules govern both direct exchanges between related parties and indirect exchanges with related parties. The rules applicable to each type of exchange vary to some extent and each set of rules deserves separate consideration. Both sets of rules are designed, however, to prevent exchangers and related parties from entering into exchanges for abusive purposes. Before examining the specific related-party rules, consider the definition of related party. This definition helps establish the applicability of the related-party exchange rules.

DEFINITION OF RELATED PARTY

A related party for purposes of section 1031 includes certain family members and certain entities. The following is a list of parties that are related for purposes of the related-party exchange rules. The definition can be quite complicated. This discussion provides an idea of the types of relationships that the section 1031 related-party exchange rules govern.

Family Members

Certain members of the exchanger's family are related to the exchanger. The exchanger's brothers and sisters (whether by whole or half blood), spouse, ancestors, and lineal descendants are related to the exchanger for purposes of section 1031. This is a broad definition of related parties. Ancestors include parents, grandparents, great grandparents, and so forth. Lineal descendants include children, grandchildren, great grandchildren, and so forth.

The breadth of the definition of family member is peculiar since the related-party exchange rules appear to be concerned with the exchanger's control over property owned by a related party. Many adults realize that they do not control their brother's or sister's property. Furthermore, as generations grow, ancestors' influence on descendants may decrease. Thus, a grandparent may have little or no control over the property of a grandchild, and vice versa. Nonetheless, the test for relatedness is a bright-line test that does not consider actual interactions between parties.

Corporations and Tax-Exempt Entities

Under the related-party definition, an exchanger may be related to a corporation of which it owns a part and to brother-sister corporations of the exchanger. Corporations are related to any individual who owns more than 50 percent of the outstanding stock of the corporation. Thus, if Erica owned 5,001 of the 10,000 outstanding shares of Doil Corp, she would own 50.01 percent of the outstanding stock of Doil Corp and would be related to Doil Corp. If, however, she owned only 5,000 of the 10,000 outstanding shares, she would not be related to Doil Corp because she would own exactly 50 percent of the outstanding shares and rules require more than 50 percent owners to establish a relationship.

Brother-sister corporations are two or more corporations that have common owners who own more than the threshold percentages. Brother-sister corporations are related for section 1031 purposes if their common owners own a sufficient percentage of the total voting power and total value of the corporations' outstanding stock. If at least one of the corporations is an S corporation, however, the brother-sister corporations are related if the common owners own more than 50 percent in value of the outstanding stock of each corporation.

Finally, a tax-exempt entity and persons who control the entity are related. Also, members of the family of a person who controls a tax-exempt entity and the tax-exempt entity are related.

Ownership Attribution

The related-party rules attribute stock ownership to certain related parties. For example, the stock ownership of an individual's family is attributed to the individual. Thus, Erica's ownership of 5,001 shares of Doil Corp is attributed to her children, Dorothy and Donald. The related-party rules would treat both Dorothy and Donald as owning Erica's 5,001 shares of Doil Corp stock. A corporation's, partnership's, estate's, and trust's ownership of stock is attributed proportionately to its shareholders, partners, or beneficiaries. Under this rule, if Travis Trust owned 5,000 shares of Doil Corp, Dorothy, the sole beneficiary of the trust, would be deemed to own all 5,000 shares.

Ownership attributed through an entity is treated as actual ownership for further attribution. Thus, Dorothy's ownership from the trust is attributed to Donald and Erica. Ownership attributed through a family member is not treated as actual ownership for further attribution. Consequently, Dorothy's husband would not be treated as owning Doil Corp stock attributed from Erica to Dorothy.

Trusts and Estates

To understand the related-party rules that apply to trusts, one must know who is the trust's grantor, beneficiary, and fiduciary. A trust's grantor is the person who funds a trust. The beneficiary is the person who receives something gratuitously from the trust. The fiduciary is the person who manages the assets of the trust. An example illustrates the parties to a trust.

Erica owns Quality Stay, a hotel. Erica's estate planner advised her to begin placing some of her assets in a trust for her children. Pursuant to that instruction, Erica transfers Quality Stay to Trusted Bank who will hold Quality Stay in trust for the benefit of Erica's daughter Dorothy. Pursuant to the trust documents, Trusted Bank is to pay a certain percentage of the income from Quality Stay to Dorothy until Dorothy turns forty years old. At that time, Trusted Bank is to distribute Quality Stay and all accumulated income to Dorothy. In this example, Erica is the trust's grantor because she transferred Quality Stay to the trust. Trusted Bank manages Quality Stay, the assets of the trust, and is the trust's fiduciary. Finally, since Dorothy gratuitously receives the benefits from the trust, she is the beneficiary. The definition of related party provides that a grantor and a fiduciary of a trust are related. Under this definition, Erica, the grantor, would be related to Trusted Bank, the fiduciary.

Fiduciaries of two trusts are related if the same person is the grantor of both trusts. If Erica transferred 5,000 shares of stock in Doil Corp to Travis Bank to hold in trust for her son Donald, both Trusted Bank and Travis Bank would be fiduciaries of trusts of which Erica is the grantor. Under the definition of related party, Trusted Bank and Travis Bank would be related parties. Thus, the section 1031 related-party rules would apply to exchanges between the two banks. Surely this rule only has application to the extent that the exchanges include assets of the trusts that Erica created.

A fiduciary of a trust and a beneficiary of the same trust are related. Thus, Trusted Bank, the fiduciary, would be related to Dorothy, the beneficiary. A fiduciary of a trust and a beneficiary of another trust are related if the same person is the grantor of both trusts. Under this definition, Donald, the beneficiary of the trust with Travis Bank, would be related to Trusted Bank because Erica is the grantor of both the Trusted Bank trust and the Travis Bank trust.

A fiduciary of a trust and a corporation are related if the trust or the grantor of the trust owns more than 50 percent of the value of the outstanding stock of the corporation. In this situation, Erica had contributed 5,000 of the 10,000 outstanding shares of Doil Corp to the trust with Travis Bank, of which Donald is the beneficiary. Because the value of the 5,000 shares is not more than 50 percent of the value of the Doil Corp outstanding stock, Travis Bank is not related to Doil Corp. The two would, however, be related if Travis Bank held 5,001 shares of Doil Corp.

Finally, an executor of an estate and a beneficiary of such estate are generally related. Thus, if Erica died and Alan, an attorney friend, became the executor of her estate, Alan would be related to the estate's beneficiaries. Assuming Erica names Donald and Dorothy as the beneficiaries, they will be related to Alan.

Partnerships

A partnership and a corporation are related if the same persons own more than 50 percent in value of the corporation's outstanding stock and more than 50 percent of the capital interest or profits interest of a partnership. Thus, if Erica owned 5,001 shares of Doil Corp's 10,000 outstanding shares and had a 51 percent profits interest in Detail Ltd, a tax partnership, Doil Corp and Detail Ltd would be related.

A partnership and a person owning more than 50 percent of the capital interest or profits interest in the partnership are related. So, if Erica owns a 51 percent profits interest in Detail Ltd, Erica and Detail Ltd will be related. Two partnerships are related if the same persons own more than 50 percent of the capital interest or profits interest in both partnerships. The attribution rules also apply to partnership ownership, so Erica's ownership in Detail Ltd would be attributed to her children.

The definition of related party helps determine the scope of the related-party exchange rules. The applicability of the rules depends upon whether an exchange is a direct or indirect exchange. As the discussion below demonstrates, in many situations section 1031 may grant nonrecognition to related-party exchanges.

DIRECT RELATED-PARTY EXCHANGES

A direct exchange between related parties will qualify for section 1031 nonrecognition if both parties to the exchange hold the exchanged properties for two years following the exchange. If, however, either party transfers an exchanged property within two years after the related-party exchange, both parties may lose the section 1031 nonrecognition. If they lose section 1031 nonrecognition, they will report the gain in the taxable year of the subsequent disposition.

Consider an example that demonstrates this rule. Erica owns all of the outstanding stock of Doil Corp, an S corporation. Erica owns Quarto Lot, and Doil Corp owns Read Lot. The two pieces of real property are like-kind and both are worth $150,000. Erica's adjusted tax basis in Quarto Lot is $50,000 and Doil Corp's adjusted tax basis in Read Lot is $150,000. On July 1, Year 1, Erica and Doil Corp exchange properties. Because the exchange qualifies for section 1031 nonrecognition, Erica defers $100,000 of gain on the exchange. After the exchange, Erica owns Read Lot and has an adjusted tax basis in Read Lot of $50,000, and Doil Corp owns Quarto Lot and has a $150,000 adjusted tax basis in Quarto Lot. (Recall from Chapter 3 that an exchanger's basis in replacement property is the basis the exchanger had in the relinquished property.) On March 12, Year 2, Doil Corp sells Quarto Lot for $150,000 to Bentley (because the exchanged properties are raw land, they do not qualify for depreciation deductions). The subsequent sale occurred within two years following the exchange, so Dorothy must recognize the gain from the transfer of Quarto Lot. The related-party rules provide that Erica must recognize the $100,000 of deferred gain during the year of the subsequent sale. Therefore, Erica must recognize the $100,000 of deferred gain in Year 2.

Direct Related-Party Exchange

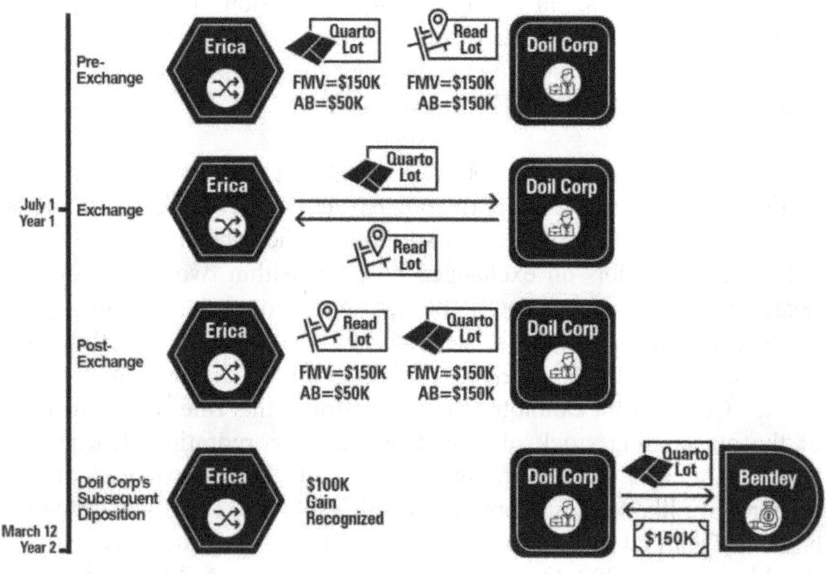

This exchange illustrates the abuse that the related-party exchange rules are designed to prevent. Without the related-party exchange rules, Erica could have shifted the high basis from Read Lot to Quarto Lot and then disposed of Quarto Lot tax free. The related-party rules apply to prevent such basis shifting and tax-free cash-out.

Basis Shifting and Tax-Free Cash Out

Assume that prior to the Erica-Doil Corp exchange that Bentley approached Erica and offered to purchase Quarto Lot for $150,000. Although Bentley was interested in acquiring Quarto Lot, he did not need to acquire it until March of Year 2. Realizing that she would recognize gain if she sold Quarto Lot directly to Bentley, Erica devised a plan to transfer Quarto Lot to Doil Corp in exchange for Read Lot. Doing this would shift the $150,000 adjusted tax basis of Read Lot to Quarto Lot.

Having shifted the adjusted tax basis of Read Lot to Quarto Lot, Erica could cause Doil Corp to sell Quarto Lot to Bentley. Because Quarto Lot would have the higher $150,000 adjusted tax basis at the time of the sale, Doil Corp would not recognize gain on the transaction but for the related-party exchange rules. The related-party exchange rules attempt to prevent the shifting of high basis to low basis property followed by a tax-free cash-out. They accomplish this by requiring gain recognition if either the exchanger or the related party sells exchange property within two years after the exchange.

INDIRECT RELATED-PARTY EXCHANGES

If the related-party rules only applied to direct exchanges, property owners could easily structure indirect exchanges to accomplish the equivalent of basis shifting and tax-free cashing out. Tax law anticipates this and imposes restrictions on indirect exchanges with related parties. Specifically, section 1031 provides that if an exchanger structures an exchange or series of exchanges to avoid a direct exchange, the related-party exchange rules will prohibit nonrecognition. Consider how Erica may otherwise structure an exchange to avoid a direct exchange of trucks with Doil Corp.

Erica may use a qualified intermediary to avoid a direct exchange, but she will be unable to avoid the related-party rules. For example, Erica may transfer Quarto Lot to Bentley through a qualified intermediary and direct Bentley to pay $150,000 to the qualified intermediary. The qualified intermediary could then use the $150,000 to acquire Read Lot from Doil Corp and transfer it to Erica. But for the rules limiting indirect related-party exchanges, neither Erica nor Doil Corp would recognize gain on this transaction; Erica would not recognize gain because she would be deemed to have done an exchange with the qualified intermediary; Doil Corp would not recognize gain because it would sell the property for cash equal to its adjusted tax basis in Read Lot.

Indirect Related-Party Exchange

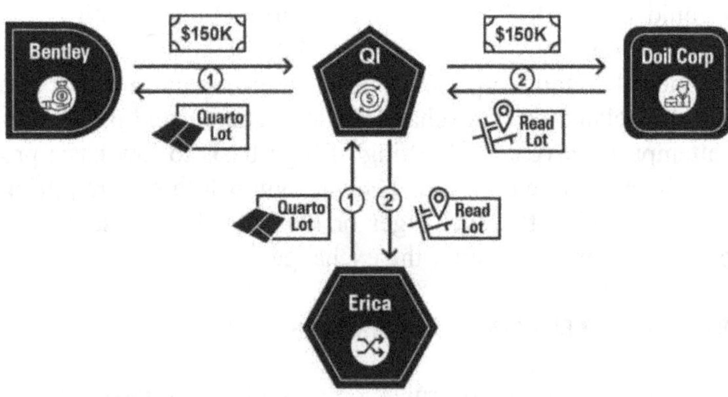

If section 1031 did not require Erica to recognize gain on this transaction, she would be able to avoid the related-party rules by merely creating an exchange structure that avoided the direct exchange with Doil Corp. Such a tax result would be inappropriate because the outcome of the indirect exchange is identical to the outcome of the direct exchange followed by Doil Corp's sale of Quarto Lot. In either situation, Erica ends up with Read Lot and Doil Corp ends up with cash. Thus, the tax result of both the direct exchange and indirect exchange should be the same. The indirect exchange rules, by requiring Erica to recognize gain, obtain this result. Several cases establish that the IRS and courts apply the related-party rules to acquisitions of replacement property from a related party anytime the related party's tax liability is less than the tax the exchanger would have owed on the taxable sale of the relinquished property.

EXCEPTIONS TO THE RELATED-PARTY RULES

Two important exceptions apply to the general related-party exchange rules. The first exception provides that the exchanger does not have to recognize gain on certain subsequent dispositions. The second exception provides that the exchanger does not have to recognize gain if the exchanger can establish that tax avoidance was not a principal purpose for structuring the exchange with the related party.

Excepted Subsequent Dispositions

The first exception provides that the related-party rules do not apply if a subsequent transfer occurs because of the death of the exchanger or the related-party. This exception is appropriate because a related-party exchange is abusive only if the parties exchange property and subsequently transfer one of the exchange properties as part of a plan to shift basis and cash out tax free. It would be a morbid thought indeed to consider a structure that requires an exchange of property with related parties and the subsequent death of one of the parties as part of a plan to shift basis and avoid taxation. If a party dies after an exchange, the rules assume that the death was not planned or integrated into the exchange.

Another exception provides that transfers by involuntary conversion or compulsory transfers are excepted from the related-party rules. Thus, if a governmental entity takes property under eminent domain, such a transfer would not trigger the related-party rules, as long as the exchange occurred before the threat or imminence of such transfer. The legislative history of section 1031 indicates that subsequent tax-free transfers (such as a tax-free contribution to other entities) may also be excepted.

Because this exception to the related-party rules focuses on the subsequent transfer, it applies mainly to direct related-party exchanges. With most, if not all, indirect related-party exchanges, one of the exchange properties has been transferred to an unrelated party. The retained property would have a low basis if the parties attempted to use section 1031 to avoid gain recognition. A subsequent transfer of that property would, in a taxable transaction, trigger deferred gain, and the subsequent transfer exception would have diminished utility. If the subsequent transfer were tax free, the transferor would retain the low basis and deferred gain in the newly acquired property. Thus, the excepted subsequent disposition applies principally to direct exchanges.

Non-Tax-Avoidance Motive

The related-party rules do not trigger gain if an exchanger can show that neither the exchange nor the subsequent disposition had a principal purpose of avoiding income tax. Interestingly, there is little, if any, real guidance from Congress, the courts, or the IRS regarding what constitutes a tax-avoidance motive. Absent such authority, exchangers must consider the purpose of the related-party rules and extrapolate what might be a tax-avoidance motive. That would help identify transactions that may not have a tax-avoidance motive.

As stated above, the related-party rules are designed to prevent basis shifting and tax-free cashing out. This purpose indicates that a transaction that shifts basis and allows the exchanger and related party to receive cash tax free has a tax-avoidance motive. The basis shifting principle makes sense only if it refers to shifting basis from high-basis property to low-basis property. For instance, but for the related-party exchange rules, Erica might attempt to shift the high basis of Read Lot to Quarto Lot and then cause Doil Corp to sell Quarto Lot.

If, on the other hand, a transaction with a related party does not shift high-basis property to low-basis property, a subsequent disposition would not be a tax-free cash out. For example, Erica received Read Lot and shifted Quarto Lot 's low basis to Read Lot. If Erica were to sell Read Lot within two years after the exchange, she would recognize

$100,000 of gain on the transaction ($150,000 amount realized minus the $50,000 adjusted tax basis she would have taken in Read Lot). Because Erica recognizes all of the deferred gain on the subsequent disposition, Erica apparently did not structure the exchange and subsequent disposition to avoid tax. Therefore, the non-tax-avoidance exception should apply to the transaction.

With the simple facts just presented Erica's subsequent sale of Read Lot would trigger all of the deferred gain. That gain recognition should clearly establish that the exchange was not tax motivated. The issue becomes troubling, however, if Doil Corp transfers Rest Lot to Erica in the exchange instead of Read Lot. If Doil Corp has a $50,000 adjusted tax basis in Rest Lot, the exchange of Quarto Lot for Rest Lot will defer $200,000 of gain ($100,000 of gain on Quarto Lot and $100,000 of gain on Rest Lot). The gain from the subsequent sale of either lot would trigger only $100,000 gain, which is less than the total gain deferred, if the related-party exchange rules do not apply. Nonetheless, the exchange and subsequent disposition do not appear to be tax motivated.

Remember that a related-party exchange is probably tax motivated if the exchange shifts high-basis property to low-basis property (e.g., the original Erica-Doil Corp exchange shifted $150,000 adjusted tax basis to Quarto Lot, which formerly had a $50,000 adjusted tax basis). But for the related-party exchange rules, a property owner could use that shift to avoid taxable gain on the disposition of Quarto Lot. If, however, the exchange properties have identical adjusted tax bases, exchanging them would not accomplish favorable tax treatment. For instance, instead of exchanging Quarto Lot for Rest Lot, Erica could simply sell Quarto Lot for $150,000 and recognize $100,000 of gain. Because the tax result from the direct sale is the same as that of the Erica-Doil Corp exchange followed by a disposition of Rest Lot, the exchange does not provide a tax benefit. Therefore, it does not appear to be tax motivated. That being the case, the related-party exchange rules generally should not apply to an exchange that does not shift high adjusted tax basis to low-basis property or to an exchange followed by a subsequent disposition of low-basis property.

The IRS has privately ruled that an acquisition of property from a related party can be part of a section 1031exchange if the related party uses the proceeds from the sale of its property to do a section 1031exchange. This type of transaction allows the exchanger and related party to string exchanges together and effectively extend the identification and exchange periods.

The IRS has privately ruled that an exchange with a related party qualifies for section 1031 nonrecognition if the exchanger transfers relinquished property to a related-party who pays cash for the property, and the exchanger, through a qualified intermediary, uses the cash to acquire like-kind replacement property. With such transactions, the related party takes a section 1012 cost basis in the relinquished property, so there is no basis shifting.

This discussion of related party exchanges provides a caveat to exchangers and exchange advisors. Failure to account for these rules when planning an exchange may prove disastrous. Trying to plan within the exceptions with related parties may also present difficulties. Because the authority addressing the exceptions is so sparse, one cannot know for certain the extent of an exception's scope. As time passes, more guidance should be forthcoming from the courts and the IRS regarding related-party exchanges. Until then, analogy and policy should direct exchangers and their advisors.

CHAPTER 10: DSTS, TIC INTERESTS, AND TRIPLE-NET PROPERTIES

Many property owners face the challenge of finding suitable replacement property and acquiring it within the section 1031 time limitations. Exchangers also often seek replacement property that is financially sound but does not require active management by the owner. Real estate syndicators recognized this problem and set out to develop a product that would be like-kind to real property, available for identification and acquisition with short notice, and a quality investment for the owner. Investors also often want to acquire class A property, diversify their investments, and not participate in the management of the property. The products of the syndicators' efforts to satisfy the investors' needs are Delaware Statutory Trusts (DSTs) and tenancy-in-common interests (TICs). Triple-net properties can also provide a passive source of income, and such properties are a popular form of replacement property for many investors.

Although investors in both TICs and DSTs can be treated as owning interests in the underlying property of the arrangement, TICs and DSTs are legally distinct arrangements. A DST is a legal entity that owns the property. The fundamental tax-classification question with a DST is whether such an arrangement is a trust or a business entity. If the arrangement is a business entity, it will be a tax partnership, and interests in the DST will not qualify as valid section 1031 exchange property. A TIC, on the other hand, is not a separate legal entity. Instead, it is an aggregate of its owners, each of whom owns an undivided interest in the property. The fundamental tax-classification question with a TIC is whether such an arrangement is a tax partnership. If the arrangement is a tax partnership, an interest in the arrangement will not qualify as valid section 1031 exchange property. (Chapter 3 discusses disqualified assets.)

INTERESTS IN DELAWARE STATUTORY TRUSTS (DSTS)

Definition of DST

A DST is a form of business entity created under state law. DSTs grant their beneficiaries (i.e., owners) limited liability protection, allow for pooling of proceeds from various exchanges, and allow for professional management separate from ownership. DSTs can be disregarded for federal income tax purposes. Tax law treats the owners of interests in a disregarded DST as owning the underlying property of the DST, so DST interests can be transferred or acquired as part of section 1031 exchanges. To obtain disregarded status, DSTs must limit their activity and restrict transfers of DST interests. In fact, the DST must convert to a regarded entity or sell the property, if it becomes in need of renovations, loses a primary tenant, or must be refinanced. Due to those restrictions, DSTs typically acquire and hold new property for extended periods with investors remaining invested in the property during such periods.

Although DST interests can be treated as real property for tax purposes, they are most likely securities under securities laws, so they are typically marketed by securities brokers.

A significant industry exists to provide, market, and promote DST investments. Most professionals who work in the section 1031 space are familiar with DST brokers and others who provide DST investments. The IRS treats DSTs as entities separate from their owners, so they are either trusts or business entities for tax purposes. If a DST is a business entity with multiple beneficiaries (i.e., members), it would be classified as a tax partnership, and interests in the DST would not be eligible section 1031 relinquished or replacement property. If a DST is an investment trust, it can be disregarded for federal income tax purposes, and interests in the DST can be treated as interests in the underlying property.

To be a disregarded trust, the trust agreement of a DST must ensure there is no power to vary the investment of the beneficiaries (fixed-investment requirement). A DST's activities must be significantly limited to ensure that the DST does not violate the fixed-investment requirement. Thus, DSTs generally cannot refinance, renovate, re-lease, or sale their property. Consequently, investors in DSTs typically buy into the DST investment for the long-term and hold their DST interests until the property is sold.

The IRS provided guidance for structuring disregarded DSTs in Revenue Ruling 2004-86. The ruling identifies restrictions imposed on DSTs that have come to be known as the "seven deadly sins."

Seven Deadly Sins
Actions that Jeopardize DST Disregarded Status

The following seven deadly sins will jeopardize the disregarded status of a DST:

1. *Selling and then acquiring or exchanging property*
2. *Purchasing assets other than short-term obligations*
3. *Accepting additional contributions of assets*
4. *Renegotiating terms of debt*
5. *Refinancing Debt*
6. *Renegotiating or entering into new leases*
7. *Making more than minor non-structural modifications to property (except as required by law)*

Investors should realize that, because of the seven deadly sins, investments in DSTs are static. A DST typically will not sell, renovate, or refinance property it owns. If the property falls into disrepair, the DST can sell the property to allow another owner to perform the renovations or convert the DST into an entity taxed as a partnership and complete the renovations as a tax partnership.

If a DST sells its property, the owners of the DST interests can use their shares of the sale to exchange into other like-kind property. A

DST can convert into a tax partnership (e.g., a limited liability company) tax-free with the DST members taking interests in the tax partnership. If the DST converts to a tax partnership, the members cannot exchange out of their interests in the tax partnership. For members of a tax partnership to participate in an exchange of property owned by the tax partnership, the tax partnership would have to sell the property and acquire like-kind replacement property or do a drop-and-swap (Chapter 8 discusses drop-and-swaps).

TENANCY-IN-COMMON INTERESTS (TICS)

Definition of TIC Interest

A TIC interest is a tenancy-in-common interest in real property. The holder of a TIC interest owns an undivided interest in property with one or more other TIC owners. TICs have become prevalent with the common use of drop-and-swap transactions discussed in Chapter8. In the early 2000s TIC sponsors syndicated property and sold TIC interests to exchangers looking for replacement property. Syndicated TIC interests can be real property interests, but they also appear to be securities under federal and state security laws, so securities brokers generally market and sell syndicated TIC interests.

In the early 2000s, the syndicated-TIC industry grew from several million dollars of sales to billions of dollars of sales each year. TIC sponsors raised approximately $5 billion of equity in 2006, the highwater mark for the syndicated TIC industry. The Financial Crisis of 2008 hit the TIC industry hard and the number of TIC sponsors declined dramatically thereafter. As the economy recovered following the 2008 financial crisis, DSTs largely filled the space once filled by TICs. Even though syndicated TICs are still to be found, DSTs have become the primary syndicated replacement property.

Although syndicated TICs are not prevalent, many exchanges involve TICs. For instance, drop-and-swap transactions often start with a distribution of TIC interests to members of tax partnerships who then exchange out of those TIC interests (see Chapter 8). TIC arrangements also provide opportunities for section 1031 investors to join real estate funds through investments in TIC interests of the managed property. Thus, TICs remain a meaningful part of the section 1031 industry.

Primary Tax Concern with TIC Interests

An exchanger considering a TIC interest as replacement property must determine whether tax law treats the interest as an interest in property, which may qualify as like-kind replacement property, or a partnership interest, which will not qualify as like-kind replacement property. A person doing a drop-and-swap also must ensure that a distributed interest is a TIC interest and not a continuation of the old partnership or the formation of a new one. This question turns on whether the arrangement is a tax partnership. Whether an arrangement is a tax partnership is a question of federal tax law, not state law. Unfortunately, federal tax law does not provide a concrete definition of tax partnership.

Definition of Tax Partnership

Defining tax partnership is one of tax law's greatest challenges. Courts have considered whether an arrangement is a tax partnership in an estimated 150 cases. Those cases do not provide a concrete definition of tax partnership. They merely provide rough guidance regarding this important question. In considering a TIC interest, the question is whether an arrangement is a tax partnership or a co-ownership. Perhaps the most significant factor in answering this question is the type of services the co-owners provide and the means they use to provide the services. If co-owners hire a manager to provide customary tenant services (e.g., provide utilities, maintain rented facilities, provide garbage disposal, etc.) and pay the manager a fair market rate for the services, the arrangement should not be a tax partnership. If co-owners provide the services themselves or share the net income with the service provider, the arrangement may look more like a tax partnership.

Because the definition of tax partnership is so indefinite, exchangers probably will not be able to obtain a "will" opinion that a specific TIC arrangement is not a partnership. The level of comfort will be higher if the property is raw land or other non-income producing property, and the tenants-in-common provide no service with respect to such property. Co-owning property that produces income, such as rental property, is more likely to be a tax partnership because of the requirement to provide services. If provided incorrectly, those services could result in tax partnership classification. Most TIC arrangements are for rental property, so they run the risk of not qualifying as section 1031 like-kind replacement property. Exchangers can seek advice from tax advisors about whether a TIC arrangement is a tax partnership, but rarely can they obtain complete assurance. Thus, acquiring a TIC interest as part of a section 1031 exchange typically involves some tax risk. Nonetheless, exchangers continue to look for TIC interest replacement property.

Rev. Proc. 2002-22

As TIC interests began to gain popularity in the early 2000s, syndicators requested that the IRS rule whether particular arrangements are tenancies-in-common or tax partnerships. After privately ruling with respect to one such arrangement, the IRS stated that it would not rule in advance whether such arrangements were tax partnerships until it had considered the issue further. The result of that further consideration is Rev. Proc. 2002-22. In that revenue procedure, the IRS provides guidelines for taxpayers seeking advanced rulings on whether co-ownership arrangements are tax partnerships. The IRS listed fifteen conditions that taxpayers generally must satisfy to obtain a favorable advanced ruling. Thus, the guidelines do not provide a safe harbor.

Although merely guidelines for obtaining advanced rulings, the conditions are worth considering, and many advisors consider Rev. Proc. 2002-22 to be a safe harbor. Under that view, any TIC arrangement that satisfies all the conditions would not be a tax partnership. The rules governing TIC classification apply to both syndicated and closely held TICs.

Condition 1: Tenancy-in-common ownership. Each co-owner must hold title to the underlying property directly or indirectly through an entity disregarded for federal income tax purposes and must be a tenant-in-common under local law. Most lenders in syndicated TIC arrangements require that each TIC interest be owned in a single-asset, bankruptcy-remote entity. Thus, most TIC interests are owned by single-member limited liability companies or another type of disregarded entity.

Condition 2: Limited number of co-owners. The revenue procedure limits the number of co-owners per TIC arrangement to no more than 35 persons. This number appears to derive from state and federal securities laws. Federal tax law imposes no such limit on the number of persons who can co-own property. The definition of "person" found in section 7701(a)(1) applies for the purpose of this condition, but a husband and wife are treated as a single person and all persons who acquire an interest from a co-owner by inheritance are treated as a single person. Even though separate co-owners are treated as a single owner for this purpose, the TIC arrangement may require each co-owner to create a separate entity to hold their respective interests.

Condition 3: Co-ownership not an entity. The co-ownership may not (i) file a partnership or corporate tax return; (ii) conduct business under a common name; (iii) execute an agreement identifying any or all of the co-owners as partners, shareholders, or members of a business entity; or (iv) otherwise hold itself out as a partnership or other form of business entity. Courts have used these factors in the past to assess parties' intent, so each factor is an indicium that the parties intended an arrangement to be a partnership.

The IRS generally will not issue a ruling under the revenue procedure if the co-owners held interests in the property through a partnership or a corporation immediately prior to the formation of the co-ownership arrangement. This condition may cause concern for parties doing a distribution followed by exchanges. If a partnership distributes undivided interests in property to its members, the co-ownership could be a tax partnership under the tax rules following the distribution. In

Miles H. Mason, however, the Tax Court granted section 1031 nonrecognition to an exchange of undivided interests immediately following a distribution. Thus, partnership classification of post-distribution TIC arrangements is not automatic.

Condition 4: Co-ownership agreement. Co-owners cannot have a partnership or operating agreement, but they may enter into a co-ownership agreement that runs with the land, subjecting subsequent co-owners to the terms of the agreement. The revenue procedure allows a co-ownership agreement to require a co-owner to offer a TIC interest for sale to the other co-owners, the TIC sponsor, or the lessee at fair market value before exercising the right to partition the property or to transfer the interest to a third party (see Condition 6). Furthermore, a co-ownership agreement will typically address voting rights of the co-owners (see Condition 5).

Condition 5: Voting. The revenue procedure requires co-owners to unanimously approve (i) the hiring of any manager, (ii) the sale or other disposition of the property, (iii) leases of any portion or all of the property, or (iv) the creation or modification of a blanket lien. The IRS has privately ruled that co-owners may vote once a year on the parameters of certain types of leases. Such annual approval of parameters is critical for some TIC arrangements of apartments. It enables the property manager to enter into leases with tenants without obtaining approval from the co-owners for each lease. Other TIC arrangements of apartments lease the property to a master tenant who then subleases units to tenants. Co-owners may also agree that approval is granted if a co-owner receives written notice and fails to reply within a pre-established period, such as 15 days.

This condition does not prohibit the co-owners agreeing to grant call options to any other person, including co-owners (see Condition 10). A carelessly drafted call option may vest a minority-interest owner with power to force the sale of the property by exercising the option to acquire all other interests in the property and then selling the property to a third party. With proper drafting, co-owners can ensure that the call options are exercisable only with approval from a certain percentage of co-owners. If the call options are exercisable with anything other than the unanimous consent of all the co-owners, the call options nullify the requirement for unanimous consent to sell the property.

Condition 5 also provides that for all actions on behalf of the co-owners, other than those requiring unanimous consent, the co-owners may agree to be bound by the vote of those holding more than 50 percent (or some higher percentage) of the undivided interests in the property. The IRS has privately ruled that failure to object within a specified period after notice can be consent for this purpose. Co-owners may not, however, provide the manager or another person with a global power of attorney or proxy to make decisions for them.

Condition 6: Right to alienate. The revenue procedure requires each co-owner to retain the right (which may be subject to a right of first offer granted to another co-owner, the sponsor, or the lessee) to transfer, partition, or encumber the co-owner's interest in the property without agreement or approval of any other person. The right of first offer in this Condition 6 and the right of first refusal in Condition 4, if used properly, may accomplish the same goal as a buy-sell agreement in the partnership or corporate context. Thus, the revenue procedure elevates form over substance with this rule. Furthermore, it allows restrictions on the right to transfer, partition, or encumber an interest in the property, if a lender requires them and they are consistent with customary commercial lending practices.

Condition 7: Split on property sale. If the co-owners sell the property, they must use the proceeds first to satisfy any debts secured by a blanket lien; they must distribute the remaining sale proceeds to the co-owners in proportion to their ownership interests. This condition prohibits TIC arrangements from continuing after the disposition of the property.

Condition 8: Proportionate sharing of profits and losses. The revenue procedure requires co-owners to share in all revenues generated by the property and in all costs associated with the property in proportion to their undivided interest in the property. Co-owners, the syndicator, and the manager may advance funds to another co-owner to meet expenses associated with the property. Such advances must be recourse to the borrower and cannot exceed a thirty-one-day period. Advances must be recourse to the owner of a disregarded entity that owns a TIC in trust.

Condition 9: Proportionate sharing of certain debt. The co-owners must proportionally share in any debt secured by a blanket lien. A blanket lien is any lien that is recorded against the property as a whole. This rule subjects all interests in a TIC arrangement to blanket liens. Thus, exchangers investing in such arrangements must acquire encumbered property.

Condition 10: Options. The revenue procedure requires the exercise price for a call option to equal the co-owner's percentage interest in the property multiplied by the fair market value of the whole property. The revenue procedure prohibits a co-owner from acquiring a put option to sell the property to the sponsor, the lessee, another co-owner, the lender, or any person related to the sponsor, the lessee, another co-owner, or the lender. The prohibition against put options makes TIC interests unattractive to investors who wish to acquire a TIC interest with a guaranteed exit strategy. In the absence of put options, co-owners must rely upon market demand to sell their interests.

Condition 11: No business activities. The revenue procedure limits the co-owners' activities to those customarily performed in connection with the maintenance of rental property. Customary activities generally include providing heat, air conditioning, hot and cold water, unattended parking, normal repairs, trash removal, and up-keep of public areas. The activities of a co-owner's agent or any person related to the co-owner are attributed to the co-owner in determining whether the co-owner performs prohibited services. Thus, co-owners can perform only limited services with respect to the property. If an arrangement requires non-customary services, leasing the property to a master lessee may be the only way to satisfy this condition. The master lessee can provide the services and sublease the property to tenants.

Condition 12: Management and brokerage agreements. The revenue procedure allows co-owners to enter into management and brokerage agreements with one or more agents (who cannot be a lessee of the property), but the activities of any agent acting on behalf of the TICs may not exceed the activities allowed under Condition 11. Any such agreement, although renewable, must terminate at least annually. Co-owners may authorize the manager to perform nominal accounting and clerical functions, but the manager must disburse to the co-owners their shares of net revenues within three months from the date of receipt of those revenues. This prohibits the TIC arrangement from accumulating an earnings reserve of any significance. Finally, co-owners must pay managers fair market value for management and brokerage services. The revenue procedure prohibits the manager from sharing in the net income or profits derived from the property.

Condition 13: Leasing agreements. All leasing agreements must be bona fide leases under federal tax law. Rents must reflect a fair market value for the use of the property and cannot depend, in whole or in part, on the income or profits of the lessee.

Condition 14: Loan agreements. The revenue procedure prohibits any person related to any co-owner, the sponsor, the manager, or any lessee from lending money to acquire an undivided interest in the property or securing a loan with the entire property.

Condition 15: Payments to syndicator. The revenue procedure generally prohibits the sponsor from sharing in the net profits from the property and requires that fees paid to the sponsor must reflect fair market value of the acquired interest or services rendered.

These are the conditions the IRS generally imposes on anyone seeking an advanced ruling about whether a TIC arrangement is a tax partnership. Property owners will recognize that these guidelines present restrictions that other ownership forms do not present. Because the source of many of the restrictions is unknown, tax advisors will be hard-pressed to suitably explain to their clients the rationale for some of the conditions.

Not surprisingly, few taxpayers have requested rulings under the revenue procedure, and the IRS has privately ruled on the revenue procedure on only a few occasions. One reason for so few ruling requests is the time required to obtain a private letter ruling. Exchangers have only 180 days to complete an exchange. Obtaining a private letter ruling in that amount of time will generally be impossible since ruling requests require significant time and effort to draft and the IRS may need several weeks or even a few months to reply to the request. Thus, requesting a ruling under the revenue procedure is infeasible in many situations.

Another reason the IRS has ruled so few times under the revenue procedure is that sponsors would be ideal parties to request the ruling, but such rulings have little value. Only the person to whom a private letter ruling is issued may rely on it as authority for a reporting position. Exchangers are concerned about the classification of a TIC arrangement. Exchangers may not, however, rely upon a ruling that is issued to a sponsor as legal precedent. Furthermore, private letter rulings only apply to specific transactions. The rulings that the IRS has issued under the revenue procedure do not apply to specific transactions, making them inapplicable to any particular taxpayer. Consequently, no taxpayers can rely upon the rulings, and their value is limited to the reasoning and IRS insight expressed in the rulings.

With so few rulings published under the revenue procedure, its utility is questionable. The revenue procedure merely sets forth guidelines for requesting rulings. Therefore, it does not set forth substantive law. That being the case, technically it is not a safe harbor. An arrangement that satisfies all of the conditions may still be a tax partnership, but it is difficult to imagine that the IRS would challenge the classification of a TIC that satisfied all of the conditions. And an arrangement that does not satisfy all of the conditions may not be a tax partnership. In fact, the IRS's private rulings under the revenue procedure provided that some arrangements that do not satisfy all of the conditions are not tax partnerships. Commentators have been critical of the revenue procedure for these reasons. Nonetheless, it has sparked significant growth of the TIC industry, and provided comfort to many parties who enter into closely-held TICs.

With the absence of significant rulings in this area, TIC investors turn to tax advisors for guidance. Often, investors will rely upon opinion letters written by the sponsor's attorney, which provide a legal opinion with respect to the classification of the TIC arrangement. Generally, such opinions are at the "should" level, and investors should be cautious when investing in a deal that has received only a "more likely than not" opinion. The sponsor's tax opinion is not substantial authority that the arrangement is not a tax partnership. The investor must be comfortable with the TIC structure before making an investment and taking a position that a TIC interest qualifies as section 1031 replacement property.

TRIPLE-NET PROPERTIES

A triple-net property is a property that is subject to a triple-net lease. A triple-net lease is a lease that requires the tenant to maintain the property and pay most expenses associated with the property. Thus, the owner of a triple-net property has little responsibility related to the property and expects to receive regular rental income with no management responsibilities. Triple-net properties are popular replacement property for exchangers who wish to exchange into property with a regular and predictable income stream and no management responsibilities. Some exchangers use triple-net properties to diversify their holdings. Such exchangers sell property in one location and buy multiple triple-net properties in different parts of the country.

Triple-net properties also allow exchangers to change the financial characteristics of their investment. An exchanger who owns a property that has generated tax deductions and has increased in value with nominal cash flow may wish to exchange out of such property into a triple-net property that generates a steady and predictable cash flow. While triple-net properties generally attract real estate investors who are looking for passive income, developers and others may consider acquiring a triple-net property to hold until the next development project materializes. If the developer acquires a triple-net property to hold for investment, the property should qualify as valid exchange property.

Most triple-net properties are marketed nationally, so exchangers can compare the financial variables of properties in various geographic areas with various types of tenants. Variables such as location, tenant creditworthiness, and remaining term of the lease can affect the value of triple-net properties. Prospective buyers of a triple-net property should carefully analyze the financial aspects of the property. National databases of such tiple-net properties can help prospective buyers compare the financial aspects of all triple-net properties on the market at any given time.

DSTs AND TIC INTEREST AND SECURITIES LAWS

A property owner who is comfortable that a syndicated DST or TIC interest is not a tax partnership must consider non-tax issues before acquiring the interest. Perhaps most significantly, one must consider whether a DST or TIC interest is a security under state and federal securities law. Most practitioners agree that the definition of security is broad enough to include most DST and TIC interests (with few exceptions, syndicated DST and TIC interests are sold as securities). That classification is significant because securities laws generally prohibit the sale of unregistered securities. To avoid the general registration requirement, syndicators attempt to come within one of the registration exemptions. In particular, syndicators market their interests only to "accredited investors" (a limited class of investors who meet certain net worth requirements) in Reg. D offerings.

The securities registration rules are significant for DST and TIC investors for two reasons. First, the exemption may not apply to a DST or TIC investor's subsequent attempt to dispose of the interest. If the exemption does not apply, securities laws would prohibit the disposition of the interest. Such restrictions will obviously affect the resale value of the interest. Second, the purchaser of an unregistered security (to which no registration exemption applies) may rescind the purchase. Thus, if following the acquisition of an unregistered DST or TIC interest (to which no registration exemption applies), the interest becomes worthless, the purchaser may return the interest to the seller and demand the sales price.

Many exchangers who acquire DST and TIC interests will be unfamiliar with securities laws because their prior investments have all been in real estate and did not come within the definition of a security. Therefore, exchangers who consider acquiring a DST or TIC interest as replacement property should talk to a lawyer who is familiar with federal and state securities laws.

CHAPTER 11: EXCHANGING MIXED-USE PROPERTY

Many people use their homes as their principal residence and for business purposes. This mixed use may require the application of both section 121 and section 1031 on the disposition of the property. The IRS has published guidance that provides rules for applying both section 121 and section 1031 to the exchange of mixed-use property. Section 121 provides gain exclusion, which is better than gain deferral, so property owners prefer section 121 whenever it applies to exclude gain.

Other property owners attempt to apply section 1031 to the sale of second homes. Section 1031 does not apply to personal-use property, such as a residence, but it does apply to investment property. Thus, some second-home owners take the position that they can exchange the second home under section 1031. The IRS has published guidance regarding when a second home can qualify for section 1031 treatment.

The examination of these two types of exchanges requires an understanding of the section 121 gain exclusion. Given a choice, property owners will almost always prefer gain exclusion over gain deferral. Thus, property owners first seek to come within section 121, and if they are not successful with that attempt, they would hope to come within section 1031.

SECTION 121 GAIN EXCLUSION ON SALE OF PRINCIPAL RESIDENCE

Section 121 excludes from gross income gain from the sale of a principal residence. To qualify for this exclusion a homeowner must own and use the property as a principal residence for two of the five years immediately preceding the sale of the residence. Section 121 limits the amount of excludable gain to $250,000 for single taxpayers and $500,000 for married taxpayers filing a joint return.

Section 121 Requirements

On the sale of a principal residence, section 121 excludes up to $250,000 of gain for single taxpayers and up to $500,000 of gain for married taxpayers filing a joint return. To qualify for exclusion, property owners must own the home for two of the five years immediately preceding the disposition of the property and must use the home as a principal residence for two of the five years immediately preceding the disposition.

Gain Exclusion

Gain exclusion is the Holy Grail of income tax. Excluded gain is superior to deferred gain because a taxpayer will never have to recognize excluded gain. Recall that because of the exchanged basis rules taxpayers may one day have to recognize gain deferred under section 1031 (Chapter 3). Gain exclusion, however, is not accompanied by exchanged-basis rules. Thus, gain excluded under section 121 is permanent. The following example demonstrates gain exclusion.

Evelyn and Everett, a married couple filing a joint return, have owned a house and used it as their principal residence for the last five years. Their adjusted tax basis in the property is $100,000 (the amount they paid for it). They sell the house this year for $400,000. Because they have owned it and used it as a principal residence for more than two of the last five years and otherwise satisfy all of the requirements of section 121, they may exclude up to $500,000 of gain on the disposition. They realize $300,000 of gain ($400,000 amount realized minus $100,000 basis) on the sale. Because this amount does not exceed the section 121 exclusion limit, however, they may exclude the entire $300,000 of gain they realized on the disposition.

Section 121 excludes the entire amount of gain. This means that Evelyn and Everett may receive the cash sale proceeds and use them as they please. They are not required to reinvest the proceeds in like-kind property or to acquire another house with the proceeds. They do not have to worry about the exchanged-basis rules or other possible deferral mechanisms. They simply pocket the proceeds and exclude the gain. The absence of a reinvestment requirement and gain exclusion make section 121 superior to section 1031 from a taxpayer's perspective.

Ownership and Use Requirements

As stated above, to qualify for section 121 exclusion, the property owner must own the property for two of the five years immediately preceding the sale and must use the property as a principal residence for two of the five years immediately preceding the sale of the property. Section 121 does not require concurrent or continuous ownership and use. The following example illustrates the application of this rule.

Evelyn and Everett purchased a house on January 1, Year 1, for $100,000. At that time, they were living in an apartment and the house had tenants who wanted to stay in the house for another year. At the end of Year 1, Evelyn and Everett moved into the house. Thus, they began using it on January 1, Year 2. On July 1, Year 3, Evelyn and Everett moved to another country to fulfill a long-term business obligation. At the time they moved, they had used the house for one-and-a-half years. They rented out the house while they were gone, but returned on January 1, Year 5, and lived in the house until they sold the house on July 1, Year 5. Thus, Evelyn and Everett owned the house, for four-and-one-half years, from January 1, Year 1, to July 1, Year 5. They used the house from January 1, Year 2, until July 1, Year 3. That is one-and-one-half years of use. After being out of the country for a year and a half, they moved back into the house on January 1, Year 5, and lived there for another six months until they sold the house on July 1, Year 5. Thus, they used the house a total of two years. Because they owned and used the house for two of the five years immediately preceding the sale, they satisfy the ownership and use requirements.

In computing the amount of gain that qualifies for the exclusion under section 121, homeowners must account for periods of nonqualified use (i.e., when the property was not used as a principal residence). Evelyn and Everett only used the property as a principal residence for two of the five years they owned it, so only two-fifths of gain can be excluded under section 121. Furthermore, they would have to recognize any gain attributable to depreciation deductions. This limit on the amount of gain that qualifies for the exclusion does not apply if the nonqualified use occurred after the owner used the property as a principal residence. This rule prohibits owners from taking full advantage of the section 121 exclusion if they acquire a residence as part of a section 1031 exchange to hold as rental property and then convert it to a principal residence.

Section 121 Ownership and Use

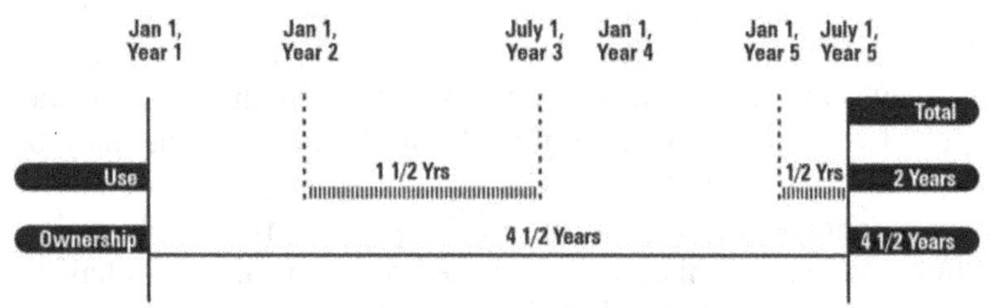

Principal Residence Requirement

Section 121 incorporates the principal residence requirement into the use requirement. Homeowners must use the house as a principal residence to satisfy the use requirement. Neither the Code nor the regulations explicitly define principal residence. Instead, the regulations provide guidelines for determining what is a principal residence when homeowners own more than one house. The regulations first provide a majority-of-time standard. Under that standard, the house the homeowners use the majority of the time generally will be the principal residence.

The majority-of-time standard is not dispositive, however. Other factors, such as where the homeowners are registered to vote, the location of the homeowners' bank, the homeowners' place of employment, the address listed on the homeowners' tax return, and the location of the homeowners' church and community organizations may determine what house is the homeowners' principal residence. Using these guidelines, homeowners with two homes must determine their principal residence.

Reduced Gain Exclusion

The section 121 gain exclusion is generally available only every two years. In certain circumstances, homeowners may use the gain exclusion more frequently or use it without satisfying the ownership and use requirements. The limit of the gain exclusion is reduced in such situations to reflect the shorter period of time owned or used.

To qualify for the reduced exclusion, a homeowner must sell the house because of a change of employment, health, or other unforeseen circumstance. Thus, if Evelyn and Everett had sold their house after using it for only one year, but sold it because Evelyn's employment took them to a different part of the country, the amount of gain they could exclude on the sale would be limited to one-half of the $500,000 general limitation available to married couples filing a joint return.

SECTION 121-SECTION 1031 TRANSACTIONS

The IRS has published guidance for applying for both sections 121 and 1031 to exchanges of property, parts of which satisfy the requirements of both sections. The guidance provides four rules for computing gain exclusion and nonrecognition: (1) apply section 121 to exclude gain before applying section 1031 to defer gain, and if gain realized is less than the amount excludable under section 121, exclude all gain realized; (2) do not apply the section 121 exclusion to gain attributable to depreciation deductions taken after May 6, 1997, but do apply section 1031 to such gain; (3) the amount excluded under section 121 is applied against cash or non-like-kind property received in the exchange to reduce the amount of section 1031 boot; and (4) apply section 1031 exchanged basis rules to compute the basis of section 1031 replacement property, but treat any gain excluded under section 121 as gain recognized by the exchanger (increase the basis by that amount). Several examples illustrate the application of these rules (some of the numbers used in these examples come from Revenue Procedure 2005-14, the IRS guidance regarding section 121-section 1031 transactions).

Principal Residence Converted to Rental Property

Elizabeth owned and used Queens House as her principal residence for five years. She then moved out and began leasing the property. At the time she began leasing Queens House, her basis in it was $210,000. She took $20,000 of depreciation deductions after converting Queens House to rental property. While she still satisfied the section 121 requirements, she sold Queens House to Barbara through a qualified intermediary for $470,000. Elizabeth then directed the qualified intermediary to use $460,000 of the exchange proceeds to acquire Rush House from Sam. The qualified intermediary distributed the remaining $10,000 of exchange proceeds to Elizabeth as boot. The transaction qualifies for both section 121 gain exclusion and section 1031 gain deferral. Elizabeth has $280,000 of gain realized on the transaction. (Chapter 3 discusses the computation of gain realized.)

Computation of Gain Realized

FMV of Rush House	*$460,000*	
Cash	*$10,000*	
Amount realized		*$470,000*
Basis in Queen's House	*$210,000*	
Depreciation after conversion	*($20,000)*	
Adjusted basis		*($190,000)*
Gain realized		*$280,000*

Elizabeth must now determine whether she may exclude or defer any portion of the gain realized. According to the IRS guidance, Elizabeth first applies the section 121 exclusion. Because she is a single taxpayer, she can exclude $250,000 of gain under section 121, but section 121 does not exclude any of the gain attributable to depreciation. The total gain realized was $280,000, thus section 121 excludes all but $30,000 of the gain. That $30,000 includes the $20,000 of depreciation deductions on Queens House that Elizabeth took before she transferred it. Therefore, Elizabeth may exclude $250,000 of gain under section 121; section 1031 defers the remaining $30,000. Section 121 excludes the gain attributable to the $10,000 of cash Elizabeth received, so she has no section 1031 boot.

Gain Excluded and Deferred

Section 121 exclusion	*$250,000 (covers the $10,000 cash)*
Section 1031 deferral	*$30,000(includes the $20,000 of depreciation)*

Having determined the gain realized, gain excluded, and gain deferred, Elizabeth must determine the adjusted tax basis she will take in Rush House. Recall that the basis in property received in a section 1031 exchange is the basis in relinquished property, increased by gain recognized and decreased by boot received (Chapter 3). The IRS provides that in a section 121-section 1031 exchange any gain excluded under section 121 increases the basis of the section 1031 replacement property. Thus, Elizabeth would have a $430,000 adjusted tax basis in Rush House.

Basis in Rush House

Exchanged basis	*$190,000*
Excluded gain	*$250,000*
Cash received	*($10,000)*
Basis in Rush House	*$430,000*

As stated earlier, the section 121 exclusion is permanent. Adding the excluded gain to basis preserves the exclusion. If Elizabeth sold Rush House immediately after the exchange for its $460,000 fair market value, she would recognize $30,000 of gain ($460,000 amount realized minus $430,000 adjusted tax basis). This is the amount she deferred under section 1031, so the IRS guidance produces the correct result.

Business-Use Property Separate from Principal Residence

If a principal residence is separate from another structure used for business, the IRS applies section 121 to the residence and section 1031 to the separate business-use structure. Eliza owns Quotient Estate, a piece of property with two separate buildings on it—a house and a guesthouse. Eliza uses the house as a principal residence and the guesthouse as a business office. The principal residence qualifies for section 121 gain exclusion. Eliza paid $420,000 for Quotient Estate, she has taken $60,000 of depreciation deductions for the guesthouse and allocates two-thirds of the property's purchase price ($280,000) to the basis of the house and one-third ($140,000) to the guesthouse. Eliza exchanges Quotient Estate for Ruby House and Ring Building, an office building. The fair market value of the residence is $480,000, and the fair market value of the business office is $240,000. The IRS treats this as two separate transactions.

Principal Residence Section 121 Gain Exclusion

With respect to the house, the IRS treats Eliza as selling the house for $480,000, the fair market value of Ruby House. Thus, Eliza would realize gain of $200,000 on the transfer of the house.

Gain Realized on Sale of House		
FMV of Ruby House	*$480,000*	
Cash	*$ 0*	
Amount realized		*$480,000*
Basis of relinquished residence (2/3 of $420,000)	*$280,000*	
Depreciation	*$ 0*	
Adjusted tax basis		*($280,000)*
Gain realized		*$200,000*

Because the IRS treats the transfer of the house as a transaction separate from the transfer of the guesthouse, section 121 only applies to the gain realized upon transfer of the house. Eliza's gain exclusion limit is $250,000, so she may exclude the entire $200,000 of gain realized on the transfer of the house. The section 121 gain exclusion does not, however, apply to any of the gain from the sale of the guest house. Eliza takes a basis in Ruby House equal to its fair market value, or $480,000.

Section 121 Gain Exclusion and Basis in Ruby House	
Section 121 exclusion	*$200,000 (the section 121 exclusion does not apply to gain from the separate building)*
Basis in Ruby House	*$480,000 (FMV)*

Guesthouse-Business Office Section 1031 Exchange

The IRS treats the transfer of the guesthouse as a separate transaction. Eliza transferred the guesthouse in exchange for Ring Building. That transaction appears to qualify for section 1031 nonrecognition: the properties are like-kind real property, Eliza held the guesthouse for productive use in a trade or business and will hold Ring

Building for productive use in a trade or business, and the transaction is an exchange. Therefore, the exchange of the guesthouse for Ring Building appears to satisfy the section 1031 requirements. Eliza will realize $160,000 of gain on the transfer of the guesthouse. Section 1031 will defer all of that gain.

Gain Realized on Guesthouse Exchange

FMV of Ring Building	*$240,000*	
Cash	*$ 0*	
Amount realized		*$240,000*
Basis of relinquished guesthouse (1/3 of $420,000)	*$140,000*	
Depreciation	*($60,000)*	
Adjusted tax basis		*($80,000)*
Gain realized		*$160,000*
Section 1031 gain deferral		*$160,000*

Under the section 1031 basis rules Eliza will take the exchanged basis in Ring Building. Since her adjusted tax basis in the guesthouse was $80,000, she will take an $80,000 basis in Ring Building, the replacement property. Because the transfer of the house is treated as a separate transaction, the amount of gain excluded under section 121 does not affect Eliza's basis in Ring Building.

Business-Use Property Part of Principal Residence

Elvis owns Quiet House. He uses two-thirds of Quiet House as a principal residence and one-third as a recording studio. Elvis paid $210,000 for Quiet House and has claimed $30,000 of depreciation deductions. Elvis has owned and used Quiet House as a principal residence for at least two of the past five years. Elvis transfers Quiet House in exchange for two separate properties: Rest Home worth

$240,000 and Recording Studio worth $120,000. The exchange of the business use portion of Quiet House for Recording Studio will qualify for section 1031 treatment. The IRS does not treat this as two separate exchanges, so Elvis must combine section 121 and section 1031 to determine gain exclusion and nonrecognition and to compute the basis of Recording Studio.

Gain Realized

Residential Portion of Quiet House

FMV of Rest Home	*$240,000*	
Cash	*$ 0*	
Amount realized		*$240,000*
Basis in residential portion		
Quiet House (2/3 of $210,000)		*($140,000)*
Gain realized on residential portion		
of Quiet House		*$100,000*

Recording Studio Portion of Quiet House

FMV of Recording Studio	*$120,000*	
Cash	*$ 0*	
Amount realized		*$120,000*
Basis in recording studio portion		
of Quiet House (1/3 of $210,000)	*$70,000*	
Depreciation	*($30,000)*	
Adjusted bas		*($40,000)*
Gain realized on recording studio portion		*$80,000*
Total Gain Realized		***$180,000***

The IRS guidance first applies the section 121 gain exclusion to all gain, other than the gain attributable to the depreciation deductions of the recording studio portion of Quiet House. Total gain realized on the transfer was $180,000, of which $30,000 is attributable to depreciation deductions. Therefore, section 121 excludes $150,000 of gain realized. Section 1031 defers the $30,000 attributable to depreciation.

Section 121 Exclusion and Section 1031 Deferral

Section 121 exclusion	*$150,000 (apply section 121 first to all gain, except to the gain attributable to depreciation)*
Section 1031 deferral	*$30,000 (amount attributed to depreciation)*

Elvis will take a basis in Rest Home equal to its fair market value (its cost to Elvis). He will compute the basis in the Recording Studio using the section 1031 exchanged basis rules and will add to that basis the amount of gain excluded under section 121.

Basis in Rest Home and Recording Studio

Basis in Rest Home	*$240,000 (FMV)*	
Basis in Recording Studio	*Exchanged basis*	*$40,000*
	121 exclusion	*$50,000*
		$90,000

The Elvis example and the Eliza example demonstrate how the rules work differently depending upon whether the business-use portion of the property is attached to the principal residence. If the business use property is not attached, the rules treat the transaction as two separate transactions and apply section 121 to the residence portion of the transaction and separately apply section 1031 to the business-use portion of the property. If the business-use property is part of the principal residence, the rules apply section 121 and section 1031 to the entire transaction, using the IRS rules stated above.

Receipt of Boot

If Recording Studio were only worth $110,000 and Elvis received $10,000 cash in addition to receiving Rest Home and Recording Studio, the amount of section 121 exclusion would cover the boot received, and Elvis would recognize no gain on the transaction.

Gain Realized

Residential Portion

FMV of Rest Home	*$240,000*	
Cash	*$ 0*	
Amount realized		*$240,000*
Basis in residential portion of Quiet House (2/3 of $210,000)		*($140,000)*
Gain realized on residential portion of Quiet House		*$100,000*

Recording Studio Portion

FMV of Recording Studio	*$110,000*	
Cash	*$10,000*	
Amount realized		*$120,000*
Basis in recording studio portion of Quiet House(1/3 of $210,000)	*$70,000*	
Depreciation	*($30,000)*	
Adjusted basis		*($40,000)*
Gain realized on recording studio portion		*$80,000*
Total Gain Realized		***$180,000***

Section 121 will exclude all gain, other than that amount attributable to depreciation, up to the $250,000 section 121 exclusion amount. Thus, section 121 will exclude up to $150,000 of Elvis's gain realized (the total $180,000 of gain realized minus the $30,000 attributable to depreciation deducted). Elvis will take a basis in Rest Home equal to Rest Home's fair market value.

Section 121 Exclusion

Section 121 exclusion	*$150,000 (covers gain, including boot, but not the amount attributable to depreciation)*
Basis in Rest Home	*Basis in Rest Home $240,000 (FMV)*

Elvis's total gain realized on the transaction was $180,000 ($100,000 from the residential portion and $80,000 from the recording studio portion). Elvis excluded $150,000 of that gain under section 121. He may defer the remaining $30,000 (amount attributable to depreciation) under section 1031.

Section 1031 Gain Deferral

Section 1031 deferral	*$30,000 (section 1031 defers the amount of gain attributable to depreciation)*

The section 1031 basis rules, modified to account for the section 121 exclusion, apply to Recording Studio. Thus, to compute his basis in Recording Studio, Elvis adds the amount of gain excluded under section 121 to his exchanged basis in Recording Studio and otherwise applies the section 1031 basis rules.

Basis in Recording Studio

Exchanged basis	*$40,000*
121 exclusion	*$50,000*
Boot	*($10,000)*
Basis in Recording Studio	*$80,000*

Total Gain Realized Exceeds Section 121 Exclusion

If the section 121 exclusion does not exclude all of the gain from the sale of the recording studio portion of Quiet House, Elvis will have to rely more heavily upon section 1031 to defer gain realized. Assume that Elvis exchanges Quiet House for Rest Home worth $360,000 and Recording Studio worth $180,000.

Gain Realized

Gain realized on transfer of residential portion

FMV of Rest Home	*$360,000*	
Cash	*$ 0*	
Amount realized		*$360,000*
Basis in residential portion of Quiet House (2/3 of $210,000)	*$140,000*	
Gain realized on residential portion of Quiet House		*$220,000*

Gain realized on transfer of recording studio portion

FMV of Recording Studio	*$180,000*	
Cash	*$ 0*	
Amount realized		*$180,000*

Basis in office portion of Quiet House (1/3 of $210,000)	*$70,000*	
Depreciation	*($30,000)*	
Adjusted basis		*($40,000)*
Gain realized on office portion of Quiet House		*$140,000*
Total Gain Realized		***$360,000***

In this example, Elvis's total gain realized is $360,000. Section 121 can exclude only $250,000 of the gain realized. That leaves $110,000 of gain realized to be deferred under section 1031. Elvis will take a basis in Rest Home equal to its fair market value.

Section 121 Exclusion

Section 121 exclusion	*$250,000 (apply section 121 exclusion capped by limit, do not apply to gain attributable to depreciation, apply to part of business gain)*

Basis in Rest Home

Basis in Rest Home	*$360,000 (FMV)*

Section 121 excluded all $220,000 of gain realized from the sale of the residential portion of Quiet House and $30,000 of gain realized from the sale of the recording studio portion of Quiet House. Section 1031 will defer the remaining $110,000 of realized gain, which includes the amount of gain attributable to depreciation.

Section 1031 Gain Deferral

Section 1031 deferral	*$110,000 (section 1031 defers remaining gain, including amount attributable to depreciation)*

The section 1031 basis rules apply to the basis Elvis will take in Recording Studio. The amount of gain realized from the sale of the recording studio portion of Quiet House and the amount of section 121 exclusion with respect to the recording studio increases the basis Elvis takes in Recording Studio.

Basis in Recording Studio

Exchanged basis	*$40,000*
121 exclusion	*$30,000*
Basis in Recording Studio	*$70,000*

Residential Gain Realized Exceeds Section 121 Exclusion

If the amount of residential gain realized exceeds the section 121 exclusion, Elvis will have to use section 1031 to defer all of the gain realized from the sale of the recording studio portion of Quiet House. He may not, however, use section 1031 to defer any of the gain realized on the transfer of the residential portion of Quiet House.

Gain Realized

Gain realized from transfer of residential portion

FMV of Rest Home	*$500,000*	
Cash	*$ 0*	
Amount realized		*$500,000*
Basis in residential portion of Quiet House (2/3 of $210,000)		*$140,000*
Gain realized on residential portion of Quiet House		*$360,000*

Gain realized from transfer of recording studio portion

FMV of Recording Studio	*$250,000*	
Cash	*$ 0*	
Amount realized		*$250,000*
Basis in recording studio portion of Quiet House (1/3 of $210,000)	*$70,000*	
Depreciation	*($30,000)*	
Adjusted basis		*$40,000*
Gain realized on recording studio portion of Quiet House		*$210,000*
Total Gain Realized		***$570,000***

The $250,000 section 121 exclusion covers only a portion of the $360,000 gain realized on the transfer of the residential portion of Quiet House. Elvis must recognize the remaining $110,000 of gain realized on the sale of that portion of Quiet House.

Section 121 Exclusion

Section 121 exclusion	*$250,000 (apply section 121 first capped by limit)*

Basis in Rest Home

Basis in Rest Home	*$500,000 (FMV)*

Section 1031 does not defer any of the gain realized from the residential portion of Quiet House because Elvis did not hold any of that portion of the house for productive use in a trade or business or for investment. He must recognize $110,000 of gain from the sale of the residential portion of Quiet House ($360,000 gain realized minus the $250,000 section 121 exclusion). Section 1031 only applies to the recording studio portion of Quiet House. Thus, Elvis may defer all $210,000 of gain realized on the transfer of the recording studio portion of Quiet House.

Section 1031 Deferral

Section 1031 deferral	*$210,000*

Elvis will use the section 1031 basis rules to determine the basis he will take in Recording Studio. Because section 121 did not exclude any portion of gain realized from the transfer of the recording studio portion of Quiet House, the amount of the section 121 exclusion will not affect Elvis's basis in Recording Studio.

Basis in Recording Studio

Exchanged basis	*$40,000*
121 exclusion	*$ 0*
Basis in Recording Studio	*$40,000*

These examples demonstrate how the IRS applies sections 121 and 1031 to dispositions of mixed-use property. The application of the rules first depends upon whether the residence and business-use property are part of the same structure. If not, section 121 and section 1031 apply separately to the different structures. If the property is a single structure, the IRS guidance applies section 121 and section 1031 concurrently to the exchange based upon the four rules in the IRS guidance presented above. The rules provide clear guidance regarding the tax treatment of such transactions. The guidance related to second homes creates an all-or-nothing rule based upon the amount of time the owner uses the property for personal use.

SECOND HOMES

Second homes may take any of a variety of forms—for example, a home on a lake that the owners use several times a year for an aggregate of several weeks, a home in the mountains that the owners use once a year for one week, a home in the country that the owners use a few times a year for no more than an aggregate of two weeks and rent to unrelated parties for several other weeks during the year, and a home by the beach that the owners acquired as an investment and visit irregularly for maintenance and upkeep purposes. Section 121 does not apply to second homes because they cannot satisfy the principal residence requirement. Thus, second-home owners often look to section 1031 to defer gain on the disposition or acquisition of such property. The owners' purpose for holding the home will affect the applicability of section 1031.

Recall that section 1031 requires the exchanger to hold relinquished property for productive use in a trade or business or for investment (Chapter 3). This requirement disqualifies personal-use property. If the owners do not rent out the second house, they do not hold it for productive use in a trade or business. For such a second house to qualify for section 1031 nonrecognition, the owners must hold the property for investment. If the property owners use the property, then it will be personal-use property, and the U.S. Tax Court has held that such property does not qualify for section 1031 treatment.

If the owners of a second home rent it out part of the year, they may have support that they held it for productive use in a trade or business, at least in part. The law provides that leasing property is a business use. In Revenue Procedure 2008-16, the IRS provided a safe harbor for second homes. Relinquished property comes within the safe harbor if the owner held it for at least 24 months prior to the exchange, the owner rents the property to another person for at least 14 days, and the owner's use does not exceed the greater of 14 days or 10 percent of the number of days it was rented for fair value during the 12-month period. Replacement property comes within the safe harbor and qualifies for section 1031 treatment if the exchanger holds it for 24 months and during each of the two 12-month periods immediately after the exchange, rents the property at fair value for at least 14 days and uses the property personally for no more than the greater of 14 days or 10 percent of the days the property is rented during the 12-month period.

Exchanging mixed-use property may present opportunities for gain exclusion and gain deferral. If the mixed-use property is both a principal residence and business-use property, section 121 may exclude part of the gain and section 1031 may defer part of the gain on the disposition of the property. If the property is a second home that the owners use personally, they can defer gain on the exchange of such property if the properties come within the safe harbor.

CHAPTER 12: DEALER PROPERTY EXCLUDED

Property owners generally would prefer that their appreciated property be a capital asset (i.e., investment property) or business-use property. Gain from the sale of investment or business-use properties can qualify for favorable long-term capital gains tax rates, if the property owner has held the property for more than one year. Gain from the sale of investment or business-use property may qualify for section 1031 nonrecognition. On the other hand, gain from the sale of dealer property is taxed at ordinary rates and does not qualify for section 1031 nonrecognition. The applicability of the favorable rates and of section 1031 turns on the definition of dealer property.

THE DEFINITIONS OF DEALER PROPERTY

Dealer property has two important definitions: the definition used to determine the applicable tax rate (the section 1221 definition) and the definition used to determine the applicability of section 1031 (the section 1031 definition). The section 1221 definition is narrower than the section 1031 definition. Thus, some property may be dealer property under the section 1031 definition, but not dealer property under the section 1221 definition. But any property that is dealer property under the section 1221 definition will be dealer property under the section 1031 definition. Property that does not come within either definition is either business-use property, investment property, or personal-use property. Gain from the sale of personal-use property may qualify for favorable capital gains tax rates but does not qualify for section 1031 nonrecognition. Gain from the sale of both business-use property and investment property may qualify for favorable capital gains tax rates and section 1031 nonrecognition. Finally, the owner of dealer property is a dealer.

The Significance of Dealer Property

There are two relevant definitions of dealer property: the section 1221 definition and the section 1031 definition. The section 1221 definition defines dealer property for the purposes of determining the character of gain realized on the disposition of property. If the property is dealer property, the gain on the sale of the property is ordinary income to the property owner. Gain from the disposition of other property may qualify for favorable long-term capital gain treatment. Section 1031 defines dealer property for the purpose of determining the scope of section 1031. Section 1031 does not apply to dealer property.

The Section 1221 Definition of Dealer Property

Section 1221 defines capital asset in the negative. It lists several assets that are not capital assets. Any asset not listed in section 1221 should be a capital asset and any gain from the sale of the asset should qualify for favorable tax rates if the property owner has held the capital asset for more than one year. First on the list of assets excluded from the definition of capital asset is inventory and "property held by the taxpayer primarily for sale to customers in the ordinary course of his trade or business." It is this latter definition of dealer property that concerns many property owners. The definition can be broken down into two main requirements—(1) the property owner must hold the property primarily for sale to customers and (2) the sale must be to customers in the ordinary course of the property owner's business. Although stated as two separate requirements, the requirements are related and concepts of each overlap. A significant body of case law addresses the definition on a case-by-case basis and provides only fairly general principles to rely upon in classifying property. The following is a broad overview of principles derived from the cases. Deciding whether to treat certain property as dealer property or as investment or business-use property will require professional judgment and involve some tax risk.

The Section 1221 Definition of Dealer

Dealer property under section 1221 is "property held by the taxpayer primarily for sale to customers in the ordinary course of his trade or business."

Held Primarily for Sale to Customers

Whether a property owner holds property primarily for sale is a question of the property owner's intent. Court's use several factors to determine the property owner's intent. A property owner's treatment of property demonstrates the purpose for holding the property. For example, if a property owner buys a large plot of land, subdivides it, and improves it, the property owner has demonstrated that it is not merely holding the property to realize an increase in its value (property held for realization in value is investment property). Instead, the activity demonstrates that the property owner acquired the property to improve and sell. The owner thus appears to hold the property primarily for sale.

Although a property owner's original purpose for acquiring property is a strong indication of the property owner's purpose for holding property, a property owner may change its purpose. For example, if a property owner acquires property to hold for investment but later improves the property and expends significant effort to sell the property, the efforts to improve and sell the property indicate the property owner has changed its holding intent. A property owner should also be able to change holding intent from primarily for sale to investment. This would probably require the owner to expend no effort improving the property and to change the way it accounts for the property (i.e., show the property on books as investment property, not inventory).

Sale to Customers in the Ordinary Course of a Trade or Business

For property to be dealer property under the section 1221 definition, the owner must hold it for sale to customers in the ordinary course of its business. This requirement examines whether the property owner is in the business of selling property. Factors such as the number of sales, the frequency of sales, the size of the sales as a percentage of the property owner's total income, and the property owner's efforts to sell the property indicate whether the property owner is in the trade or business of selling property. The cases that have addressed this issue do not provide bright-line tests for any of these factors. The general rule provides, however, that the more significant the sales activity, the more likely the property owner is a dealer and that the property will be dealer property. Thus, a property owner who spends significant time trying to sell the property, hires an agent or broker to sell the property, or otherwise significantly markets the property will look more like a person in the business of selling property. On the other hand, a property owner who merely puts a for-sale sign on property or receives unsolicited offers may not be a dealer, regardless of the size of sales.

The Section 1031 Definition

The section 1031 definition of dealer property is broader than the section 1221 definition. It provides simply that property "held primarily for sale" is dealer property and cannot be exchanged under section 1031. This definition thus excludes all section 1221 dealer property from section 1031 and excludes some properties that do not come within the section 1221 definition. The section 1031 definition looks solely at the exchanger's intent. Thus, the section 1221 factors that demonstrate that the property owner is in the trade or business of selling property are not important to the section 1031 definition of dealer property.

The Section 1031 Definition of Dealer

Section 1031 defines dealer property as "property held primarily for sale." By omitting the requirement that the property be sold to customers in the ordinary course of the property owner's trade or business, the section 1031 definition of dealer property is broader than the section 1221 definition. Thus, section 1031 excludes all section 1221 dealer property and any other property held primarily for sale.

AVOIDING DEALER PROPERTY CLASSIFICATION

Property owners may plan the acquisition, holding, and disposition of property to avoid dealer property classification. This requires generally that the property owner be able to demonstrate an intent to hold the property for investment and not for resale. This in turn requires the property owner to not develop the property and to not engage in significant marketing and sales activity with respect to the property. Property owners consider two different options to preserve investment property classification—they acquire properties in separate ownership entities and sell the property before improving it.

Separate-Entity Ownership

A dealer may hold investment property. The challenge in such a situation is to keep the investment property separate from the dealer's dealer property. This requires careful accounting records and a clear demonstration that the investment property is separate from the dealer property. Although a dealer may separate investment property from dealer property on its books, most dealers worry about having such a classification challenged.

To help reduce the likelihood that the intended investment property will be tainted by the property owner's marketing and sales activity with respect to other property, dealers can form a separate investment entity to take title to investment property. The dealer should ensure that the separate legal entity is not be disregarded for tax purposes. Thus, the dealer should ensure that the investment entity has at least two members and is recognized for tax purposes. If the separate investment entity merely holds the investment property, the dealer's marketing and sales activity with respect to property in a related entity should not taint the holding intent of the separate investment entity. Gain from the sale of property held for investment in the investment entity should also qualify for section 1031 nonrecognition if the owner can demonstrate that it did not hold the property primarily for sale.

Sale of Investment Property to Related Developer

Subdividing and developing property is often very profitable. It also indicates that the property owner holds the property primarily for sale to customers in the ordinary course of business. Once investment property converts to dealer property, all pre-conversion gain converts from capital gain to ordinary income. Thus, property owners look for techniques to preserve the pre-conversion capital gain. To preserve the investment-property classification of a piece of land, a property owner must limit its subdividing and developing activities. As a general rule, to preserve the investment-property classification, a property owner should not move dirt (i.e., the property owner should not begin developing the property). Property owners may be able to preserve the investment intent and still participate in developing property if they separate the ownership of investment property from the development of dealer property. They can do this by forming separate entities to own and develop property. With such a structure, the ownership entity may transfer the property to the developer which would develop and sell the property.

The following example demonstrates how property owners may preserve gain from investment property and still develop it. Assume a number of individuals own Investment Partnership. The individuals also own Developer Corp, an S corporation that develops property and sells individual lots to numerous buyers. Several years ago, Investment Partnership acquired Quantity Land, a large tract of land. The owners bought the land to hold for investment and sale when it had appreciated significantly in value. The city has now grown out to Quantity Land and it has appreciated significantly. The owners of Investment Partnership want to realize the appreciation in Quantity Land. The individual owners also want to subdivide Quantity Land and sell individual lots to realize the additional value from subdividing the property. They do not, however, want to lose favorable long-term capital gains treatment on the sale of Quantity Land. They know that if Investment Partnership subdivides and sells Quantity Land, it will become dealer property and all of the gain on the disposition will be taxed at ordinary income rates. They also know that if Investment Partnership sells Quantity Land as a single unit in one sale without subdividing or developing it, the gain from such a sale should qualify for favorable long-term capital gain treatment. If Investment Partnership sells Quantity Land to an unrelated party, the owners will lose the gain from subdividing the property.

To ensure that Quantity Land does not lose its investment-property classification, the owners have Investment Partnership transfer Quantity Land to Developer Corp. Developer Corp then subdivides Quantity Land and sells individual lots to buyers. If the transaction is properly structured, the gain Investment Partnership recognizes should be long-term capital gain and subject to favorable tax rates. The gain Developer Corp recognizes should be taxed at ordinary income rates. The structure thus allows the owners to lock in pre-conversion gain as long-term capital gain. Any post-conversion gain will be taxed at ordinary income.

To illustrate, if Investment Partnership had purchased Quantity Land for $1,000,000, it would recognize $4,000,000 of gain by selling the land to Developer Corp for $5,000,000. If Developer Corp spent another $1,500,000 subdividing and developing Quantity Land, its basis in the property would become $6,500,00. Upon sale of that property for $7,500,000, Developer Corp would recognize $1,000,000 of gain, which would be taxed as ordinary income. For the lock-in to be respected, the sales price to the developer entity must be fair market value.

Sale of Investment Property to Related Developer

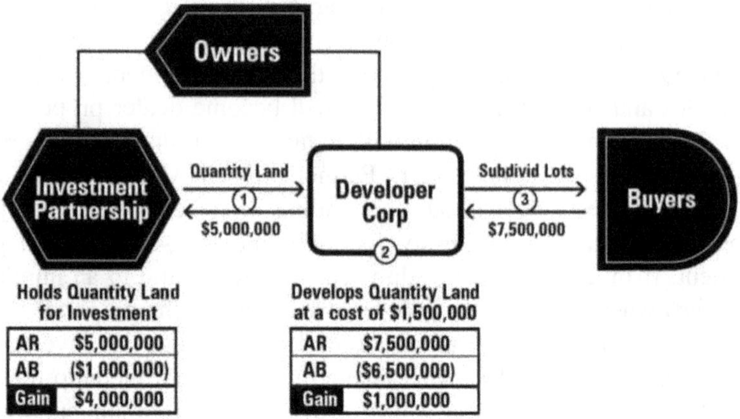

Owners

Investment Partnership

Quantity Land
1
$5,000,000

Developer Corp
2

Subdivid Lots
3
$7,500,000

Buyers

Holds Quantity Land for Investment

AR	$5,000,000
AB	($1,000,000)
Gain	$4,000,000

Develops Quantity Land at a cost of $1,500,000

AR	$7,500,000
AB	($6,500,000)
Gain	$1,000,000

A court has blessed this type of transaction. Therefore, property owners should be able to use it to help preserve capital gains. In doing so, however, the property owners must plan carefully. For example, the developer entity must be a tax corporation (either an S corporation or a C corporation); it cannot be a tax partnership if the investment entity is a partnership. If the investment entity and the developer entity are both partnerships and controlled by the same parties, the gain on the sale to the developer entity will be taxed at ordinary income rates. Thus, the developer must be a corporation.

The sales price the developer corporation pays for the property should reflect the fair market value of the property on the date of transfer. Thus, that sales price should not reflect the improved value of the property. Some property owners will want the sales price paid by the developer to include some of the value of the improvements will create. This would reduce the amount of gain subject to the ordinary income rates. Such property owners should, however, remember the adage that pigs get fat and hogs get slaughtered. If the sales price does not reflect the property's fair market value, the IRS may disregard the transfer to the developer corporation and treat the entire gain as ordinary income.

To avoid this outcome, property owners should ensure that the sales price paid by the developer reflects fair market value.

Section 1031 Implications

Some property owners will want to use section 1031 to defer the gain on the sale of property to a related developer corporation. This would require the property owners to transfer property through a qualified intermediary to a developer. The qualified intermediary would receive the sale proceeds from the developer corporation and acquire property for the exchanger. In such transactions, the developer corporation will often be related to the exchanger. This requires examining the related-party exchange rules. The related-party exchange rules clearly apply if an exchanger receives high basis replacement property from a related party (Chapter 9). The IRS has privately ruled, however, that transfers of property to a related party as part of a multi-party exchange can qualify for section 1031 nonrecognition. Thus, the exchange, which transfers investment property to a related developer corporation, may qualify for section 1031 nonrecognition. To be extra cautious, the parties who own the investment property may transfer the property to an unrelated developer corporation. They can do this by changing the ownership structure of the developer corporation to ensure that owners of the investment property own no more than 50 percent of the developer corporation. This structure would allow the exchanger to avoid ordinary income treatment and defer gain recognition. This is yet another example of how proper planning can produce favorable tax results under section 1031.

CONCLUSION

As a tax-planning tool, section 1031 provides significant opportunities for property owners to preserve investment net worth. By exchanging into other like-kind property tax-free, property owners avoid taxes that would otherwise diminish their net worth. Property owners and tax advisors have become creative in finding ways to structure transactions to come within section 1031 and benefit from its tax-saving offerings. Courts and the IRS have blessed many of the structures that property owners use, but they require that such transactions satisfy formalistic requirements.

The continued-investment purpose of section 1031 supports both the lenient use of exchange structures and the elevation of form over substance. A transaction is a continuation of an investment if, after a transaction, the exchanger is invested in property that is similar to property the exchanger transferred. The involvement of multiple parties in the exchange should not affect this application of the continued-investment purpose. For an investment to continue uninterrupted, however, the exchanger must not receive cash or non-like-kind property. The formalistic requirements of section 1031 and the numerous exchange structures focus primarily on ensuring that the exchange does not interrupt the investment. Thus, the continued-investment purpose inspired section 1031 and has inspired its evolution.

The several section 1031 developments over the past four decades have spurred a growth of both the use of section 1031 by property owners and the growth of the section 1031 industry. The section 1031 industry, through handling exchanges estimated in the hundreds of thousands, has developed efficiencies that make section 1031 nonrecognition available to a broad cross section of property owners. Large property owners continue to find beneficial applications of section 1031 and small property owners find that they can preserve net worth with simple exchange structures.

If the past is prologue, section 1031 has a bright future. Even though section 1031 repeal appears from time to time in legislative proposals, it has thus far survived such proposals. For the sake of the real estate and general economy, legislators should ensure that it remains a part of our tax laws. Property owners will continue to use it to defer gain recognition, tax advisors will continue to explore the limits of its application, and the exchange industry will continue to become more sophisticated. The ability to exchange out of one property into another tax free, allows property owners to specialize in specific ownership functions and allows property to be put to its highest and best use. Exchange companies will continue to look for ways to provide better service to exchangers, and the Federation of Exchange Accommodators and other professional organizations will demand more of their members. All this will continue to move section 1031 forward. Section 1031 provides ballast to the real estate market.

APPENDIX A: GLOSSARY

95% rule A replacement property rule providing that if the exchanger violates both the three-property rule and the 200% rule it may nonetheless satisfy the identification rules by acquiring identified replacement property the total value of which is at least 95 percent of the total value of identified replacement properties.

200% rule A replacement property identification rule providing that the exchanger may identify any number of replacement properties so long as the aggregate value of the identified replacement properties does not exceed 200 percent of the aggregate value of the relinquished property.

Accommodation titleholder An exchange accommodator that holds property to facilitate reverse and improvements exchanges. Accommodation titleholder refers generally to any party who holds property to facilitate an exchange. It may refer to exchange accommodation titleholders under Rev. Proc. 2000-37 or any other titleholder.

Accommodator-facilitated improvements exchange An exchange structure employing the following steps: (1) an accommodation titleholder acquires property from a party who is not related to the exchanger, (2) the accommodation titleholder constructs improvements on the property, (3) the exchanger transfers relinquished property through a qualified intermediary, and (4) the exchanger acquires the improved property from the exchange accommodation titleholder through the qualified intermediary as replacement property.

Actual receipt The receipt of money or property through taking possession or legal title.

Adjusted tax basis The basis of property used to compute gain realized on the sale or other disposition of property. The starting point in computing adjusted tax basis is generally the cost of the property. That amount is increased by the amount of any improvements to the property and decreased by the amount of allowable depreciation deductions and certain other items.

Agent of an exchanger For purposes of determining whether a person is a disqualified person, the regulations define agent of an exchanger as any person who has acted as the exchanger's employee, attorney, accountant, investment banker or broker, or real estate agent or broker within the two years prior to the exchange. Such persons are not agents of the exchanger, however, if they only provide services with respect to section 1031 exchanges or provide only routine financial, title insurance, escrow, or trust services for the exchanger.

Amount realized The amount of money and the fair market value of property received plus the amount of liability relief upon the sale or other disposition of property.

Audit lottery The notion is based on the fact that the IRS has limited resources and audits only a limited number of returns each year. The limited resources result in a low audit rate. Audit lottery is the risk a taxpayer takes that it will not be audited due to the low audit rate. Taxpayers may be tempted to play the audit lottery by taking a position on a tax return and hoping they will not be audited based upon the IRS's low audit rate. No one can accurately predict the odds of being audited because numerous factors affect the IRS's decision to audit certain returns. Return preparers have a duty to ensure tax return positions are supported by the proper quantity of legal authority.

Basis shifting The result of a related-party exchange which shifts high basis from one property to another property that formerly had low basis. The related-party rules are designed to prevent basis shifting and the subsequent tax-free disposition of property.

Beneficial owner The party tax law treats as owning property. Tax law considers several factors in determining the owner of property. Possession of legal title is one factor, but it is not dispositive. Thus, a party other than the person holding legal title may be the beneficial owner of property.

Boot Money, non-like-kind property, and certain liability relief that an exchanger receives in exchange for relinquished property. The receipt of boot triggers gain under section 1031 to the extent of boot received or gain realized, whichever is lower.

Business transaction Any number of different transactions that affect the ownership of a business entity, including of the following transactions: contribution to a business entity, distribution from a business entity, merger or consolidation of business entities, division of a business entity, and termination of a business entity.

Buyer A party to an exchange who purchases the exchanger's relinquished property directly from the exchanger or through a qualified intermediary or other exchange facilitator.

Buyer-facilitated exchange An indirect exchange requiring the buyer to acquire replacement property from another party and transfer it to the exchanger in exchange for relinquished property.

Capital asset Property that a property owner holds to realize appreciation in value.

Capital gain Gain a property owner recognizes from the sale of a capital asset or other property that qualifies for capital-gain treatment.

Case law or common law The body of law found in judicial decisions. Courts create law by interpreting statutes and deciding other disputed legal questions.

Chain of title The parties of record who have held legal title to a piece of property. The chain of title shows a property's original owner of record and the subsequent transfers and owners of the property.

Constructive receipt A tax fiction that treats a person as receiving money or property even though another party takes possession of the money or property or receives legal title to it.

Corporation A legal entity generally formed under state law by filing articles of incorporation with the secretary of state. The owners of a corporation are shareholders who generally have the right to elect a board of directors. The board of directors appoints officers to manage the corporation. For tax purposes, corporations are either C corporations or S corporations. C corporations are subject to corporate income tax. S corporations are not subject to corporate income tax, but transferring property to or from a corporation may be a taxable event. Because of a corporation's negative tax treatment, property owners generally choose to hold property in a legal form other than a corporation. The name of a corporation generally includes one of the following: "Inc," "Corp," or "Co."

Dealer Property For purposes of determining the applicable tax rate, dealer property is property held primarily for sale to customers in the ordinary course of a trade or business. For purposes of determining the applicability of section 1031, dealer property is property held primarily for sale.

Deferred exchange A transfer of relinquished property and subsequent acquisition of replacement property.

Deferred improvements exchange An exchange that utilizes exchange proceeds to finance the construction of replacement property improvements. The exchanger transfers relinquished property through a qualified intermediary and the qualified intermediary receives the exchange proceeds and finances construction of improvements on property held by the exchange accommodation titleholder. The exchanger then acquires the improved replacement property through the qualified intermediary to complete the exchange.

Depreciation A tax deduction allowed for the wear and tear of property. Used colloquially, depreciation may refer to diminution in value of property. Depreciation for tax purposes, however, does not necessarily reflect a reduction in the value of an asset. It is a mere cost recovery system that allows a property owner to deduct the cost of property over a period of time.

Depreciation recapture The amount of gain attributable to depreciation deductions that a property owner must recognize on the sale or other disposition of property. Depreciation recaptured on the sale of personal property and some section 1245 real property is taxed at ordinary income rates. To avoid depreciation recapture on a section 1031 exchange, an exchanger must acquire section 1245 real property to replace any transferred section 1245 real property. Because personal property does not qualify for section 1031 nonrecognition, section 1031 cannot defer depreciation recapture realized on personal property. Depreciation taken on real property often results in recognition of unrecaptured section 1250 gain on the taxable sale of real property, but such gain can be deferred in a section 1031 exchange.

Direct deeding The transfer of legal title as part of an indirect exchange from the exchanger to the buyer and from the seller to the exchanger. If the exchanger properly structures the transaction, the IRS will, for federal income tax purposes, treat an exchange facilitator as acquiring the relinquished property from the exchanger and transferring it to the buyer and acquiring the replacement property from the seller and transferring it to the exchanger, even though the exchange facilitator does not take legal title to either property.

Direct exchange An exchange between two parties. The exchanger transfers relinquished property to another person in exchange for property the other person owns.

Direct related-party exchange A direct exchange between related parties—the exchanger transfers relinquished property to a related party and acquires replacement property from the related party.

Disqualified assets Assets section 1031 specifically excludes from nonrecognition treatment, which include property held primarily for sale.

Disqualified person A disqualified person is any person who is related to an exchanger, the agent of an exchanger, or related to the agent of an exchanger. A disqualified person may not serve as qualified intermediary, trustee of a qualified trust, holder of a qualified escrow account, or exchange accommodation titleholder.

Disregarded entity A legal entity that income tax law disregards. Any non-corporate entity that has a single member is generally disregarded. Thus, a single-member limited liability company is a disregarded entity. The owner of a disregarded entity reports the tax activities of the entity and owns all of the entity's property for tax purposes. A disregarded entity may elect to be a tax corporation, and thus forfeit its disregarded status. Properly structured DSTs can also be disregarded.

Disregarded partnership A partnership that has a single member for tax purposes and does not elect to be a tax corporation. A person may form a disregarded partnership by becoming the partnership's sole limited partner and creating a limited liability company to be the general partner of a limited partnership. That person becomes the sole member of the limited partnership. Because the limited liability company is disregarded for tax purposes, a single person is both the general partner and limited partner. Because the partnership has a single member, tax law disregards it.

DST (Deferred Sales Trust) A deferred sales trust (DST) results from a sales transaction that occurs outside the scope of section 1031. The general structure of a deferred sales trust requires a property owner to sale property to an intermediary in exchange for an installment note issued by the intermediary. The intermediary then sells the property and takes possession of the proceeds. The benefit of a properly structured deferred sales trust is that the property owner can defer gain recognition under the installment method and only recognize gain when payments are received under the installment note. The disadvantage of a deferred sales trust is that the property owner gives up access to sale proceeds in exchange for the note. To obtain the desired tax result, the property owner cannot have a security interest in the proceeds. Thus, the cost of obtaining the tax benefit is giving up financial security.

DST (Delaware Statutory Trust) A Delaware statutory trust (DST) is a legal entity formed under the laws of the state of Delaware. If properly structured, a DST will be disregarded for federal income tax purposes, and the owners of interests in the DST will be treated as owning interests in the DST's underlying property. Exchangers commonly acquire interests in DSTs as replacement property for their section 1031 exchanges.

DST dealer A licensed securities dealer who specializes in selling DST interests.

DST interest An interest in a Delaware statutory trust, which federal income tax law may treat as an interest in the trust's underlying property.

DST promoter A real estate syndicator who organizes Delaware statutory trusts. A DST promoter typically forms a DST, acquires DST property, and sells interests in the DST to parties looking to acquire DST interests.

Exchange accommodation titleholder An exchange facilitator that holds property for an exchanger doing a reverse or improvements exchange under Rev. Proc. 2000-37.

Exchange agreement An agreement entered into between an exchanger and a qualified intermediary or other facilitator. The exchange agreement provides details of the obligations of the exchanger and the facilitator. If a qualified intermediary facilitates an exchange, the exchange agreement must contain the (g)(6) restrictions and other language that establishes the qualified intermediary.

Exchange costs The costs an exchanger incurs in doing an exchange. Exchange costs include monetary costs such as attorney fees, CPA fees, and exchange facilitator fees. Exchange costs may also include non-monetary costs such as tax risk and effort required to satisfy the section 1031 requirements.

Exchange facilitator A generic term covering any party that facilitates an exchange. Qualified intermediaries, exchange accommodation titleholders, and any other party who facilitates on exchange are exchange facilitators.

Exchange-first reverse exchange A title-parking reverse exchange structure under which the exchanger transfers relinquished property to the accommodation titleholder in exchange for replacement property. The accommodation titleholder later sells the relinquished property to the buyer. Because the exchange occurs before the accommodation titleholder acquires the relinquished property, the transaction is referred to as an exchange-first reverse exchange.

Exchange-last reverse exchange A title-parking reverse exchange structure under which the accommodation titleholder acquires and holds replacement property. The exchanger subsequently transfers relinquished property in exchange for the parked replacement property. Because the exchange occurs after the accommodation titleholder has held the replacement property, the transaction is referred to as an exchange-last reverse exchange.

Exchange proceeds The consideration a buyer pays to acquire relinquished property from the exchanger.

Exchanged basis The basis an exchanger takes in replacement property under section 1031. The exchanged basis is equal to the basis the exchanger had in the relinquished property increased by the amount of any gain the exchanger recognizes on the exchange and decreased by the amount of boot the exchanger receives and the amount of any loss the exchanger recognizes on the exchange.

Exchanger A party seeking section 1031 nonrecognition through the exchange of property. An exchanger transfers relinquished property and acquires replacement property.

Federation of Exchange Accommodators A professional association of parties that act as qualified intermediaries and exchange accommodation titleholders. The FEA's website is www.1031.org.

(g)(6) restrictions Restrictions imposed by the section 1031 safe harbor regulations on all deferred exchange safe harbors. The (g)(6) restrictions limit the exchanger's right to receive, pledge, borrow or otherwise obtain the benefits of money or non-like-kind property held under a safe harbor arrangement.

Gain deferral A federal income tax mechanism that defers unrecognized gain until some future time. Section 1031 defers gain through its exchanged-basis rules. The exchanger, by taking exchanged basis in replacement property, will recognize deferred gain when it subsequently disposes of the replacement property in a taxable transaction.

Gain exclusion The permanent elimination of gain from income. For example, section 121 provides that some gain from the sale of a principal residence is excluded from income. The seller who qualifies for section 121 gain exclusion will never encounter the excluded gain again.

Gain realized The economic gain resulting from the sale or other disposition of property. Gain realized is the amount realized minus the adjusted tax basis of the property.

Gain recognized The amount of gain realized an exchanger must include in gross income and report on a tax return. Generally all gain realized must be recognized. Section 1031 provides, however, that gain realized on the exchange of like-kind property does not have to be recognized.

Holding requirement The requirement that the exchanger hold relinquished property as the tax owner before an exchange and hold replacement property as the tax owner after an exchange.

Identification period The 45-day period beginning the day following the transfer of relinquished property and ending at midnight on the 45th day after the transfer. During the identification period, the exchanger must identify replacement property.

Improvements exchange An exchange employing exchange proceeds to construct replacement property before the exchanger acquires it. There are at least five improvements exchanges: (1) the seller-facilitated improvements exchange, (2) the accommodator-facilitated improvements exchange, (3) the leasehold improvements exchange, (4) the improvements exchange on exchanger-owned property, and (5) the deferred improvements exchange.

Improvements exchange on exchanger-owned property A transaction that occurs as follows: (1) the exchanger transfers an interest in property to an accommodation titleholder, (2) the accommodation titleholder constructs improvements on the property, (3) the exchanger transfers relinquished property through a qualified intermediary, and (4) the exchanger acquires the improved property from the accommodation titleholder. The IRS has stated that the reverse exchange safe harbor will not apply to this type of transaction. Thus, all such exchanges will be non-safe harbor exchanges.

Indirect exchange An exchange whereby one party (the buyer) acquires the exchanger's relinquished property and the exchanger acquires another party's (the seller) property as replacement property. Generally a qualified intermediary will facilitate an indirect exchange, but an exchanger can also structure an indirect exchange as a buyer-facilitated exchange or seller-facilitated exchange.

Indirect related-party exchange An exchange in which the exchanger transfers relinquished property through a qualified intermediary and acquires replacement property from a related party through a qualified intermediary.

Installment method A gain-deferral method providing that a person who sells property for an installment note shall recognize gain on receipt of the installment payments. The installment method applies only if the installment note requires at least one payment be made in the taxable year following the year of the sale.

Installment note A promissory note requiring the maker to make payments on the note over time.

Intangible property Property that cannot be touched. Intangible property includes such things as copyrights, stock, partnership interests, patents, trademarks, and licenses. Section 1031 does not apply to intangible property.

Interest and growth factors A deferred exchange safe harbor that provides that an exchanger will not be deemed to be in actual or constructive receipt of boot held under a safe harbor arrangement even though the exchanger receives interest or some other growth factor based on the period of time the safe harbor arrangement holds the boot. The safe harbor provides that the exchanger may not receive such interest or growth factor until after the expiration of the (g)(6) restrictions.

Intermediary-facilitated exchange An exchange structure that requires an intermediary to actually or constructively acquire relinquished property from the exchanger and transfer it to the buyer and to actually or constructively acquire replacement property from the seller and transfer it to the exchanger.

Internal Revenue Code The body of federal statutory tax law.

Leasehold improvements exchange A transaction that occurs as follows: (1) a party related to the exchanger leases property to the accommodation titleholder, (2) the accommodation titleholder constructs improvements on the leased property, (3) the exchanger transfers relinquished property through a qualified intermediary, and (4) the exchanger acquires the leasehold interest (which must have at least thirty years to run at the time) and improvements through the qualified intermediary to complete the exchange.

Legal entity An entity recognized for state-law purposes. The following are examples of legal entities: corporations, partnerships, and limited liability companies.

Liability assumed The liability a person incurs to acquire property or the amount of liability to which property is subject at the time a person acquires the property.

Liability relief The amount by which a property owner's liability decreases on the sale or other disposition of property. Liability relief includes the amount of debt to which transferred property is subject.

Like-kind property Property that satisfies the section 1031 definition of like-kind.

Limited Liability Company A type of state-law entity that provides limited liability to its members and significant management flexibility. Limited liability companies are taxed as partnerships unless their owners elect for them to be taxed as corporations.

Long-term capital gain Gain a property owner recognizes from the sale of a capital asset that the property owner has held for more than one year.

Loss The adjusted tax basis of property minus the amount realized on the sale or other disposition of property. Taxpayers generally must recognize all realized loss. Section 1031, however, prohibits loss recognition on exchanges of like-kind property.

Merger The combining of one entity into another. State law generally provides rules for merging one legal entity into another. Tax law also provides rules that define when entities have merged. A tax merger may occur without a legal merger.

Midstream business transaction A business transaction that occurs while an exchange is pending (i.e., between the transfer of the relinquished property and acquisition of the replacement property).

Net worth The difference between a person's total asset value and total liabilities. Many property owners measure their financial success by tracking net worth over time and consider how transactions may affect their net worth. By deferring gain and tax on the exchange of the property, section 1031 helps preserve net worth. Net worth is not a technical tax term.

Mixed-use property Property the owner uses for dual purposes. Mixed-use property includes a residence, part of which the owner uses as an office, and vacation homes that the owners rent out and use for personal purposes.

Multi-party exchange An exchange involving at least three parties. In a typical multi-party exchange, the exchanger transfers relinquished property through a qualified intermediary to a buyer. Later the exchanger acquires replacement property through the qualified intermediary from a seller.

Nondepreciable tangible personal property Tangible personal property for which the owner may not take depreciation deductions. Such property includes artwork and collectibles.

Non-like-kind property Property that is not like-kind to relinquished property.

Non-safe harbor reverse exchange A reverse exchange structured outside the title-parking safe harbor in Rev. Proc. 2000-37 Generally an exchanger will structure a non-safe harbor reverse exchange if it will not be able to complete the exchange within the 180-day time period in the title-parking safe harbor.

Parked property Property, the title of which, an accommodation titleholder holds. Exchangers park title with accommodation titleholders to structure reverse exchanges and improvements exchanges.

Partnership A legal entity with two or more co-owners engaged in business for profit. Business or property owners may form a general partnership without filing documents with the state. In fact, some owners form general partnerships through their actions, unaware of such formation and its legal implications. A general partnership does not provide liability protection to its members. By filing articles of organization, business or property owners may form a limited partnership. A limited partnership must have at least one limited partner and one general partner. A limited partnership provides liability protection to the limited partners, but not to the general partner. General partners typically are other legal entities, such as a limited liability company, to provide liability protection to the owner of the general partner. The name of a limited partnership generally includes "Ltd" or "LP." Both general partnerships and limited partnerships are subject to partnership tax rules. Most property owners prefer an entity that is subject to partnership tax rules because those rules provide leeway for planning. A partnership may, however, elect to be taxed as a corporation.

Pending exchange An incomplete exchange. A situation created by a property owner transferring relinquished property in anticipation of acquiring replacement property in exchange.

Personal property Property that is not real property. Personal property includes such things as equipment, automobiles, computers, machinery, artwork, and collectibles. It also includes intangible personal property. Section 1031 does not apply to personal property.

Potential tax liability The tax liability a property owner would owe in the absence of a section 1031 exchange. Property owners compare their potential tax liability to the costs of doing an exchange to decide whether to sell or exchange property.

Principal residence The residence a person lives in and owns. If a person owns two residences, the principal residence generally is the residence that the person uses the majority of the time but can be the residence that reflects the locus of the person's existence (i.e., the place where the person is registered to vote, licenses vehicles, attend religious activities, etc.). A property owner who satisfies several requirements may exclude some or all of the gain realized on the sale of a principal residence.

Property-for-property requirement An element of the section 1031 exchange requirement providing that an exchanger must transfer property and acquire property, as opposed to money, to qualify for section 1031 nonrecognition.

Proximate business restructuring A business transaction that occurs before or after an exchange or while an exchange is pending. Business transactions include contributions to a business entity, distributions from a business entity, mergers and consolidations of businesses, divisions of businesses, and terminations of businesses.

Pure reverse exchange A reverse exchange supported in tax theory but not direct legal authority under which an exchanger acquires and holds replacement property before transferring relinquished property. Because no direct authority supports such exchanges, exchangers structure reverse exchanges as title-parking reverse exchanges.

Qualified escrow account A deferred exchange safe harbor providing that an exchanger will not be in actual or constructive receipt of boot placed in a qualified escrow account to secure the buyer's obligation to transfer replacement property to the exchanger. To be a qualified escrow account, an arrangement must satisfy several requirements in the regulations.

Qualified intermediary A deferred exchange safe harbor. A qualified intermediary is a person who does not come within the regulatory definition of disqualified person, whom an exchanger hires to facilitate an exchange, and who enters into an agreement with the exchanger that satisfies all of the requirements in the regulations. Pursuant to the safe harbor, a qualified intermediary will not be deemed to be the exchanger's agent (and thus incapable of facilitating an exchange) if the exchanger and qualified intermediary satisfy all of the requirements in the regulations.

Qualified trust A deferred exchange safe harbor providing that an exchanger will not be in actual or constructive receipt of boot placed in a qualified trust to secure the buyer's obligation to transfer replacement property to the exchanger. To be a qualified trust, an arrangement must satisfy several requirements in the regulations.

Real property Property that is tangible, immovable, and provides the owner perpetual rights in the property. Real property includes land, buildings, improvements, and fixtures.

Reciprocal requirement An element of the section 1031 exchange requirement providing that the person who transfers relinquished property must acquire replacement property.

Regulations The body of regulatory rules promulgated by an administrative agency. In the case of tax law, Treasury and IRS promulgate Income Tax Regulations that interpret or supplement provisions of the Internal Revenue Code. Regulations are valid law only if they reasonably interpret or supplement provisions of the Internal Revenue Code.

Related party Any person who bears a relationship to the exchanger defined in either the Internal Revenue Code or regulations. The definition of related party is important for determining whether a party is a disqualified person for purposes of the qualified intermediary and other safe harbors and the applicability of the related-party exchange rules. For both purposes, certain family members are related to the exchanger. For purposes of determining whether a party is a disqualified person, certain entities are related to the exchanger if the exchanger owns more than 10 percent of the entity, and certain entities are related to each other if the same persons own more than 10 percent of each. For purposes of determining whether the related-party rules apply, certain entities are related to the exchanger if the exchanger owns more than 50 percent of the entity, and certain entities are related to each other if the same persons own more than 50 percent of each.

Related-party exchange An exchange in which the exchanger transfers relinquished property to or acquires replacement property from a related party. Section 1031 nonrecognition is not available to certain types of related-party exchanges. Section 1031 provides rules governing direct and indirect related-party exchanges.

Relinquished property Property an exchanger transfers as part of a section 1031 exchange.

Replacement property Property an exchanger acquires as part of a section 1031 exchange.

Revenue procedure An IRS publication in which the IRS publishes its procedural stance on specific tax issues.

Revenue ruling An IRS publication in which the IRS rules on a specific substantive area of tax law.

Reverse exchange An exchange under which the exchanger acquires replacement property and subsequently transfers relinquished property. The IRS has published a safe harbor for title-parking reverse exchanges, (Rev. Proc. 2000-37). Pure reverse exchanges may find support in tax theory, but not in direct legal authority. To avoid pure reverse exchanges, exchangers use title-parking reverse exchanges and avoid holding relinquished property and replacement property simultaneously.

Safe harbor A set of guidelines or rules that if followed will produce a specific tax result. For example, the IRS provides the qualified intermediary safe harbor. If a transaction satisfies the safe harbor requirements, the qualified intermediary will not be treated as the exchanger's agent.

Section 121 A provision of the Internal Revenue Code which excludes some or all of the gain realized on the sale of a principal residence.

Section 1031 A provision of the Internal Revenue Code providing that no gain or loss shall be recognized on the exchange of real property held for the productive use in a trade or business or for investment for like-kind property to be held for the productive use in a trade or business or for investment.

Section 1031 nonrecognition The result of satisfying all of the requirements of section 1031. A party who satisfies the section 1031 requirements does not recognize gain or loss on the exchange of the relinquished property for like-kind replacement property. Section 1031 nonrecognition is not optional, so nonrecognition results if a transaction satisfies all of the section 1031 requirements.

Section 1221 The provision of the Internal Revenue Code that defines capital asset.

Section 1245 recapture The portion of gain attributable to depreciation previously taken on section 1245 property. Section 1245 recapture is recognized on the transfer of section 1245 property and is taxed at ordinary rates, unless it is exchanged for like-kind replacement section 1245 property. Because section 1031 only applies to real property, both the relinquished and replacement section 1245 properties must be real property for the exchanger to avoid section 1245 recapture on the transfer of section 1245 property.

Section 1250 gain Gain recognized on the sale of real property attributable to depreciation that is subject to a tax rate higher than the long-term capital gains tax rate.

Security A property interest subject to the U.S. or state securities laws. Common examples of securities include corporate stocks and bonds. TIC interests are also probably securities.

Security or guarantee arrangement A deferred exchange safe harbor providing that an exchanger shall not be deemed to be in actual or constructive receipt of boot, even though the exchanger retains a security interest in the relinquished property, a third party guarantees the buyer's obligation to acquire and transfer replacement property, or a standby letter of credit secures the buyer's obligation to acquire and transfer replacement property. This safe harbor ceases as soon as the exchanger has the right to receive boot pursuant to the security or guarantee arrangement.

Seller A party to an exchange who sells the replacement property that the exchanger ultimately requires.

Seller-facilitated exchange An exchange structure requiring the seller to acquire relinquished property from the exchanger in exchange for the replacement property, after which the seller transfers the relinquished property to the buyer.

Seller-facilitated improvements exchange An exchange in which the replacement property seller constructs improvements on the replacement property before transferring it to the exchanger.

Sixteenth Amendment The Sixteenth Amendment of the United States Constitution, granting Congress the authority to impose an income tax on individuals without apportionment among the several states and without regard to any census or enumeration. The Sixteenth Amendment was ratified on February 3, 1913.

Tax liability The amount of tax a person owes the federal government or other taxing authority. Tax liability is computed by multiplying taxable income by a tax rate.

Tax risk The likelihood that a court will reject a return position based on its merits. In the section 1031 context, tax risk is the likelihood that a court will hold that a transaction does not qualify for section 1031 nonrecognition. Determining that likelihood requires the professional judgment of a competent lawyer or CPA.

Tenancy-in-common (TIC) A co-ownership arrangement in which multiple parties own undivided interests in a single piece of property. TIC interests have become popular replacement property for section 1031 exchangers.

Three-property rule A rule governing the identification of replacement property and providing that the exchanger may identify any three properties regardless of the properties' fair market value.

TIC agreement An agreement between co-owners of a piece of property that specifies the co-owners' rights in the property.

TIC dealer A licensed securities dealer who specializes in selling TIC interests.

TIC interest A tenancy-in-common interest in property.

TIC promoter A real estate syndicator who organizes TIC arrangements. A TIC promoter will acquire TIC property or put it under contract and sell interests in the property or assign rights in the contract to parties interested in acquiring TIC interests.

Title-parking reverse exchange A reverse exchange facilitated by an exchange accommodator who takes title to either replacement property or relinquished property to ensure that the exchanger does not hold both properties simultaneously.

Title-parking safe harbor The safe harbor in Rev. Proc. 2000-37 providing that the IRS will treat the exchange accommodation titleholder as the beneficial owner of parked property for tax purposes if the arrangement between the exchanger and exchange accommodation titleholder satisfies all of the safe harbor requirements. Often the most difficult requirement to satisfy is the holding-period limitation which allows the exchange accommodation titleholder to hold property for only 180 days.

Triple-net lease A lease on property pursuant to which the tenant agrees to pay rent to the landlord, manage the property, and pay other costs associated with the property such as real estate taxes and insurance.

Triple-net property Property subject to a triple-net lease. Triple-net properties are commonly a part of section 1031 exchanges. They are attractive as replacement property because the owner has little, if any, management responsibilities related to the property.

Use requirement The requirement that the exchanger hold exchange property for the productive use in a trade or business or for investment.

APPENDIX B: WORKSHEETS FOR ESTIMATING TAX LIABILITY

Computing Amount Realized

Amount of money received	$ ________
Plus	
Fair market value of property received	$ ________
Plus	
Liability relief	$ ________
Minus	
Costs incurred to sell property	($ ________)
Equals	
Amount realized	$ ________

Computing Adjusted Tax Basis

Property acquired by purchase

Amount paid for property	
Amount of cash paid	$ ________
Plus	
Amount of liability assumed or incurred	$ ________
Total amount paid for the property	$ ________
Plus	
Costs incurred to acquire the property	$ ________
Plus	
Cost of improvements to the property	$ ________
Minus	
Depreciation deductions	($ ________)
Equals	
Adjusted tax basis of property acquired by purchase	$ ________

Property acquired through section 1031 exchange

Adjusted tax basis of relinquished property	$________
Increased by	
Gain recognized on exchange	$ ________
Or decreased by	
Loss recognized	($ ________)
Decreased by	
Boot received	($ ________)
Equals	
Exchanged basis of property acquired through section 1031 exchange	$ ________
Plus	
Cost of improvements	$ ________
Minus	
Depreciation deductions	($ ________)
Equals	
Adjusted tax basis of property acquired through section 1031 exchange	$________

Estimating Deferrable Tax

Amount realized	$ ________
Minus	
Adjusted tax basis	($ ________)
Equals	
Gain realized	$ ________

<u>Potential tax liability</u>

Depreciation recapture	$ ________	× ordinary rate = $ ________
Plus		
Short-term capital gain	$ ________	× ordinary rate = $ ________
Plus		
Section 1250 gain	$ ________	× 25% = $ ________
Plus		
Long-term capital gain	$ ________	× 20% = $ ________
Plus		

NII Tax	$ ________ × 3.8% =	$ __________
Plus		
State and local taxes	$ _________ × rate =	$ __________
Equals		
Total potential tax liability		$ __________

APPENDIX C: FORM 8824

Form **8824**

Department of the Treasury
Internal Revenue Service

Like-Kind Exchanges
(and section 1043 conflict-of-interest sales)
▶ Attach to your tax return.
▶ Go to www.irs.gov/Form8824 for instructions and the latest information.

OMB No. 1545-1190
2020
Attachment Sequence No. **109**

Name(s) shown on tax return | Identifying number

Part I **Information on the Like-Kind Exchange**

Note: Generally, only real property should be described on lines 1 and 2. However, you may describe personal property transferred prior to January 1, 2018, as part of an exchange subject to the like-kind exchange transition rule described in the instructions, and/or real property on lines 1 and 2, if you are filing this form to report the disposition of property exchanged in a previously reported related party like-kind exchange. If the property described on line 1 or line 2 is real or personal property located outside the United States, indicate the country.

1 Description of like-kind property given up:

2 Description of like-kind property received:

3	Date like-kind property given up was originally acquired (month, day, year)	3	MM/DD/YYYY
4	Date you actually transferred your property to the other party (month, day, year)	4	MM/DD/YYYY
5	Date like-kind property you received was identified by written notice to another party (month, day, year). See instructions for 45-day written identification requirement	5	MM/DD/YYYY
6	Date you actually received the like-kind property from other party (month, day, year). See instructions	6	MM/DD/YYYY

7 Was the exchange of the property given up or received made with a related party, either directly or indirectly (such as through an intermediary)? See instructions. If "Yes," complete Part II. If "No," go to Part III . . . ☐ **Yes** ☐ **No**

Note: Do not file this form if a related party sold property into the exchange, directly or indirectly (such as through an intermediary); that property became your replacement property; and none of the exceptions in line 11 applies to the exchange. Instead, report the disposition of the property as if the exchange had been a sale. If one of the exceptions on line 11 applies to the exchange, complete Part II.

Part II **Related Party Exchange Information**

8	Name of related party	Relationship to you	Related party's identifying number
	Address (no., street, and apt., room, or suite no.; city or town; state; and ZIP code)		

9 During this tax year (and before the date that is 2 years after the last transfer of property that was part of the exchange), did the related party sell or dispose of any part of the like-kind property received from you (or an intermediary) in the exchange? . . . . ☐ **Yes** ☐ **No**

10 During this tax year (and before the date that is 2 years after the last transfer of property that was part of the exchange), did you sell or dispose of any part of the like-kind property you received? . . . . ☐ **Yes** ☐ **No**

*If both lines 9 and 10 are "No" and this is the year of the exchange, go to Part III. If both lines 9 and 10 are "No" and this is **not** the year of the exchange, stop here. If either line 9 or line 10 is "Yes," complete Part III and report on this year's tax return the deferred gain or (loss) from line 24 **unless** one of the exceptions on line 11 applies.*

11 If one of the exceptions below applies to the disposition, check the applicable box.

a ☐ The disposition was after the death of either of the related parties.

b ☐ The disposition was an involuntary conversion, and the threat of conversion occurred after the exchange.

c ☐ You can establish to the satisfaction of the IRS that neither the exchange nor the disposition had tax avoidance as one of its principal purposes. If this box is checked, attach an explanation. See instructions.

For Paperwork Reduction Act Notice, see the instructions. Cat. No. 12311A Form **8824** (2020)

Form 8824 (2020) Page 2

Name(s) shown on tax return. Do not enter name and social security number if shown on other side. | Your social security number

Part III **Realized Gain or (Loss), Recognized Gain, and Basis of Like-Kind Property Received**

Caution: If you transferred **and** received **(a)** more than one group of like-kind properties or **(b)** cash or other (not like-kind) property, see ***Reporting of multi-asset exchanges*** in the instructions.

Note: Complete lines 12 through 14 **only** if you gave up property that was not like-kind. Otherwise, go to line 15.

12	Fair market value (FMV) of other property given up	12	
13	Adjusted basis of other property given up	13	
14	Gain or (loss) recognized on other property given up. Subtract line 13 from line 12. Report the gain or (loss) in the same manner as if the exchange had been a sale	14	
	Caution: If the property given up was used previously or partly as a home, see ***Property used as home*** in the instructions.		
15	Cash received, FMV of other property received, plus net liabilities assumed by other party, reduced (but not below zero) by any exchange expenses you incurred. See instructions	15	
16	FMV of like-kind property you received	16	
17	Add lines 15 and 16	17	
18	Adjusted basis of like-kind property you gave up, net amounts paid to other party, plus any exchange expenses **not** used on line 15. See instructions	18	
19	**Realized gain or (loss).** Subtract line 18 from line 17	19	
20	Enter the smaller of line 15 or line 19, but not less than zero	20	
21	Ordinary income under recapture rules. Enter here and on Form 4797, line 16. See instructions . .	21	
22	Subtract line 21 from line 20. If zero or less, enter -0-. If more than zero, enter here and on Schedule D or Form 4797, unless the installment method applies. See instructions	22	
23	**Recognized gain.** Add lines 21 and 22	23	
24	Deferred gain or (loss). Subtract line 23 from line 19. If a related party exchange, see instructions . .	24	
25	**Basis of like-kind property received.** Subtract line 15 from the sum of lines 18 and 23	25	

Part IV **Deferral of Gain From Section 1043 Conflict-of-Interest Sales**

Note: This part is to be used **only** by officers or employees of the executive branch of the federal government or judicial officers of the federal government (including certain spouses, minor or dependent children, and trustees as described in section 1043) for reporting nonrecognition of gain under section 1043 on the sale of property to comply with the conflict-of-interest requirements. This part can be used **only** if the cost of the replacement property is more than the basis of the divested property.

26	Enter the number from the upper right corner of your certificate of divestiture. (**Do not** attach a copy of your certificate. Keep the certificate with your records.) . . . . ▶		____ -
27	Description of divested property ▶ ____________________		
28	Description of replacement property ▶ ____________________		
29	Date divested property was sold (month, day, year)	29	MM/DD/YYYY
30	Sales price of divested property. See instructions	30	
31	Basis of divested property	31	
32	**Realized gain.** Subtract line 31 from line 30	32	
33	Cost of replacement property purchased within 60 days after date of sale .	33	
34	Subtract line 33 from line 30. If zero or less, enter -0-	34	
35	Ordinary income under recapture rules. Enter here and on Form 4797, line 10. See instructions . .	35	
36	Subtract line 35 from line 34. If zero or less, enter -0-. If more than zero, enter here and on Schedule D or Form 4797. See instructions	36	
37	**Deferred gain.** Subtract the sum of lines 35 and 36 from line 32	37	
38	**Basis of replacement property.** Subtract line 37 from line 33	38	

Form **8824** (2020)

APPENDIX D: ADDITIONAL SECTION 1031 RESOURCES

Section 1031 Treatises

Bradley T. Borden, TAX-FREE LIKE-KIND EXCHANGES (Civic Research Institute 2d ed. 2015)

Bradley T. Borden, *How to Structure Like-Kind Exchanges*, TAX ADVISORS PLANNING SERIES (RIA)

Howard J. Levine Aaron S. Gaynor, *Taxfree Exchanges Under Section 1031*, BNA TAX MANAGEMENT PORTFOLIO, 567-5th T.M.

Jeremiah M. Long & Mary B. Foster, TAX-FREE EXCHANGES UNDER § 1031 (Thompson Publishing, updated annually)

CHAPTER 1: THE HISTORY OF TAX-FREE EXCHANGES

Bradley T. Borden, *The Like-Kind Exchange Equity Conundrum*, 60 FLA. L. REV. 643 (2008)

Bradley T. Borden, *Reverse Like-kind Exchanges: A Principled Approach*, 20 VA. TAX REV. 659 (Spring 2001)

Erik M. Jensen, *The Uneasy Justification for Special Treatment of Like-Kind Exchanges*, 4 AM. J. TAX. POL'Y 193 (1985)

Marjorie Kornhauser, *Section 1031: We Don't Need Another Hero*, 60 S. CAL. L. REV. 397 (1987)

Martin J. McMahon, Jr., *Rollover is Better Than Section 1031, But Why Stop There?*, 92 TAX NOTES 1111 (2001)

CHAPTER 2: THE SECTION 1031 PLAYERS

Bradley T. Borden, *Twenty Things Real Estate Attorneys Can Do to Not Mess Up a Section 1031 Exchange*, 36 PRAC. REAL EST. LAW. 30 (September 2020)

Bradley T. Borden, *Section 1031 Qualified Intermediaries in the New Economy*, 27 J. TAX'N INV. 86 (Fall 2009)

Bradley T. Borden, *Safe Harbors and Careful Planning Make Deferred Exchanges a Valuable Tool*, 25 J. TAX'N INV. 43 (Spring 2008)

Kelly E. Alton and Louis S. Weller, *Treatment of Section 1031 Exchange Intermediaries as Borrowers Under New Prop. Reg. 1.468B-6*, 104 J. TAX'N 338 (June 2006)

Bradley T. Borden, Paul L. B. McKenney, and David Shechtman, *Like-Kind Exchanges and Qualified Intermediaries*, 124 TAX NOTES 55 (July 6, 2009)

Terrence Floyd Cuff, *Deferred Exchanges and How to Become a Millionaire*, 27 J. REAL ESTATE TAX'N 324 (Summer 2000)

Terrence Floyd Cuff, *Structuring a Simple Forward Real Estate Exchange*, 34 REAL ESTATE TAX'N 77 (1st Quarter 2007)

John Stark, *Investors in Court to Recover Cash: Lack of Safeguards Cited in Tax-Deferral Strategy*, THE BELLINGHAM HERALD (December 5, 2006)

E. John Wagner, II, *Ruling Paves the way for Professionals to Operate Section 1031 Exchange Intermediaries*, 99 J. TAX'N 349 (December 2003)

CHAPTER 3: DECIDING WHETHER TO HOLD, SELL, OR EXCHANGE

Commissioner v. Chrichton, 122 F.2d 181 (5th Cir. 1941)

Regals Realty v. Commissioner, 127 F.2d 3931 (2d Cir. 1942)

Oregon Lumber Co. v. Commissioner, 20 T.C. 192 (1953)

Wagneson v. Commissioner, 74 T.C. 653 (1980)

Cottle v. Commissioner, 89 T.C. 467 (1981)

Click v. Commissioner, 78 T.C. 225 (1982)

Lindsley v. Commissioner, 47 T.C.M. (CCH) 540 (1983)

Chase v. Commissioner, 92 T.C. 874 (1989)

Neal T. Baker Enterprises Inc. v. Commissioner, 76 T.C.M. (CCH) 301 (1998)

Peabody Natural Resources Co. v. Commissioner, 126 T.C. 261 (2006)

Bradley T. Borden & Todd D. Keator, *Workout-Driven Exchanges*, 25 TAX MGMT. REAL EST. J. 23 (February 4, 2009)

Bradley T. Borden, *Tax Issues for Real Estate Investors Considering a Mortgage Defeasance as Part of a Section 1031 Exchange*, 28 J. TAX'N INV. 3 (Winter 2011)

Bradley T. Borden, *Code Sec. 1031, the Code Sec. 199A and Bonus Depreciation Regulations, and Ozone Drop-Swap Cash-Outs,* 22 J. PASSTHROUGH ENT. 13 (January-February 2019)

Kelly E. Alton, Louis S. Weller, *Does State Law Really Determine Whether Property is Real Estate for Section 1031 Purposes?* 32 REAL ESTATE TAX'N 30 (4th Quarter, 2004)

Kelly E. Alton, Bradley T. Borden, *Section 1031Tax Alchemy: Transforming Personal Tangible and Intangible Property into Real Property*, 34 REAL ESTATE TAX'N 52 (1st Quarter 2007)

Bradley T. Borden, *The Whole Truth About Using Partial Real Estate Interests in Section 1031 Exchanges*, 31 REAL ESTATE TAX'N 19, (4th Quarter, 2003)

Terrence Floyd Cuff, *Issues in Cashing Out of an Exchange*, 28 J. REAL ESTATE TAX'N 68 (Fall 2000)

Terrence Floyd Cuff, *Liabilities in Section 1031 Exchanges*, 27 J. REAL ESTATE TAX'N 119 (Winter 2000)

Terrence Floyd Cuff, *Some Comments on Structuring a Simple Forward Real Estate Exchange* (forthcoming)

Richard M. Lipton, Michael T. Donovan, and Daniel F. Cullen *Tax Court's* Peabody *Decision Clarifies When Real Property Interests are Like-Kind*, 105 J. TAX'N 90 (August 2006)

Richard M. Lipton, *The 'State of the Art' in Like-Kind Exchanges, 2006*, 104 J. TAX'N 138 (March 2006)

CHAPTER 4: EXCHANGE STRUCTURES: DIRECT AND INDIRECT EXCHANGES

Mercantile Trust Co. v. Commissioner, 32 B.T.A. 82 (1935)

Hayden v. Commissioner, 165 F.2d 588 (5th Cir. 1948)

Carlton v. Commissioner, 395 F.2d 238 (5th Cir. 1967)

Halpern v. Commissioner, 286 F. Supp. 255 (N.D. Ga. 1968)

Biggs v. Commisioner, 632 F.2d 1171 (5th Cir. 1980)

Rev. Rul. 57-244, 1957-1 C.B. 247

CHAPTER 5: EXCHANGE STRUCTURES: DEFERRED EXCHANGES

Starker v. United States, 602 F.2d 1241 (9th Cir. 1979)

Bradley T. Borden, *Universal Deadline Extensions Draw Attention to Section 1031 Periods*, 167 TAX NOTES FED. 603 (April 27, 2020)

Bradley T. Borden, *Section 1031 Qualified Intermediaries in the New Economy*, 27 J. TAX'N INV. 86 (Fall 2009)

Terrence Floyd Cuff, *Some Comments on Structuring a Simple Forward Real Estate Exchange* (forthcoming)

Terrence Floyd Cuff, *Identification of Multiple Replacement Properties in a Deferred Exchange*, 25 J. REAL ESTATE TAX'N 165 (Winter 1998)

Howard J. Levine, *Premature Distributions From 1031 Exchange Accounts—New Ruling Provides Guidance*, 93 J. TAX'N 7 (July 2000)

Howard J. Levine, David Weintraub, *Tax and Reporting Rules for Escrows and Trusts used in Deferred Like-Kind Exchanges*, 90 J. TAX'N 332 (June 1999)

Richard M. Lipton, *The 'State of the Art' in Like-Kind Exchanges, 2006)*, 104 J. TAX'N 138 (March 2006)

Richard M. Lipton, *The 'State of the Art' in Like-Kind Exchanges, Revisited*, 96 J. TAX'N 334 (June 2003)

CHAPTER 6: EXCHANGE STRUCTURES: REVERSE EXCHANGES

Bloomington Coca-Cola Bottling Co. v. Commissioner, 189 F.2d 14 (7th Cir. 1951)

Coastal Terminals v. United States, 320 F.2d 333 (4th Cir. 1963)

Rutherford v. Commissioner, 37 T.C.M. (CCH) 1851-77 (1978)

Grodt & McKay, Inc. v. Commissioner, 77 T.C. 1221 (1981)

Bezdjian v. Commissioner, 845 f.2d 217 (9th Cir. 1988)

DeCleene v. Commissioner, 115 T.C. 34 (2000)

Estate of Bartell v. Commissioner, 147 T.C. 140 (2016)

Rev. Proc. 2004-51, 2004-2 C.B. 294

Rev. Proc. 2000-37, 2000-2 C.B. 308

Bradley T. Borden, Bartell *and the Expansion of Facilitated Exchanges*, 20 J. PASSTHROUGH ENT. 13 (January-February 2017)

Bradley T. Borden, *Reverse Like-kind Exchanges: A Principled Approach*, 20 VA. TAX REV. 659 (Spring 2001)

Bradley T. Borden, *New Safe Harbor Promotes Reverse Exchanges*, 66 PRAC. TAX STRAT. 68 (February 2001); 11 J. OF CONST. ACTG. AND TAX'N 3 (March/April 2001); TAX IDEAS

Mary B. Foster, *New Tool in the Real Estate Biz; A Tale of Parked Properties and Reverse Exchanges*, 11 BUS. LAW TODAY 26 (January–February 2002)

Mary B. Foster, *Reverse Exchanges after Rev. Proc. 2000-37*, 4 J PASSTHROUGH ENTITIES 24 (January–February 2001)

Howard J. Levine, *Long-Awaited IRS Guidance on "Parking Arrangements" Facilitates Like-Kind Exchanges*, 28 J. REAL ESTATE TAX'N 91 (Winter 2001)

CHAPTER 7: EXCHANGE STRUCTURES: IMPROVEMENTS EXCHANGES

Coastal Terminals v. United States, 320 F.2d 333 (4th Cir. 1963)

Estate of Bartell v. Commissioner, 147 T.C. 140 (2016)

Rev. Proc. 2004-51, 2004-2 C.B. 294

Bradley T. Borden, Bartell *and the Expansion of Facilitated Exchanges*, 20 J. PASSTHROUGH ENT. 13 (January-February. 2017)

Bradley T. Borden, Alan S. Lederman, Glenn Spear, *Build-to-Suit Ruling Breaks New Ground for Taxpayers Seeking Swap Treatment*, 98 J. TAX'N 22 (2003)

Bradley T. Borden, *Recent Developments in Build-to-Suit Exchanges*, 44 TAX MGT. MEMO. 19 (January 2003)

Kelly E. Alton, Bradley T. Borden, and Alan S. Lederman, *Rev. Proc. 2004-51: The IRS Strikes Back*, 83 TAXES 17 (February 2005)

Mary B. Foster, *Construction Exchanges Under Code Sec.1031 Five Years after Issuance of Rev. Proc. 2000-37*, 9 J. PASSTHROUGH ENTITIES 31 (March–April 2006)

Comments Regarding Rev. Proc. 2000-37 Safe Harbor Build-to-Suit Exchanges Involving Leasehold Improvements, 2004 TNT 90-85 (May 10, 2004) (principal authors: Kelly S. Alton, Bradley T. Borden, and David Shechtman)

CHAPTER 8: EXCHANGES AND PROXIMATE BUSINESS RESTRUCTURINGS

Commissioner v. Court Holding Co., 324 U.S. 331 (1945)

Magneson v. Commissioner, 753 F.2d 1490 (9th Cir. 1985)

Bolker v. Commissioner, 760 F.2d 1039 (9th Cir. 1985)

Miles H. Mason v. Commissioner, 55 T.C.M. (CCH) 1134 (1988)

Maloney v. Commissioner, 93 T.C. 89 (1989)

Rev. Rul. 75-292, 1975-2 C.B. 333

Rev. Rul. 77-337, 1977-2 C.B. 305

Bradley T. Borden, *S-Corporation Cash-Out Break-Ups and Code Sec. 1031 Exchanges*, 21 J. PASSTHROUGH ENT. 21 (September-October 2018)

Bradley T. Borden, *Code Sec. 1031 Drop-Swap Cash-Outs and Unrecaptured Section 1250 Gain*, 19 J. PASSTHROUGH ENT. 27 (September-October 2016)

Bradley T. Borden, *Section 1031 Drop-and-Swaps Thirty Years After* Magneson, 19 J. PASSTHROUGH ENT. 11 (January-February 2016)

Bradley T. Borden, *Section 1031 Drop-and-Swaps Thirty Years After* Bolker, 18 J. PASSTHROUGH ENT. 21 (September-October 2015)

Saul B. Abrams, Mary B. Foster, *One Question, Two Answers—An Inconsistency in Disregards?*, 20 PRAC. TAX LAW. 19 (Summer 2006)

Bradley T. Borden, *Section 1031 and Proximate and Midstream Business Transactions*, 19 TAX MGT. REAL ESTATE J. 307 (November 2003)

Bradley T. Borden, *What You Should Know About Mergers and Divisions of Partnerships*, 17 PRAC. TAX LAW. 45 (Winter 2003)

Mary B. Foster et al. *American Bar Association - Bar Section: Joint Report on §1031 Open Issues Involving Partnerships*, 42 TAX MGM'T MEMO. 43 (January 29, 2001)

Howard J. Levine, David A. Weintraub, *Two-Member LLC can be Disregarded in 1031 Exchange Where one Member has no Economic Interest*, 90 J. TAX'N 138 (March 1999)

Richard M. Lipton, *Multi-Year Deferred Like-Kind Exchanges by Partnerships—Is the New Rev. Rul. a Trojan Horse?*, 99 J. TAX'N 69 (August 2003)

CHAPTER 9: RELATED-PARTY EXCHANGES

I.R.C. § 1031(f)

Teruya Brothers v. Commissioner, 580 F.3d 1038 (9th Cir. 2009)

Ocmulgee Fields v. Commissioner, 613 F.3d 1360 (11th Cir. 2010)

North Central Rental & Leasing v. U.S., 779 F.3d 738 (8th Cir. 2015)

Malulani Group, Ltd. v. Commissioner, 112 T.C.M. (CCH) 530 (2016)

Rev. Rul. 2002-83, 2002-2 C.B. 927

Bradley T. Borden, Malulani *and the Entrenchment of Mechanical Analysis of Related-Party Exchange Rules*, 20 J. PASSTHROUGH ENT. 15 (May-June 2017)

Bradley T. Borden, North Central *and the Expansion of Code Sec. 1031(f) Related-Party Exchange Rules*, 18 J. PASSTHROUGH ENT. 19 (May-June 2015)

Bradley T. Borden & Alan S. Lederman, *Section 1031 Exchanges: Death of a Related-Party Exchange—Did "Butler" Do it?*, 75 DAILY TAX REP. J-1 (April 20, 2015)

Kelly E. Alton, Bradley T. Borden & Alan S. Lederman, *Do Serial Exchangers Get the Cash, with Extra Time to Boot, Under New Letter Ruling?*, 114 J. TAX'N 153 (March 2011)

Kelly E. Alton, Bradley T. Borden & Alan S. Lederman, *Related Party Like-Kind Exchanges:* Teruya Brothers *and Beyond*, 111 J. TAX'N 324 (December 2009)

Kelly E. Alton, Bradley T. Borden & Alan S. Lederman, *Related-Party Like-Kind Exchanges*, 115 TAX NOTES 467 (April 30, 2007)

Bradley T. Borden, Alan S. Lederman, Glenn Spear, *Build-to-Suit Ruling Breaks New Ground for Taxpayers Seeking Swap Treatment*, 98 J. TAX'N 22 (2003)

Bradley T. Borden, *Recent Developments in Build-to-Suit Exchanges*, 44 TAX MGT. MEMO. 19 (January 2003)

Terrence Floyd Cuff, *Teruya Brothers and Related-Party Exchanges—How Much More Do We Know Now?*, 102 J. TAX'N 220 (April 2005)

Terrence Floyd Cuff, *Related-Party Exchanges—an examination of Technical Advice Memorandum 9748006*, 26 J. REAL ESTATE TAX'N 155 (Winter 1999)

CHAPTER 10: DSTS, TIC INTEREST, AND TRIPLE-NET PROPERTIES

Rev. Rul. 2004-86, 2004-2 C.B. 191

Rev. Proc. 2002-22, 2002-1 C.B. 733

Bradley T. Borden, *Open Tenancies in Common*, 39 SETON HALL L. REV. 387 (2009)

Bradley T. Borden, *The Federal Definition of Tax Partnership*, 43 HOUS. L. REV. 925 (2006)

Bradley T. Borden, *Exchanges Involving Tenancy-in-Common Interests can be Tax-Free*, 70 PRAC. TAX STRAT. 4 (January 2003); TAX IDEAS

Bradley T. Borden, *Revisiting the Federal Tax Definition of Partnership and the § 761(a)(1) Election in the TIC Environment*, 47 TAX MGT. MEMO. 51 (February 6, 2006)

Bradley T. Borden, Sandra Favelukes, and Todd Molz, *A History and Analysis of the Co-Ownership-Partnership Question*, 106 TAX NOTES 1175 (March 7, 2005)

Bradley T. Borden, Todd D. Keator, *Tax Opinions in TIC Offerings and Reverse TIC Exchanges*, 23 TAX MGM'T REAL ESTATE J 83 (March 7, 2007)

Bradley T. Borden, W. Richey Wyatt, *Syndicated Tenancy-in-Common Arrangements: How Tax-Motivated Real Estate Transactions Raise Serious Non-Tax Issues,* 18 PROB. AND PROP. 18, (September/October 2004)

Terrence Floyd Cuff, *Research Can Prevent an Investment in a Ticky Tacky TIC*, 33 REAL ESTATE TAX'N 170 (4th Quarter 2006)

Richard M. Lipton, *"Securities" and Like-Kind Exchanges*, 9 J. PASSTHROUGH ENTITIES, 5 (July-August 2006)

Richard M. Lipton, *New Rules Likely to Increase Use of Tenancy-in-Common Ownership in Like-Kind Exchanges*, 96 J. TAX'N 303 (May 2002)

Richard M. Lipton and Daniel F. Cullen, *Tenancy-in-Common Interests: A Valuable Addition to the Financial Planner's Toolkit*, 6 J. Prac. EST. PLAN. 21 (October-November 2004)

Richard M. Lipton, Arnold Harrison, and Todd Golub *The Intersection of Delaware Statutory Trusts and Tenancies-In-Common*, 32 REAL ESTATE TAX'N 76 (1st Quarter 2006)

Richard M. Lipton, Todd Golub, and Daniel F. Cullen, *Delaware Statutory Trusts and 1031: A Marriage Made in Heaven or Just a Pipe Dream?*, 101 J. TAX'N 140 (September 2004)

Alex R. Pederson, *The Rejuvenation of the Tenancy-in-Common Form for Like-Kind Exchanges and its Impact on Lenders*, 24 ANN. REV. BANKING & FIN. L. 467 (2005)

CHAPTER 11: EXCHANGING MIXED-USE PROPERTY

I.R.C. § 280A(a), (d)(1)

Rev. Proc. 2005-14, 2005-1 C.B. 528

Rev. Proc. 2008-16, 2008-1 C.B. 547

Bradley T. Borden & Alex Hamrick, *Like-Kind Exchanges of Personal-Use Residences*, 119 TAX NOTES 1253 (June 23, 2008)

CHAPTER 12: THE PROHIBITION OF DEALER PROPERTY

I.R.C. § 1221

Estate of Barrios v. Commissioner, 265 F.2d 517 (5th Cir. 1959)

Malat v. Riddell, 383 U.S. 569 (1966)

Bynum v. Commissioner, 46 T.C. 295 (1966)

United States v. Winthrop, 417 F.2d 905 (5th Cir. 1969)

Cary v. Commissioner, 32 T.C.M. (CCH) 913 (1973)

Biedenharn Realty Co., Inc. v. United States, 526 F.2d 409 (5th Cir. 1975)

Suburban Realty Co. v. United States, 615 F.2d 171 (5th Cir. 1980)

Buono v. Commissioner, 74 T.C. 187 (1980)

Graves v. Commissioner, 867 F.2d 199 (4th Cir. 1989)

Bramblett v. Commissioner, 960 F.2d 526 (5th Cir. 1992)

Bradley T. Borden, Nathan R. Brown & E. John Wagner, II, *A Case for Simpler Gain Bifurcation for Real Estate Developers*, 16 FLA. TAX REV. 279 (2014)

Bradley T. Borden & Matthew E. Rappaport, *Accounting for Pre-Transfer Development in* Bramblett *Transactions*, 41 REAL EST. TAX'N 162 (3rd Quarter, 2014)

Terrence Floyd Cuff, *Dirt Isn't Dirt: Exchanges of Property Held for Sale*—Neal T. Barker Enterprises, 26 J. REAL ESTATE TAX'N 304 (Summer 1999)

INDEX

CPSIA information can be obtained
at www.ICGtesting.com
Printed in the USA
BVHW031323251022
650238BV00015B/568

9 781600 425394